ISRAEL IN EXILE

RANEN OMER-SHERMAN

Israel in Exile

JEWISH WRITING AND THE DESERT

UNIVERSITY OF ILLINOIS PRESS
URBANA AND CHICAGO

Manufactured in the United States of America
∞ This book is printed on acid-free paper.
C 5 4 3 2 1

Library of Congress Cataloging-in-Publication Data
Omer-Sherman, Ranen.
Israel in exile : Jewish writing and the desert / Ranen Omer-Sherman.
p. cm.
Includes bibliographical references and index.
ISBN-13: 978-0-252-03043-7 (cloth : alk. paper)
ISBN-10: 0-252-03043-5 (cloth : alk. paper)
1. Wilderness areas in literature. 2. Israeli literature—History and criticism. 3. Jewish literature—History and criticism. 4. Identity (Philosophical concept) in literature. 5. Bible. O.T.—Criticism, interpretation, etc. I. Title.
PJ5012.W54044 2006
892.4'0932154—dc22 2005021530

For my mother, Betty

Whose home I have made the wilderness,
the salt land his dwelling-place
Amused by the tumult of the city,
Oblivious to the demands of a taskmaster,
Roaming the mountains for pastures;
And seeking every green thing.

—Job 39:6–8

God Himself has spoken from these shores . . .
the desert still seems
struck dumb with terror, and one would say that it has
still not been
able to break the silence since it heard the voice of the
eternal.

—François-René de Chateaubriand

If grass is the question of life sand is perhaps its answer.
Then I would have devoted my life to pestering the desert.

—Edmond Jabès

Contents

Preface

> Then Abram journeyed by stages through the Negeb.
>
> —Genesis:12:9

> Wilderness is a necessary condition for every revelation, for every internalization of the Torah's teaching: "Whoever would wish to acquire Torah, must make himself ownerless like the wilderness."
>
> —Midrash Rabba

> The experience of the desert is both the place of the Word—where it is supremely word—and the non-place where it loses itself in the infinite.
>
> —Edmond Jabès

The spirit of this project is much indebted to my first encounter many years ago with lines written by Maurice Blanchot observing Kafka's strange attraction and repulsion toward Zionism: "his wandering does not consist in nearing Canaan, but in nearing the desert, the truth of the desert—in going always further in that direction."[1] Challenged by the prospect of testing that notion in relation to other prophetic Jewish writers, my excitement grew as I encountered the vivid ways that strange paradigm manifests itself in contemporary Israeli narratives as well as literature from the Diaspora. This book was in part inspired by and written for a new generation of Jews, including a growing number of young rabbis, striving to reinvigorate Judaism, in its myriad communal and individual forms, by exploring the neglected close spiritual and political relationship between Judaism's sacred texts and nature and the wilderness. My book describes how, in Jewish narratives, the desert becomes a metaphysical idea that is both a process and a place that raises compelling questions about justice and national identity. Contemporary Jewish writing often tries to validate the grumblings and rebellions in the wilderness of Exodus, finding that subversive spirit as important as the official trajectory toward liberation and homecoming. In this regard, my literary/cultural study builds on Walter Brueggemann's insightful analysis of how the Mosaic tradition born in the desert experience "tends to be a movement of protest . . . situated among the disinherited and which articulates its theological vision in terms of a God who decisively intrudes, even against seemingly impenetrable institutions." In contrast, "the Davidic tradition tends to be a movement of consolidation . . . situated among the established and secure, and which articulates its theological vision in terms of a God who faithfully abides and sustains on behalf of the present order" (202). In my study, I examine the ancient tension between these clashing paradigms as a healthy dynamic that still reverberates in secular Jewish literature.

I suppose that the true origins of this book must be traced to my first encounter with the desert as a perhaps excessively fervent sixteen-year-old. In the relatively halcyon era of the 1970s it was easy to have a guiltless, non-critical stance toward Israel simply because the conflict with the Palestinians was not yet something that most Jewish Americans were aware of (let alone those of my age). Raised on the relatively sentimental and morally uncomplicated narratives of Israel's struggle for survival that were and still are woefully typical of Jewish American pedagogy, I was altogether uncritically caught up in the essential justness of the Jewish national cause. In 1975, the year I made my monumental decision not only to immigrate but to help establish a kibbutz in Israel's southern borderlands, I had been in Israel only on one previous occasion. But even then, on a youth program that toured borders, army bases, and kibbutzim not long after the traumatic Yom Kippur War, I had already begun to weave Israel into my own personal fantasy of fulfillment. As a young and sometimes lonely teenager suddenly numbed by the overwhelming spatial and cultural distance I had traveled from an indolent California adolescence to the unknown perils of the three years of military service which loomed just ahead, I was still baffled by the Hebrew language and not fully at ease in the noisy congestion, tense undercurrents, and frenetic pace of life in Israel's cities. It was with profound relief and even a sense of revelation that I first became acquainted with the isolated southern settlements of the Negev, Arava, and the even greater expanses of the Sinai Peninsula (in those years still in Israel's control). In contrast to the dizzying cultural commotion of Israel's urban life, I was attracted to the desert's pure air, its serenely radiant mornings and evenings, and the extraordinary clarity which it mysteriously seemed to bestow on both external appearances as well as one's own internal landscape.

How did I see the desert then? Perhaps more than anything as a fantastic realm of the unknown, a beckoning emptiness that meant limitless potential. Its expanses had a personal meaning to me—everything seemed possible. Leaving the trendy and material (yet for all that seemingly unreal) San Fernando Valley for the tawny luminosity of the Negev was to experience a condition of perpetual ferment, shivering in anticipation for my real life to begin. I knew nothing at that time of the early Zionist "Canaanite" movement which had loathed traditional forms of historical Judaism. But, recalling my indifference to the tepid variety of liberal Judaism with which I had been raised in America, it now seems as if I had unconsciously echoed that early Zionist generation's fervent quest for an "authentic," indigenous core that would demonstrate one's essential at-homeness in the exotic landscape as much as the Bedouin of whom one caught occasional glimpses, no matter where one came from. That 1950s ideology, prevalent in a number of important literary modernist Hebrew works, advocated a return to the origins of premonotheistic Near Eastern culture as a more satisfying and unified framework, an alternative to the divisive nationalisms of the region. And as Rachel Brenner points out, "though the Canaanites failed as a political movement, their ideological position influenced the formation of the native Israeli" (*Inextricably Bonded* 294).[2] Like them I was drawn to an imaginary "East," a spiritual geography that somehow seemed more immediate than the monotheistic religions it had birthed. My *aliyah* (immigration) to Israel was much informed by years of immersion in Jewish education and a growing awareness of the Holocaust. But settling into that primordial place as a young person gave me a giddy sense that I could unravel myself from the weight of all that historical trauma. Liberated from actually coming to terms with Jewish complexity (and religious tradition), I would bypass history and establish a new identity in the pure expanses of stone and sand. Processes of habitation, acculturation, and exploitation crept into that archaic world too, but it seemed at a geological pace.

Unmarked, unmeasured, and wild, the Negev was still a place in which the relentlessly anxious and insecure outlook of the Jewish state was not the measure of all things. In my early exposure to a place in which one's sensory experience often seemed reduced to the beating of the hot sun on one's skin, worries and complex intellectual thought processes easily melted away. These were so much ephemeral vapor in the great furnace-blast of a white sun. The kibbutz I helped create nestled in a stunning environment of distant smoky gray and charcoal black granite peaks and rosy sandstone that made mundane life seem intensely epic and even cinematic. Kibbutz life in the 1970s, especially juxtaposed with my exploratory ventures into the desert, now seems to have been an astounding amalgam of romantic, ruralist, pantheist, and occasionally Jewish beliefs and experience. In retrospect, I find that my impression of what that encounter did to me is viscerally captured by Craig Childs, a North American naturalist and fellow desert rat who in his evocative *Soul of Nowhere* notes of the desert that "there's no rest here. It pulls your soul inside out. Sort of a dry washing machine and you're never clean until you're turned to sand and wind." Looking back now, it seems that I experienced something akin to what Childs describes; a sort of blissful lethargy in which all forms of doubt and inquiry vanished on the untrammeled road to "authenticity." This contemplative quiet inspired a deeper form of consciousness, a clarity that, if not exactly "revelation," seemed like an unprecedented momentum toward new truths.

In the beginning, we were an assortment of very intense, perhaps just slightly crazed individuals. What immediately struck me, as I worked as a desert guide and ranger for the Nature Reserves Authority among the sparsely populated desert communities inhabited by maverick and occasionally anarchic Israelis, was that everyone I encountered seemed somehow more filled with idealistic purpose, indeed more radiant and intensely alive, than any people I had ever known. Surely this was a fallacy on a scale of grandiose proportions, but so it seemed to me in those days. It should be noted that kibbutz life, even at its best, is always a community whose idealistic individuals often experience acute social claustrophobia and a restless desire for privacy that proves all too elusive. Yet the southern Arava that I helped settle proved a rewarding environment for exploring that intrinsic tension of kibbutz life, between the rigors of creating a unique social experiment with others and seeking a greater sense of one's own self. Just at the borders of our green lawns and cowsheds beckoned a little-explored desert vastness of ochre hills, cliffs, dunes, and flint-strewn flatlands.[3] It was as though we were formed by the heightening effects of isolation, the wilderness's mysterious contrasts, of blinding light and deep somber shadows, as much as by the experience of living in a boisterous community (and as my analysis of how Shulamith Hareven and Simone Zelitch reveals, this is often understood by modern Jewish writers as a crucial dimension of what happened to the Israelites at Mount Sinai). However presumptively, we excited youngsters in our early twenties felt our adventure was aligned to the way the Exodus story of liberation went out to the world as an epic reverberating with universal hope. After all, we were on the cusp of agricultural innovations and discoveries (desert irrigation; new crops; sun-baked land that had never been tilled) that would benefit humanity in the famines of Africa or anywhere that drought or desertification threatened. And of course because we had consciously chosen the empty desert over occupying Palestinian lands (the triumphal Settler Judaism of Gush Emunim was then ascendant), we saw ourselves sincerely striving for true equality and social responsibility.

The Arava desert seemed to us an optimum space for realizing the egalitarian idealism of kibbutz life; the limitless desert expanses implicitly contested the notion of a material center or mastery over property which is intrinsic to the American insularity of middle-class domesticity that so many of us fled from in the early seventies.[4] Moreover, it complicated received notions of the Jewish relation to place in the modern state of Israel for, as Orthodox rabbis often commented (when it came to biblical and talmudic injunctions regarding the treatment of agriculture and livestock in the land bequeathed to Abraham's descendants), the Arava, a region just outside the southern borders of the Land, is *not* "Eretz Yisrael" in the ancient sense. For this and less visible reasons, the energetic questioning that the desert helped provoke in all of us was the antithesis of that early mental torpor.

After my desert sojourn I am easily persuaded by the clear sense of Sven Lindqvist's own experience in the remote Sahara: "the best part of suddenly encountering solitude is that it provides training: you discover your life when you have to start using its long-since forgotten and atrophied muscles" (35). And today I also recognize what Paul Bowles, author of *The Sheltering Sky,* meant when he said that someone who has been in the desert is never the same again. My great joy in those years was to set out from the confines of kibbutz life into the relatively unmapped spaces of the surrounding expanses. My own desert aesthetic was not always easily sustained because in solitary moments I became aware that the desert is filled with voices and the same landscape that could inspire would sometimes evoke the revulsion, loneliness, and fear in me that it produced in many others, whether visitors or those who dwell there. I grew to understand the strange fateful moments of disquiet experienced by the estranged protagonist of Amos Oz's *A Perfect Peace.* Alone in the desert on certain occasions, I learned that the individual has to exert a great deal of self-control, for unease and nameless dread are always spinning about the margins of one's rational control. The desert humbles one in numerous ways, reducing the intellectual to unprecedented awareness of bodily identity (through thirst, heatstroke, and hallucinations). And people do perish there all the time. It was my sense of the radical vulnerability of the individual in the desert that led me to appreciate the fact that human identity as a whole owes much more to its desert experience than to its dreams of Eden in the forms of restful gardens (however soothing and welcome such spaces are in contemporary urban life). Both of course are necessary, but we, Jews and others, often lose sight of the value of the former.

Today, like many of the writers examined in this study, I vastly prefer the wild God of the desert, that is, monotheism's terrifyingly unknowable and ambiguous deity, to the God of certainty that emerges from the radical political messianism of the fundamentalist Right. In the desert one invariably returns to uncertainty, is less likely to be converted by the violence that accompanies such claims as "God is on our side." But in such uncertainty rests a redemptive clarity, a sense of moving from childhood fantasy to a spiritual plane made for those adults who appreciate that God must be held responsible for the tragic as well as the "good" dimensions of reality, and that the divine truly dwells separate from humankind. This journey has not caused me too much anguish for if I am an optimist today I think it might just owe to the memory of living for years with clear horizons under cloudless skies in seemingly limitless space—and witnessing life flourish under adversity. If we are to speak at all of the "messianic," it should be with an awareness that the Negev beckons with greater urgency than ever, as an alternative national space, patiently awaiting the day when an Israeli government of sufficient vision and courage will dismantle the illegal settlements that have proved so costly for the societies of both Palestinians and Israelis and settle its uninhabited expanses.

Over the years, I have been delighted to observe the powerful undercurrents of dissent and questioning the desert seems to inspire emerge in exciting ways in the imaginative worlds of contemporary Jewish writing which is the focus of this book. Today, my years as a desert guide and ranger for the Nature Reserves Authority are far behind me and I often miss the days of annual gazelle counts in the Negev, discovering the forlorn remains of ancient campfires, dwellings, and burial sites, investigating the lairs of hyenas, and leading rabbinic students to the summit of Mount Moses in the southern Sinai. But I would like to think that as a professor in comparative literature classrooms, that passion has successfully metamorphosed into new forms of textual exploration that I hope other readers interested in the myths, metaphors, and material reality of desert space will welcome. That this too will prove to be a rich and complicated journey, ambitiously encompassing linear and non-linear plots, structures, and motifs as well as the imaginative mapping of settled and unsettled landscapes, including their discrete metaphoric functions, from writer to writer. The line between writing and the desert is substantial and direct, but negotiating between these essential components requires attention to aesthetic as well as ideological structures of the text. For the literature explored here suggests that for the individual artist, this indeterminate and resistant space has a way of thwarting the tendentious ways that the Jewish nation in Israel and abroad has tried to shape and incorporate it within its collective fantasy of place and belonging. And yet at the same time it cannot be ignored that these ostensibly individual treks are mapped over the palimpsest of collective Jewish memory—the emancipatory Exodus from Egypt and the communal acceptance of the Torah at the base of a desert mountain. Hence, the limits of my study are, on the one hand, the desert as ancient system of imaginative geography in the biblical writer's grasp of reality, and on the other hand, the desert as a site of moral awakenings and stirrings of conscience, whose uncanny intrusions, whether into the settled life of Jewish dwellers of Israeli cities and kibbutzim or the far-flung Diaspora, have contemporary relevance for the modern writer's relation to society and pressing questions of justice.

In his exposition of the quotation cited above from Midrash Numbers Rabba, R. Issachar Katz of Szczebrzesyn remarks that "ownerless" means to be "lowly and humble to learn from everybody and to teach everybody."[5] In my own life I have had the good fortune to learn from many wonderful teachers and colleagues whose brilliance has often humbled me while inspiring the development of my own ideas. Nevertheless, in spite of much encouragement from gifted individuals there were times I felt perhaps too humble. At such moments, I felt compelled to reconsider the meaning of this project; beset by doubt, I wondered whether there was indeed a tangible purpose inherent in my project or whether, like some of the characters that fascinated me, I was poised on the edge of a precipice overlooking the abyss, at a point where the slightest misstep would push me into nothingness or absurdity.

Once, some years ago when I was still a novice ranger struggling to come to terms with the perils of driving a jeep across relatively unknown desert terrain with an old friend, we suddenly found ourselves poised on the edge of a real precipice. We were beginning to slide down a treacherous slope and it seemed clear that the jeep might teeter over any moment into the boulder-strewn depths of the wadi below. *"Oh no!"* I groaned quite audibly, genuinely alarmed at the prospect of losing control. To which my friend, out of some mysterious reserve of calm which I still find uncanny, rejoined, "Either do it or don't do it. But don't say 'oh no.'" Macho Israeli army officer that he was, there was little doubt toward which alternative he leaned. Needless to say, I let it rip and we exulted in the thrill of unsafe vehicular acceleration over a precarious slope of tumbling rock.

In a mysterious way, the guiding principle of that momentous command, its instant of absurd lucidity, now seems to me to have influenced the outcome of the early days of this project. Having wavered and vacillated, thinking too much about the perils of taking what has certainly proved an unconventional approach to literature, I suddenly remembered his words and took the plunge. For this memorable episode and his companionship on memorable desert treks in the Negev and Sinai, I am grateful to Yonaton Gold. Other generous hiking companions for whose company I feel blessed include Ellis Shuman (stalwart companion on my trek to Petra), Nancy Melrose, Nancy Sampson, and numerous veteran members of Samar, Yotvata, and the other southern Arava settlements. I was very fortunate to be mentored by some of Israel's most accomplished and knowledgeable desert guides and naturalists: Avner Goren, Giora Ilani, Menahem Marcus, Eli Roz, and Beni Shalmon. I owe a similar debt to Kibbutz Mitzpe Shalem, Kibbutz Yahel, the Eilat Field School, and the Israel Nature Reserves Authority, all for the years of desert training—and immense happiness—they afforded me at various times. It is through those experiences that I feel emboldened to embark on a project that probes the permeable boundaries between literary analysis and lived experience.

At the University of Miami, I have enjoyed teaching a number of courses focusing on Jewish literatures of "place," as well as the Israeli-Palestinian conflict, to enthusiastic students, and I am grateful for their lively and thoughtful responses which have often stimulated the interpretive work of these chapters. Portions of the reading of Oz appeared in the *Journal of Modern Literature.* I am thankful to the Lucius N. Littauer Foundation for their support of this project. A special thanks to Lane Sherman for her strong support over the years. The University of Miami has generously supported my work through timely awards of faculty-enhancement grants. I would also like to thank my supportive colleagues who participated in the Twentieth Anniversary Research Colloquium of CrossCurrents: the Association for Religion and Intellectual Life, which met at Columbia University during the summer of 2003. I am also indebted to the friendly and knowledgeable library staffs of Columbia University and the Jewish Theological Seminary. Thanks also go to the lively and erudite participants in the inaugural Brandeis University Summer Institute for Israel Studies in 2004. At an early stage of this project, Lindsay Tucker offered warm support and critical suggestions which helped me to think about both the subtleties of feminist criticism and the tyrannical potential of myth. Paula M. Cohen's and Bernard Horn's enthusiastic responses to early versions of various chapters encouraged me to embark on what has proved to be one of the most fruitful journeys of my intellectual life and career. Yael Feldman, one of the true luminaries of modern Hebrew literary criticism, provided invaluable criticism and corrections of errors in my chapter on Shulamith Hareven and was exceptionally gracious and patient during a difficult time. Special thanks also go to Mehnaz Afridi, Samantha Baskind, Ira Dworkin, Stephen Fredman, Daniel Greene, and Jennifer Ratner-Rosenhagen for thoughtful critiques that led to significant revisions. Finally, I would like to thank Gilat and Kesem for their love and support.

ISRAEL IN EXILE

1 *Representing Desert Wilderness in Jewish Narrative: Poetics and Politics*

> "Thus says, the Lord,
> I remember the devotion of your youth, your love as a bride, how you
> Followed me in the wilderness, in a land not sown."
> —Jeremiah 2:2

> My name is Solomon Levi,
> The desert is my home,
> My mother's breast was thorny,
> And father I had none.
>
> The sands whispered, *Be separate,*
> The stones taught me, *Be hard.*
> I dance, for the joy of surviving,
> On the edge of the road.
> —Stanley Kunitz, *The Testing Tree*

The Jewish textual and physical encounter with the desert is surely one of humanity's most imaginative, spiritual, and in some ways mysterious adventures. The journey that began in Mesopotamia, traversed the Fertile Crescent, descended into the Nile, and culminated in a mysterious encounter with a demanding deity at the base of an unknown desert mountain would have expansive reverberations in humanity's relation to the sacred throughout the centuries that followed. Site of privation as well as inspiration, the desert was a formidable presence in the moral vision of the Jewish prophets, a paradigm that would later prove intrinsic to some of Jewish literature's most imaginative approaches to the ethical dimensions of exile and homecoming, dispossession and occupation.[1] Yet the present study is written out of a deep conviction that just as most of Western humanity is now oblivious to its nomadic origins, the vast majority of Jewish readers and critics have given little consideration to the immense relation between the stark, spare landscape of the desert and the most profound expressions of the Jewish ethical and literary imagination, beginning with the Hebrew Bible. Nevertheless, as a French scholar of ancient texts ironically notes, "the symbol of the desert is one of the most fertile in the Bible" (Chevalier and Gheerbrant 187).[2] Of late, there have been vital indicators that the field of Jewish Studies, joining disciplines such as critical anthropology, human geography, and political science, has begun to respond to the compelling need to intensify the exploration of the relationship between place and identity.[3] This path offers exciting ways to transcend the well-worn binary opposition of Diaspora[4] versus Israel that has often dominated discussions of contemporary Jewish identity.[5] I welcome these efforts to consider the Jewish relation to crucial dimensions of spatial identity that transcend the neat antithesis between homeland and exile.

Since undertaking my own project it has become clear to me that the desert experience carries its own permutations of wandering; the Jewish imagination never strays far from the threat and promise of peripatetic movement of one kind or another. In the chapters that follow, I undertake to illuminate how the universality of desert space serves as an urgent reminder to many Jewish writers that exile and alienation remain the essential human condition in spite of the ostensible transformations wrought by Zionism and other territorial nationalisms. Beginning with Gaston Bachelard's *The Poetics of Space* (1964) and as recently as Susan Brind Morrow's remarkable meditation on language and the desolate spaces of Egypt and the Sudan in *The Names of Things* (1997), contemporary philosophers and poets have proposed exciting paradigms of what in essence is a notion of non-human space as haunted by an imaginative process that converts the world into emotionally and figuratively endowed geographies often in mysterious ways that transcend empirical or positive forms of knowledge. Indebted in part to these and other non-Jewish sources the reader will encounter in the chapters that follow, my work must also wrestle with the ways that nature is overwritten by the human. Similarly, though technically speaking a literary study, I adopt a flexible approach by referencing important non-literary sources. Therefore I hope to complement some of the most innovative recent cultural and theoretical work being done in Israel Studies, including Oz Almog's *The Sabra,* Meron Benvenisti's *Sacred Landscape,* Ilan Troen's *Imagining Zion,* and Yael Zerubavel's *Recovered Roots.* The question of space, place, and identity in Jewish culture has lately received critical attention in these and other important works.

My own theoretical point of departure is that ever since the composition of Exodus, many outstanding Jewish writers have "listened" to the desert silence, interpreting the void—as if responding to the challenge of Chateaubriand's perception of the "mute" landscape (which serves as one of the epigraphs to this study) in order to situate the Jewish self in relation to place. For it has often been posited that monotheism's origins were dependent on the vast expanses and simple oneness of desert and that the latter lends itself to resisting the tyranny of the image.[6] For instance, one finds the theologian Belden Lane linking the "aniconic images" of cloud, desert, mountain, to a revolutionary discourse that stirs us to "question the overconfidence in words that sometimes characterizes the theological enterprise" as well as expressing "the deepest, virtually indescribable, human experiences of pain and joy" (4). Or as Israeli anthropologist Zali Gurevitch says so evocatively, "Between the place and the world lies the non-place, the desert, wherefrom the voice comes and where the book is given" (210). In the struggle of such writers to articulate an ancient mystery, it is clear that the desert of Exodus still provokes its interpreters, disengaging from any sentimental notion of the earth as merely nurturer and healer. Most significantly, in terms of the contemporary Jewish literary imagination, it is important to note that the desert experience is much more than an aberrant hiatus between slavery and the return to territorial possession. Indeed, it is a constituent of the earliest antiroyal strand of Israelite history which rejected any sovereign other than God. Hence, to a large extent, this study considers the dilemmas of present time against the desert and wilderness narratives of the past, investigating neglected intersections between geography and cultural production.

As if beckoning back toward Abraham's radically complete dependence on God's will, Moses and Joshua lead the people into an austere environment that necessitates the organic growth of the people under divine guidance.[7] Unlike many other religious narratives of place and revolution, the Hebraic narration of the receiving of the Law in the desert exhibits no interest in ecstatic experience. Instead, Moses, who in his encounter with God sees only God's back or perhaps only the wake of God's passing, must return to engage the people with the concrete realities of a new social and ethical vision. When contemporary readers revisit the complaints of the Israelites (especially from the perspectives of their own deeply troubled age), they are reacquainted with the earth as a hostile and indifferent place in which human beings, if they survive, must do so as ethical beings in relation to other ethical beings.

After a silence encompassing four weighty centuries of slavery and oppression, the voice which spoke to Abraham now greets Moses, outside the constraints of empire, in the desert. When Moses encounters the burning bush, he is told by a disembodied voice: "Put off thy shoes from off thy feet, for the place whereon thou standest is holy ground" (Exod. 3:5). In spite of this tangible suggestion of sacred ground, the desert of Exodus offers a stern rebuke to those who would fetishize place. As Gurevitch points out, the site of holiness is "an arbitrary unrecognized piece of land" destined for obscurity immediately after the voice departs (212). In the monumental absence of the voice, one of the most critical spaces in the mythic mapping of Jewish destiny is not dignified as "holy" (nor, for that matter, does the Pentateuch ascribe "holiness" to Canaan itself). As for Moses, he is fated to remain in the desert, outside the contours of his own story as it were. In Gurevitch's nuanced reading:

> Moses . . . is held back in non-place. He is never allowed to enter the place: "Yet thou shalt see the land before thee; but thou shalt not go thither unto the land which I give the children of Israel" (Deut. 32:52). The voice must remain in the desert, and is never to be placed, to be embodied in the land as locality—country, kindred, father's house. The place is of the voice and not vice versa. Only the voice must remain holy, not the land. Thus, the voice that delivers the Israelites from slavery to bring them into the promised land, remains in the desert to keep the desert a living essence of the myth. (212)

This book invites the reader into several of the pivotal literary texts of the recent Jewish engagement with the desert, the implications of "non-place" for Zionist consolidation of space and territory,[8] as well as diasporic considerations of power and powerlessness. For a striking range of modern Jewish writers, it would seem that the prospect of a world that permanently overcomes its desert spaces is apparently undesirable.

Even in the critical and often awkward phase of early-twentieth-century formulations of modern American Jewish identity, an influential Zionist essayist like Josephine Lazarus (sister of the poet Emma Lazarus) expressed the conviction that the spiritual and ethically beneficent legacy of the Eastern desert would be transmitted to the West if the latter was sufficiently open to the contributions of its Jewish Others. Through "interdependence and interchange of gifts spiritual and material" Lazarus argued that the Jew would only achieve at-homeness in America by reclaiming a distant origin in the desert sands, the ethos of which would redeem the host nation:

> The West has never originated any great religion. It has only adapted and elaborated theologies and systems of philosophy, fitting or misfitting them to Western forms and purposes. But we Jews still carry in our hearts the divine spark—the day star of the Orient. . . . We still bear in our soul the soul of the desert—the wide, vast spaces, the great silence, the great solitude, the silent watches of the night under the calm, large stars of the East, the flight of the alone to the Alone. (268)

As this grandiose passage suggests, Lazarus's desert ethos struggles to transcend the smooth materialism of American democracy for a more inchoate spiritual essence of the "East." But as this study demonstrates, a far more fraught and consequential struggle ensues in the more recent literary works, the cultural products of the uneasy Zionist return to the desert. For instance, Abraham Shlonsky (1900–1973), one of the leading poets after Hayim Nahman Bialik, produced a vision of the desert that radiates a stridently Orientalist hostility in which the "Eastern" desert is desolate absence when juxtaposed with the "Western" program of industrious Zionism:

> Many, many, many generations
> The sands lay still like ivories,
> Latent, their rebellion quelled:
> None approach
> To disrupt them.
>
> . . . . . .
> Suddenly the all-conquering shovel glimmered
> And the sand herds bleat
>
> . . . .
> I have vanquished you on this day
> Languishing camel:
> It is you who shall bring the mortar
> For the cement.

The hostile struggle against the desert's obdurate futility ("With a psalm of victory I desecrated/Your seed-hating desolation") eventually culminates in this triumphant image: "Thus a road—oh, bridle straps! Houses upon houses—like fists in the void!"[9] As Ariel Hirschfeld suggests, there is little room to doubt the ominous "ethnic identity" of Shlonsky's threatening wastes:

> Now I know: the wasteland
> Howls by night a prayer of vengeance.
> And from afar,
> Above the high domed roof of the mosque:
> A crescent moon moves,
> Like a scimitar. (1022)

In sharp contrast we find another militant Zionist poet, Shaul Tchernichovsky (1875–1943), crafting a sequence of seven quasi-pagan sonnets that expresses a decidedly exuberant embrace of the Eastern desert as a wellspring for the poet's imagination (perhaps because he was still far removed from the scene of Palestine in his native Russia):

> In my heart the dew yet lodges that descends on Edom's steppes
> And moistens the sand in the desert of God,
> And in my ears lives the song that comes with shadow's coming
> And a gentle star glitters to primeval ways.[10]

In these lines, the poet evokes the biblical term for the eastern borderlands of ancient Israel as well as Jacob's desert sojourn on his return home from Aram. The scene delineated here and in the succeeding stanza seems to embrace the "primitive" origin of the modernist Jewish poet's imagination. As Arnold Band observes, the imagery is "not from Greece or Canaan" but Sinai (Mintz 87) expressing a fervent attraction to the desert origins of the Jewish story.

One of my chief concerns is to demonstrate how the Jewish struggle for a coherent identity is intensified by existential as well as political debates over territorialism and occupation. In this regard it must be stressed that the significance that recent Hebrew writers assign to the symbolic geography of the desert is much more critical than it might be in other cultural contexts. To begin with, literary novels and their authors are taken very seriously in Israel. As Smadar Lavie notes, "Israelis have one of the highest rates in the world for readership of literature" and "literature plays a key role in forming Israeli national identity . . . Hebrew literature, in the revived biblical language, has been central to imagining the new Israeli national identity" ("Blowups in the Borderzones" 59). The desert of Exodus endures as a particularly inspiring template for the modern Jewish writer's provocative interrogation of the limits of both the individual and the collective. I would like to think that this owes in part to the fact that, as Douglas Rushkoff observes, the talmudic imagination stresses that Sinai was a place where "God was experienced differently by everybody. Accordingly, the Israelites who witnessed him "directly" at Mount Sinai, each saw a different image of God" (28). I see this as a difference that would resist the tyranny of the same, inaugurating an imaginative bridge between the individual and the official narrative unprecedented in previous spiritual and social constructions of reality. More often than not, the writers explored in the following chapters set their narratives in Sinai, perhaps because even today it is a stubbornly intangible and uninhabitable space that somehow always seems to transcend a conventional national identity, no matter which nation controls it.

Particularly in the final decades of the twentieth century, the renewal of writing about the desert's empty spaces enabled an exuberantly performed expression of the Israeli writer's religious, cultural, and political ambivalences. However, even in the diasporic perspective, it seems apt that French Jewish historians Jean-Christophe Attias and Esther Benbassa should declare in their compelling study of the role of geography in Jewish cultural and political discourse that "the fundamental experience of wandering in the desert is no less central in Jewish memory than is possessing and then losing the land" (19). Indeed, a number of scholars of the Hebrew Bible have gone so far as to insist that in certain books, notably Hosea, the desert is represented as the "ideal period in Israel's history."[11] And yet for all this, in our time the desert still remains a much neglected, little understood trope in the mythic and symbolic construction of Jewish space. Whereas, among critics of contemporary Hebrew literature, there seems to be general agreement that "desert psychology has a prominent role in Israeli literature" (Joseph Cohen 135), little has been done to demonstrate either its pervasiveness or exactly how it functions. Yet it remains, a stubborn enigma that disrupts the supposed clarity of the past, rupturing into the present. As I will demonstrate in subsequent chapters, the appearance of the desert in the Israeli imagination has the startling capacity to rouse the unwelcome specter of "Diaspora" that Zionist teleology had repudiated.

It is not difficult to discern just why the paradigm of the desert experience has so often been understood as the site of a revolutionary consciousness. Deuteronomy reveals to us that the ancient Israelite imagination's invention of a bodiless deity seemed to require the emptiness and vacancy of the Middle East's most desolate spaces:

> The Lord spoke to you out of the fire; you heard the sound of words but perceived no shape—nothing but a voice. . . . For your own sake, therefore, be most careful—since you saw no shape when the Lord your God spoke to you at Horeb out of the fire—not to act wickedly and make for yourselves a sculptured image in any likeness whatever: the form of a man or a woman, the form of any beast on the earth. . . . Take care, then, not to forget the covenant that the Lord your God concluded with you and not to make for yourselves a sculptured image in any likeness, against which the Lord your God has enjoined you. For the Lord your God is a consuming fire, an impassioned God. (Deut. 4:12–24)

Here at least one highly suggestive reason emerges to explain why the desert was so critical to the spiritual perception and ethical innovations of monotheism. A disembodied God (whose "impassioned" voice is yet inimitable) seems essential to delegitimization of the royal authority and kingship that had been embodied in the representations of plastic art. But Joseph Cohen's intriguing concept of "desert psychology" in later Jewish literature gains even greater coherence if we turn to yet another ancient text, the rather curious episode of Isaac's sojourn among the Philistines (Gen. 25:19–28:9). There, attempting to assert himself by reclaiming his father Abraham's wells, the wandering patriarch meets hostile resistance:

> But when Isaac's servants, digging in the wadi, found there a well of spring water, the herdsmen of Gerar quarreled with Isaac's herdsmen, saying "The water is ours." He named that well Esek, because they contended with him. And when they dug another well, they disputed over that one also; so he named it Sitnah. He moved from there and dug yet another well, and they did not quarrel over it; so he called it Rehoboth, saying, "Now at last the Lord has granted us ample space to increase in the land." (Gen. 26:17–22)

It would be difficult to imagine activities less helpful to a program of territorial conquest than this strange account of a series of submissive accommodations and withdrawals. Born to a zealous nomad perhaps existentially paralyzed following his near-sacrifice, Isaac is often dismissed as the most passive of the patriarchs, unhelpfully stalling the inexorable momentum of conquest and possession that otherwise distinguishes the trajectory of the Five Books of Moses. But from another perspective, this patient patriarch of the second generation might best be appreciated as one who consistently seeks to resolve disputes with local tribes over the rights to various wells and grazing lands rather than pursuing an agenda to conquer territory and subdue others. An ethic and ethos born of the desert experience, Isaac's ancient form of diasporic accommodation contrasts sharply with the territorial and occasionally fanatic rootedness in the landscape that possesses Shlonsky—and the contemporary Jewish nation. It seems noteworthy that Isaac's restrained, nomadic maneuvers are rewarded, for immediately after this episode, God visits Isaac in a dream that very night, which assures him the blessings of fertility and divine protection.[12] This neglected narrative is worth the modern reader's attention, I would argue, because the desert's traditional association with challenging the complacency of political hegemony still reverberates for Jewish writers.[13]

In later centuries, representations of the desert were woven into such a varied range of Jewish literary and religious texts that it is impractical to attempt to explore more than a representative number of texts in the space of a single study.[14] Accordingly, to demonstrate the decisive impact of physical geography on the Jewish narrative of time, space, and culture, I have selected works that will demonstrate how the desert, rather than preserving itself as a "timeless reality" in a platonic sense, continues to emerge, evolve, metamorphose, and even generate parodies of itself in ways that profoundly invigorate the Jewish literary tradition in both Israel and the Diaspora. We will encounter narratives in which the Zionist dream of Israel is marked by confinement and stagnation, whereas the desert beckons as an eternally youthful and creative realm.

Such textual varieties of ambivalence and nostalgia have actually been manifest ever since the great new moral and intellectual freedom that accompanied the Israelites' flight into the wilderness as we observe in Jeremiah's reading of the desert relationship of God and the people as an idealized one, "a new bride unquestioningly trusting her groom and following Him, even in the wilderness" (D. Boyarin 42).[15] But rather than argue that the desert (whether as root metaphor or reality) occupies a privileged, self-defining, independent, and autonomous place, I consider how, just like other imaginative geographies, the desert is culturally constituted as well as constitutive of culture, contributing to a general Jewish sense of reality. For Jewish writing, the scene of wilderness serves not just as an austere retreat from civilization but as a discursive battleground for the exploration of conflicts that divide the Jewish self. Most importantly, in our anxious and violent present, desert narratives offer edgy and spirited contrasts to the uniform and linear structure of the Zionist narrative's mooring of Israeli identity in space as well as its teleological thrust. As Miri Talmon argues, in Israeli culture, "'place' is never taken for granted. Instead, it must be appropriated over and over again, bearing both the ambivalence and the contradiction of 'otherness' and 'alienation/difference' that cannot be resolved into 'assimilation' and unified belonging" (191). Where in other world literatures the desert plays a crucial role in narratives that destabilize the existential limits of identity, nationality, and borders, in the contemporary Israeli situation, the transformative topography of the desert (its shifting sands and other erosive features of the landscape), mirrors a national reality that is itself in more radical flux than is often acknowledged. In short, the desert is often the catalyst for complex ideological positions.

My guiding premise is that this cultural complexity has its origins in the Hebrew Bible, which departs in such striking ways from the seamless dichotomy of other cultural texts of antiquity where the desert is singularly a place of violence, barbarity, and deprivation. Indeed, this is a crucial dimension of the ancient/modern Jewish text's idiosyncratic relation to space. World literature and the texts of religious antiquity express a common mistrust of the desert and have produced sharply etched negative images of its essential hostility toward settled human culture. Whether dwelling in cities or the rustic agrarian sites of fertile river valleys, the ancients imagined the earth's ostensibly empty spaces as havens for darkness and death.[16] Christianity's desert howls with evil spirits that threaten God's hegemony (Williams 11) and Islamic deserts are often haunted by dangerous spirits called djinns that subvert human will and destiny.

The Christian spatial imagination links Cain's atrocity, the punishment of wandering for his primal denial of human community, to earlier events in Genesis and the prevailing sense that the Adamic fall would bring about the further moral decay or desertification of God's creation (Gen. 3:17).[17] Human sin is projected into landscapes that do not conform to the pastoral. In contrast, the same Hebrew prophet who might curse the people with the fate of the "barrenness" of the wilderness might also recognize it as a site of an exalted spiritual state, glancing back enviously toward the forty years of wandering as a period in which the people shared a special intimacy with the deity who accompanied them. The prophet Jeremiah nostalgically recalls the days of Israel's "youth" in the wilderness, and Hosea even dreams of a day in which God will bring the nation of Israel back to the desert to renew the covenant. In this regard, whatever else might link it to the other major monotheistic traditions, the prophetic Hebraic worldview also shares a certain ground with ancient pre-Islamic Arabic poems (frequently committed to memory and recited by Bedouin tribes), an early form of diasporic nostalgia that often laments the desert encampment or oasis that has been abandoned.

For the prophets, the exilic sojourn in the Sinai is filled with death and tribal disorder, and yet this condition also blesses the people with God's redemptive love and undivided interest in their growth as a people. In a much later period, the mysterious apocalyptic community of the Essenes (whose apocalyptic imagination continues to churn scholarly controversies) created Qumran, a monastic community on the shores of the Dead Sea, apparently to escape the corruptions of the decadent city. Adolfo Roitman, a Dead Sea Scrolls scholar and curator of Jerusalem's Shrine of the Book, argues that the mysterious Qumranites sought the desert because "the origin of the people of Israel was in the desert, and so perhaps they felt that their salvation would also come in the desert."[18]

To trek through the Hebrew Bible's representations of the desert invariably means to move from a literal geography toward increasingly metaphoric geography. But it remains a concrete enough realm to emerge as a vital alternative to the corruptions of sovereignty, such as when Elijah flees Baal to meet God in the wilderness (1 Kings 19:3–18). Most importantly, when considering the contemporary moral imagination of secular writers, it is important to note that desert translates as one of the Hebraic imagination's most pervasive symbols of universality. As one midrashic commentary on the Book of Exodus has it, the Torah was given in the desert, "for if it had been given in the land of Israel, the nations of the world could have said, 'We have no portion in it.' Therefore it was given in the wilderness, publicly and openly, and in a place to which no one had any claim. Everyone who desires to accept it, let him come and accept it."[19] If we consider this early rabbinic approach to the spiritual logic of scripture, we find that an idealized notion of "wilderness" often forms the central prism that guides the dominant approach to social iniquities. Expressions of this bold universality are also abundant in later, secular literature. Certainly it engenders the concept of physical suffering that is later exchanged for metaphysical enlightenment, most visibly in securing the right to inhabit the Holy Land of Canaan after the long and painful journey out of Egypt.

Ever since, the ways that Jews envision the liberating journey toward peace and responsibility—in both its collective and individual fulfillments, remains linked to the terrain of difficult torments of risks wherein both God and humanity uttered curses and threats to one another. For the French Jewish intellectual Emmanuel Levinas (1906–1995), that most commanding voice of postmodern Jewish thought, the desert nomadism of Abraham, seen as one who goes out from his home to an alien land, never allowing even his servants to return, is illustrative of Judaism's prophetic openness to the divine, its disregard for the utilitarian consequences of the journey ("Trace of the Other" 346–49). In Levinas's post-Holocaust thought, Abraham's desert wanderings have important implications for prophetic Judaism's emphasis on the human Other as well:

> Above all Abraham is the one who knows how to receive and feed men, the one whose tent was open to the four winds. Through all these openings he watched out for passersby he could welcome. The meal offered by Abraham? We know of one above all: the meal he had offered to the three angels. Without being aware that they were angels . . . Abraham must have taken the three passers-by for three Bedouins, three nomads from the Negev desert—three Arabs indeed! He runs to meet them and calls them "My Lords." Abraham's descendents are men to whom their ancestor bequeathed a difficult tradition of duties toward the other, which we have never finished fulfilling, an order from which we are never released, but where duty takes on above all the form of obligation toward the body, the duty to feed and shelter. . . . Abraham's descendents are men of all nations: every man who is truly a man is probably a descendent of Abraham. (*Du sacré au saint* 19)

It is this study's primary purpose to demonstrate that such hopeful universality also surfaces in the urgency with which pressing questions of justice and oppression are framed in contemporary literary narratives. But before turning to those, it is worth elaborating further on the Levinasian approach to archetypal wanderings. A crucial current running through his philosophy critiques Western philosophy's horror of the Other—"an insurmountable allergy" manifested in Greek culture's Ulysses. Contrasting Greek and Hebraic modes of wandering, Levinas says that whereas Ulysses returns home to himself, a one-way movement embodying the West's perpetual self-sufficiency and self-satisfaction, the Abraham of Genesis leaves his homeland forever for the unknown, thus embodying a movement without return.[20] The difference, Adriaan Peperzak declares, is between "the exodus of the just" and "the odyssey of the hero" (67–68). Whereas Ulysses returns essentially unchanged to Ithaca, Abraham and Moses set out on desert journeys to leave the comforts and riches of national origin behind.[21] For Levinas, this means a life led in deferment of self-gratification, in loss, indifferent to the quantitative or utilitarian measurement of the relation with the Other.

In approaching texts that address the plight of the Palestinian people, I am particularly interested in Levinas's provocative essay "Meaning and Sense," which clarifies the proper orientation to the other's vulnerability as a radical "movement of the Same towards the Other which never returns to the Same" (91). At such moments, Levinas seems more interested in what transpired *before* the collective journey of the people under the tutelage of Moses; Abraham's desert self-exile from Ur embodies the brave individuation of one who transcends the concept of the tribe into which he was born.[22] Yet revelation in the desert continues to provoke an ethical orientation toward alterity, toward the Other, even in Moses' strange encounter with the divine. According to Levinas, when Moses pleads to witness God's transcendent glory but is permitted only to glimpse the passing, or wake, of His back, "The God who has passed by is not the model whose face would be the image. To be in the image of God does not signify being the icon of God, but finding oneself in His trace. The revealed God of our Judeo-Christian spirituality keeps the whole infinite of His absence which is the personal order itself. He shows himself only through his trace, as in Exodus 33. To go toward Him is not to follow this trace, which is not a sign, but to go toward Others who are held in the trace" (*En découvrant l'existence* 202).

I'm excited by Levinas's affirmation that, by privileging anecdotal narratives of protest and spiritual restlessness alongside the law and ritual, the Bible credits the desert as the site of a supreme skepticism unsettling all nationalist or individualist complacency. Susan Handelman elaborates on this ethos in her own reading of Levinas: "The 'non-site' of desert . . . is an opening up as an exposure to the outside—to the other . . . it is the ultimate openness and exposure to the other as ethics and responsibility for the other" (*Fragments of Redemption* 296). In remarkably similar terms, Jonathan Sacks, chief rabbi of Britain, writes that "We encounter God in the face of a stranger. That, I believe, is the Hebrew Bible's single greatest and counterintuitive contribution to ethics. God creates difference; therefore it is in one-who-is-different that we meet God. Abraham encounters God when he invites three strangers into his tent. Jacob meets God when he wrestles with an unnamed adversary alone at night" (59–60). Here I would add that Theodor Adorno's famous injunction that "it is part of morality not to be at home in one's home" is as indebted to this ancient desert skepticism as it is to the Jewish experience in modernity. Persuaded that powerful residual traces of Abrahamic estrangement still linger in the Jewish imagination, the question I will consider throughout this study is just how this paradigm continues to inspire bold transgressions of the comforting limitations of "home" and "identity." As readers will see, I often find that such a critique is best furthered by juxtaposing ancient with modernist and postmodern retellings. For instance, I trace the strange cultural aftereffects of a talmudic legend that stir a poetic epic by the modernist poet Bialik and then again many decades later by the contemporary novelist David Grossman. In part, this study demonstrates how, with varying degrees of social critique, the novels of Grossman, Amos Oz, and the late Shulamith Hareven at times repudiate the enduring ethics of such nomadic destabilization in the daunting face of extreme political realities, and in other instances retreat from the radical disengagement from national life inherent to the condition of exile. By way of contrast, a later chapter offers an examination of the strategic representations of the desert in the works of two diasporic writers.

Though inspired by the premise that when identity and place brush up against each other they create exciting new alignments, this study does not ignore the fact that the construction of desert narratives took place in varying contexts that influenced their disparate rhetoric, style, and content. Acknowledging differing perspectives on Jewish identity, I will demonstrate that throughout the Jewish epic of time and space, the desert is employed as a potent trope to strengthen, rewrite, and reconfirm certain core values. As Levinas's post-Holocaust ethics bear witness, the powerfully lingering effects of the desert experience shaped the Jewish sensibility in times and places far removed from Sinai.

In exploring the enduring relevance of this ancient encounter with the desert to a new century of atrocities and complex global politics, there are other dimensions to consider. For one thing, in the haunted aftermath of the Holocaust, the Jewish conception of God is no more that of a loving, healing deity exclusively. More than ever before, the Jewish imagination has had to expand to accommodate the terrifying consciousness (or absence) that enables deadly force at inexplicable moments in the quotidian world. It is as if for the first time we know the stark terms of the Book of Job's portrayal of innocent suffering. Yet in some ways our most daunting visions of the alienating deity of the post-Auschwitz world are rivaled by the severely punitive divinity of the foundational desert story. Often envisioned as the material and deliberate being who guides their destiny, for most of their forty years of wandering this hostile land of struggle, death, and exile, God vacates himself from the Israelites' story. This withdrawal allows the urgent fragility of human existence and human community to speak in the reverberating silence of absence. At other times, the deity arrives on the scene to punish insurrection with plagues and earthquakes that decimate great numbers of the desert generation.

Every Jewish child, brought up with even a modicum of Jewish literacy, learns through the Passover liturgy that the Jews were condemned to wander the desert for forty years. In this collective commemoration of human liberation, the desert is a realm of enlarged spirit, affording transformations that hegemonic, constrictive Egypt with its smothering monuments cannot. As the story begins, the strong individuals who went down to Egypt with Jacob are now a "swarming" (*vayishretzu*) mass. "Fruitful and multiplying," the descendants of Jacob are also fully assimilated to their environment. Indeed, as Avivah Gottlieb Zornberg asserts, this is the primal crisis of Exodus: "how to be redeemed when Egypt, that enervating soulscape, has one in its pincer grip? From such a perspective, Israel in Egypt *cannot* be redeemed; no separation is possible—in the same way as, in terms of mythic thought, the baby held in the womb *cannot* be born, must remain monstrously but all-too-implausibly immobilized forever" (18). Zornberg's eloquent meditation is representative of a growing number of feminist and psychoanalytic biblical critics who have persuasively forged exciting ways to link the emergence of a national identity to that of a human birth, with all its attendant problems of nurture that confront a wandering population of individual adults reduced to dependence on an invisible deity in a harsh environment.

Such scholars are attentive to the manifestly material and cultural Egyptian world of buildings, the Hebrews' bodily immersion in clay, straw, mortar, and bricks, as well as the fish, melons, and abundance of the life-giving Nile. From this cultural and agrarian fecundity, the Hebrews are irretrievably removed to a transcendent space untouched by the materiality of history. If the divine mission is to expunge from them all traces of idolatrous Egypt, this would seem to be the right place. But as Ilana Pardes observes, once in the wilderness, the Hebrews' progress toward redemption is anything but assured. In her rich psychoanalytic analysis, the biblical desert is a space of fissured identities, radical skepticism, and questioning of official narratives of the nation. Unlike its anointed patriarch, the desert wanderers, unconvinced by the binds of collective identity, are "confused and fearful about homecoming": "The wandering Israelites are skeptical about the very premise that Canaan is their homeland. The only land they wish to return to is Egypt. But they end up in the wilderness, between Egypt and the Promised Land, returning to neither" (Pardes 104). It is not that wilderness skepticism is sanctified or rewarded by God. Doubting God, the desert generation is "doomed to remain forever in the arid land of the desert" (Pardes 50). Pardes observes how existentially it appears reasonable to conclude that both their God and the desert are co-conspirators in a plot to destroy the wanderers. Their complaints earn them only the threat of utter annihilation and oblivion:

> Say to them, "As I live," says the Lord, "I will do to you just as you have urged Me. In this very wilderness shall your carcasses drop. Of all of you

> who were recorded in your various lists from the age of twenty years up, you who have muttered against Me, not one shall enter the land in which I swore to settle you—save Caleb son of Jephunneh and Joshua son of Nun. Your children who, you said, would be carried off—these will I allow to enter; they shall know the land that you have rejected. But your carcasses shall drop in this wilderness, while your children roam the wilderness for forty years, suffering for your faithlessness, until the last of your carcasses is down in the wilderness." (Num. 14:28–33)

Though the children of the desert sojourners do at last survive to enter Canaan and settle, their parents are rewarded with a different fate. The dry desert will reduce their bodily remains to dust that will be unmarked by any form of lasting commemoration.[23] In talmudic discourse, the desert generation is seen as singularly unworthy of a better outcome for a variety of reasons. For example, Abraham Ibn Ezra even anticipates the ethnic psychology of Sander Gilman's famous study of "Jewish self-hatred," seeing in the people's long history of enslavement an inevitable internalization of negative images which cumulatively engender an obdurate slave mentality that ultimately renders them unfit for the responsibilities of authentic freedom.

On one level, Pardes tells us that the wilderness means little more than a site where childhood is enacted, where the people perpetually "moan and groan," yet to emerge from "a preverbal and preconscious state, unaware of God's providence" (34). The Canaan that awaits them is too intangible to console the exiles of the "howling waste" (Deut. 32:10). Here is where the triumphal God of monotheism seems little more than an ascendant pharaoh, just as likely to exterminate the exiles. Whatever the merit of this resistance in the discourse of piety, the value of this ambivalence is that it lingers, producing creative ferment in the present. In the Jewish literary imagination, "desert" serves as a geographic disjunction that disrupts the clear continuity of national narratives even today, with its recent nomadic past. And for some of the literary protagonists we will encounter, exilic ambivalence emerges as a welcome alternative to the paradigm of the settled land whose security is won via unending wars and suffering. These are some of the crucial paradigms that challenge and stimulate retellings of Exodus and the ancient desert sojourn by the Israeli as well as Diaspora-based writers we will explore.

The contemporary desert narratives that I have chosen for this study possess certain critical features that make of them a distinctive subgroup within Jewish literature. Most importantly, they offer rich variations of a solitary protagonist whose interaction with desert space causes him to depart from the practices or ideological beliefs of the community. This seems apt, for Jewish writing has always represented a tense mediation of both solitude and city; yearning for escape from the community and reconciliation with the burden of return. Characteristically, from early antiquity, Jewish narratives set in the desert are provocative separation narratives in which external conflicts and internal divisions mirror each other, often with surprisingly rich psychological (hence modern) dimensions. For instance, when at war with Esau, Jacob retreats into the wilderness where he encounters a mysterious being he must strive against until granted a strange new identity, Israel—which re-establishes his relation to the collective destiny of the people who will bear his name. Like many modern Jews, the Hebrew Bible itself is filled with nostalgic yearnings for authenticity perhaps for a sense of youthful communion with the deity, as in the wistful verse: "Renew our days as of old" (Lam. 5:21). The voice of God is temporally and geographically situated in the archaic purity, the timeless flight, of the desert experience: "A blast, an eastern wind of the Lord, shall come blowing up from the wilderness" (Hos. 13:15). And in the contemporary narratives of Hareven, Oz, Grossman, Zelitch, and Jabès, the remote wilderness, as in any narrative about quest and distance, continues to be where the protagonist discovers the other side of the self, or to be more precise, what is missing within.

More often than not, this is a vital clue that provides him the way back to human community. It is notable that the individual Israeli writers I explore neither presume the Jewish state's total assimilation of its still-sparsely populated South nor absorb the desert uncritically into their artistic egos. Instead, the desert is "lived in" (though only literally so in Oz's case) as a roomy place brimming with possibility. In contrast to the existential novels of Paul Bowles, Michael Ondaatje, and others in whose novels the desert would seem to exact a sacrifice of the ego, something much more artistically affirmative often ensues in modern Hebrew literature—with relevance for the Zionist society as a whole. Disrupting the linear time and space of the modern nation-state, the desert disturbs with its ethical otherness. Hence, when it comes to Israeli literature, even before the advent of "post-Zionist" discourse, the writer's encounter with the eternal desert disrupted certain polarities and essentializing gestures of mainstream Zionist conventions. The writer's desire to revive the open potentiality of Judaism's exilic past is veiled in narratives about contemporary Israeli wilderness sojourners. There is a unique lucidity as well as an unparalleled depth of intensity in the desert experience that permeates their various retreats from society.

At the same time, it must be appreciated that Israel's literature of the desert often achieves a greater representational complexity than that other dominant imaginative narrative form—cinema. In Nurith Gertz's astute analysis of the Israeli films of the 1940s and 1950s, she finds that the desert, often seen as inseparable from the Arab Other, represented threatening, unconquered space:

> The Arabs who inhabit Palestine . . . metaphorically represent desolation and death. . . . [They] serve as background, which emphasizes the transformation of the Jew having become an Israeli. Films such as *The Great Promise* [Dir. Joseph Leits, 1948] and *End of Evil* [Dirs. Helmar Larsky and Joseph Krungold, 1949] show the Arabs in the exposition. *End of Evil* opens with shots of a desert and Arab convoys with camels; the narrator introduces the Arabs as part of the old Palestinian landscape that the settlers have come to remake. They are "the thieves and the desert," he says. . . . They are part of "these dead hills", which the settlers have come to revive. ("From Jew to Hebrew" 188)

I am intrigued by the fact that early Israeli films often feature a protagonist who is a Holocaust survivor or immigrant who is transformed: "the films use space to remake [the protagonist] into a Hebrew" ("From Jew to Hebrew" 182). In other cinema made on the cusp and aftermath of Jewish statehood, settlements are established in the wilderness of Arabs and jackals; the revival of dry and desolate places and the exilic Jew into fertile and productive entities are strategically linked. In contrast I find that the Israeli literature of the 1970s, 1980s, and beyond is often innovative in its aesthetic and ethical departures from that cinematic Zionist narrative. In other words, the literary texts I explore have historical and cultural significance not least because they represent a substantial rupturing of the ideological elements of the classic Zionist plot that Gertz critiques in this period.[24] What I seek to demonstrate in my own study is how narratives of this later period appropriated the liminal spaces that had once been anathema, investing them with new values. The protagonists of literary narratives who venture into desert spaces often emerge with both disillusionment and new cultural wisdom.

It should also be noted that in the Western literary tradition (existentialism aside) there is an undercurrent that preserved the ancient writers' original sense of the desert as site of spiritual revelation and prophetic knowledge, and this too deserves acknowledgement as the inheritance of the contemporary Jewish writer. For instance, Blake's barbed response to the rationalistic conventions of his age expresses an exuberant metaphoric evocation of both the liberatory energies of Exodus and the prophetic tradition:

Mock on, mock on, Voltaire, Rousseau;
Mock on, mock on, 'tis all in vain!
You throw the sand against the wind,
And the wind blows it back again.

And every sand becomes a gem
Reflected in the beams divine;
Blown back they blind the mocking eye,
But still in Israel's paths they shine.

The Atoms of Democritus
And Newton's Particles of Light
Are sands upon the Red Sea shore,
Where Israel's tents do shine so bright.

More typically, in the imperialistic age that Blake prophesied against (particularly in the prose of Wilfred Thesiger, Richard Burton, Charles Doughty, and T. E. Lawrence), the archaic desert of Arabia was a place that promised heroic action of the distinctly nationalist variety. The East seduces the European interloper with a realm of adventurous exploits that while severely testing the sojourner's mental and physical capacities, beckons with a classically static landscape associated with "nobility and freedom."[25] This tradition produced a rich harvest of narratives which seem to exult in unabashed masochism, or what Thesiger called "the satisfaction which comes from hardship and the pleasure which springs from abstinence" (37). Even the idiosyncratic Disraeli succumbed to this Orientalist fetishization of "authentic" space in his novel *Tancred,* with its unabashed Victorian racialized sentimentality and professed admiration for Arabian insularity: "The decay of race is an inevitable necessity unless it lives in deserts and never mixes blood" (150). In particular (often resembling the discourse of early Zionists), the English travel writers extolled the Bedouins, whose timeless poverty transformed them into uncorrupt and mythic embodiments of the virtues of abstinence and self-denial that were rapidly decaying at home in the seat of empire:

> Even tonight, when they considered themselves well off, these men would sleep naked on the freezing sand, covered only with their flimsy loincloths. I thought, too, of the bitter wells in the furnace heat of summer, when, hour by reeling hour, they watered thirsty, thrusting camels, until at last the wells ran dry and importunate camels moaned for water which was not there. I thought how desperately hard were the lives of the Bedu in this weary land, and how gallant and how enduring was their spirit. (Thesiger 135)

For the British (often traveling as disguised Arabs), the desert imposed an ethic of renunciation (if at times uneasily coexisting with the erotic charms of Eastern boys and girls).

Interestingly, there is an analogous tradition in early modern Hebrew writing among the Jews of eastern Europe who were fascinated by what they imagined as the enchanting allure of the Middle Eastern desert (and opposed to Shlonsky's notion of a monolithically hostile realm). This is especially noteworthy in Mordechai Feuerberg's "Whither" (1899) though the young author, dead by the age of twenty-five, never set foot in Palestine. As Ehud Ben-Ezer observes, the author's "rallying cry 'Eastward! Eastward!' welled up from a desire to found a new and a pure world . . . which would be the antithesis of the corrupt Western European civilization. The clean and virgin desert was the ideal setting for a new existence" (4). During the years of Israeli occupation of the Sinai that lasted from 1967 until 1982, anthropologists and other cultural observers often remarked on the unusually warm relations between the Bedouin and the Israelis who, eagerly fleeing their claustrophobic national space, ventured into the peninsula's immense expanses of enticing mountains, beaches, and desert wadis. They commented too on the unusual nature of an emerging breed of young people, who were lured to those spaces for unexpected reasons, according to David Shipler:

> The desert drew a special breed of Israeli Jew, not one who reveled in the militant nationalism of his country's larger conflict but one who treasured more the marvels of Bedouin culture, the human contact with a people who could perform the miracle of scratching a life out of the vast, spectacular wasteland. A passion for the Bedouin was mixed into a passion for the desert: The man and his environment converged; the desert was alive; its people were part of the landscape. (362)

From the initial stages of this encounter emerged a deep romantic identification, perhaps a kind of distant willful reflection: "Israeli Jews were seduced by the mysterious beauty of the desert and were drawn into an affection and fascination for the culture of the Bedouins" (Shipler 358). Many young Israelis subsequently studied Bedouin customs, recorded oral poetry, and in some cases actively sought to mediate the more abrasive aspects of life under Israeli military rule. As the most highly regarded Israeli scholar of Bedouin life, Clinton (Yitzhak) Bailey (one of Shipler's interviewees) wistfully muses, "Among Bedouins I find a tremendous lack of materialism, and emphasis on social values, which definitely takes predominance over material values" finding correspondence and continuity with "my own biblical ancestors. . . . There's a lot of behavior in the Bible that I would say is Arab, if not Bedouin, behavior. . . . In that sense the Bible is a rather accurate record of life when the Israelites lived in the desert" (Shipler 362). Most striking here is Bailey's unspoken but implied rebuke of his own culture for its uncritical embrace of materialism and his idealistic approval of the ethics of the Other, apparently, not so unlike Jeremiah, seeing it as a bridge to an idealized Hebraic past. Sensitive young Israelis couldn't fail to be ravished by such mirroring reconstructions any more than they could resist the beautiful simplicity and profound cultural poetics of the Bedouin, whose pastoral mores, they imagined, bore little resemblance to their own deeply fissured and conflicted society:

> The fire was an eternal, civilizing ritual. One of the first things a Bedouin does when he comes to a new place is to light a little fire to make a center, a focus that structures and diminishes the vastness, that creates a circle of intimacy in the wilderness. . . . In an empty desert, with few tangible goods, the Bedouins have surrounded themselves with remarkable intricacy, a complexity amid simplicity, an edifice of mores that organizes and defines existence in a hostile, sweeping, limitless land. (360–61)

Bearing in mind this idealistic portrait, with its hints of the writer's own cultural dissatisfaction, it seems apt that in the fictions of Amos Oz (b. 1939), who since 1986 has called the small desert town of Arad home, the desert expanses, far from serving as utopian or heroic space, often raise the troubling specter of fissures in the young individual's loyal commitment to the chain of a national identity that disappoints him.

Throughout his fiction, Oz's Sabra, or native-born, characters (invariably male) are usually strangers in their own country, alienated by the sharp disparity that divides the grim reality that surrounds them and the utopian dreams with which they were nurtured. As Ehud Luz points out, "they are restless, bedeviled, and unable to live simple, normal lives. They no longer believe in the Messiah, but a world devoid of redemption is repugnant to them. Their yearning for redemption makes it difficult for them to come to terms with their homeland as it is. . . . Wanderlust is the only 'Jewish' trait Zionism has left them" (257). Identifying this current in Oz's 1983 novel *A Perfect Peace* (*Menuha nekhona,* 1982) enables us to see how the idealistic dream of a famous pioneer father to create a generation of new Jews rooted in their fertile land has somehow been lost on his disaffected son, who is inexplicably drawn to the threatening desert wastes. Not altogether unlike the nostalgic Victorian quest for purity and a "noble savage" that remained static as the world of empire accelerated, Oz's character flees homogenous insularity. Even when raised under the classic kibbutz ideology that so resembled the ever-elusive Puritan values the Victorian imagination sought in the natives of Arabia, the disenchanted subject hedonistically longs for a distinct sense of self, unreconciled to his surroundings. In Oz's novel, the desert serves a variety of ideological uses. As Joseph Cohen remarks, "nowhere has Oz written more brilliantly of the desert and its role in fomenting (and illustrating) the insanities that inhabit the Israeli psyche" than in *A Perfect Peace,* which he compares to Conrad's achievement in exploring the relation between place and the human unconscious in Marlow's bestial quest in *The Heart of Darkness:* "Oz's narrative succeeds in its ability to map the human unconscious through the mood of the desert" (173). But until now, nobody has charted the intricate relation between self and landscape in Oz's work.

Both Oz and David Grossman—one of the most exciting heirs of the 1960s generation of Israeli literature—create peculiar, depressed protagonists whose extreme loneliness seems to require a strategic withdrawal from the nation, a desert sojourn of varying duration, to overcome despair and dysfunction.[26] In my reading of these writers, I embrace the spirit of Avraham Balaban's perception that the secular Israeli writer is one "whose belief is not a solid certainty, but is only a doubtful possibility, something they hesitantly reach for." Balaban identifies this as "a technique that enables the writer to push the boundaries of human experience, to encompass unfamiliar, uncharted territories" ("Secularity and Religiosity" 76). For instance, of Oz he observes that (in spite of the writer's declarations that he is a secular Jew) "religious yearnings are among the strongest motives behind his characters' actions" (69). Like Balaban, in spite of the divisive rift between Orthodoxy and secular Israeli Jews, I would very much hope to shift the reductive perception that writers like Oz, Aharon Appelfeld, and A. B. Yehoshua are devoted solely to "secular-existential themes"—toward one sensitive to the marked presence of weighty religious subtexts relevant to urgent ethical challenges in the present. Balaban describes the startling transition, which began in the late 1950s, when

> The previously prevalent feelings of cohesion and fulfillment faded away, bringing about a dissolution of the concomitant solid code of values. The resulting vacuum gave rise to a quest for the purpose and meaning of life. The previous sense of belonging, which these writers had neither experienced as youngsters or read about in the works of their senior colleagues, only heightened and exacerbated their distress. Consequently, the quest for the lost harmony—on a personal as well as on social and metaphysical levels—became a central feature of young Israeli fiction.

> This quest, together with the search for the meaning of life, the attempt to understand "where we came from and where we are going", begot a surge of religious yearning. Such sentiments do not find expression in the enhancement and glorification of immediate reality, but rather in the quest that goes beyond its limited horizon. ("Secularity and Religiosity" 64)

In my view, this paradigm was dynamically expressed through another new trend in which the writer's external focus on the landscapes and cityscapes of settled, social realities began to be enriched by experimenting with the transcendent possibilities of the desert in a quest for a subjectivity unfettered by the claustrophobic norms of the state.

A confession. After my army service, while serving as a desert guide and ranger for the Nature Reserves Authority in the 1980s and toiling in the date plantations of a young kibbutz, I too sought "authenticity." After experiencing the ancient tradition of Bedouin hospitality—*Karwat al Deif* is the most sacred tenet of that society in which one is hosted generously, as long as three days with no questions asked—I was thrilled to realize that I had participated in a social ritual that extends back to Abraham's encounter with three wayfarers who later prove to be emissaries of God. Like most Western interlopers who romanticize the desert spaces of the Middle East in the mode of Lawrence of Arabia (it's a surprisingly enduring paradigm), my conceit was to find personal meaning in the epic desert expanse.[27] It is a place where one receives the clear sense of Jon Levenson's observation that "[g]eography is simply a visible form of theology" (116). Sojourning in the high mountains of southern Sinai, often only with a Bedouin guide for company, I was struck by the ancient Hebraic notion of *Ha-Makom;* this unspoiled terrain was the site of revelation to which I, like the wandering Israelites, anticipated access.[28] For myself and many others, Smadar Lavie's observations of her own early experiences still resonate: "I grew up with the Zionist frontier mythology—making the desert bloom, all the while mourning the eradication of desert spaces, and museumizing Negev Bedouin culture even while expropriating Bedouin land. . . . As a twelve-year-old right after the 1967 war, I was instructed by my teachers, many other Israelis, and the radio to consider the Sinai 'the last frontier'" (*Poetics of Military Occupation* 7). Lavie notes how "oddly enough, aside from establishing several settlements, the Israeli government had decided purposely to leave the South Sinai barely touched, as a safari space, a nostalgic replacement for the lost Negev wilderness perhaps—an escape from the social and spatial crowdedness of a small country" (7–8). With Lavie's probing recollections in mind, I set out to explore the additional paradox of how the desert often excludes and dispossesses in the Hebrew novel, as if to resist the symmetry of Zionist return.[29] In this regard, the political skepticism of the writer is always important to consider. In the chapters that follow, I trace the intimate intersections of place, art, and politics to analyze how writers' feelings of displacement and internal exile are projected onto the spiritual Diaspora of the desert.

Fittingly, unlike the lonely masculine egoistic quests of Oz and Grossman's subjects, this landscape has rather divergent uses in the feminist imagination. Though, for modern women writers, perhaps most famously in the poetry of Emily Dickinson, home has often a sustaining center as well as a site from which to critique the values of the surrounding culture, since the 1990s, as critic Kersten Shands argues, "critical consciousness" has been mapped out "on the run or in the wilderness . . . for those who wish to display a fashionably postcolonial, postmodernist feminist consciousness" (8). After all, for the feminist literary imagination, foremother Eve's disobedience may have led to exile and loss, but being cast out into the wilderness of the world is often represented as a catalyst for alternative modes of perception. Hence, this study begins with Shulamith Hareven's *Thirst: The Desert Trilogy,* where the desert wilderness of Exodus is a movable borderlands forming a meeting point for past and present, a spatio-temporal deconstruction of nation building and an interrogation of home and dwelling in both myth and contemporary politics.[30] Hareven is drawn to the desert as a site that allows for conceiving of the people of Israel as a moral work in progress as well as a space of heterogeneous mingling with others, uncorrupted by the constraints of the nation. For a feminist Israeli writer like Hareven, a gender-critical struggle against canonical interpretations of the original text must invariably lead toward a questioning of the stakes of ancient patriarchy as well as contemporary uses of a unified national identity. Hareven's essays and fiction (both are addressed here) deserve a much greater English-speaking audience for their unprecedented meditation on the dispossession of Others—and for their profound commentary on what she sees as the idolatrous possession of sacred space. For while she may seem to be playfully conjuring the land and myths that shaped the Hebrew people, her faint yet insistent allusions to the seeds of the present struggle between Israelis and Palestinians continually disrupt the novel's ostensible focus.

Next, in Oz's *A Perfect Peace,* a disillusioned character recalls reading "somewhere in Dostoyevsky that if a man wants to stay really honest, he'd better die before he turns forty. From forty on they're all scoundrels." Perhaps it is no accident that the cynical speaker is a kibbutznik, for the remark curiously resembles the fate of the kibbutz movement as a whole at the end of the twentieth century—and hints at the core crisis of the novel which is a young man's desperate trek out into the wilderness where he hopes to recover authenticity and meaning.[31] Oz's novel gains its powerful force and pedagogy as a powerful allegory of a clash between the individual and the collective that today seems as relevant to the present generation as it does to the second generation youth that is its ostensible focus.

Most Israelis were raised in the tradition of youth movement treks and marches in the desert and other unsettled regions of Palestine and Israel. As Oz Almog states in his seminal study *The Sabra,* from Israel's early years of independence, due to "their secrecy, risk, the sense of independence they required, and the small-scale rebelliousness they involved, these marches became, over time, an important element in the tradition of Sabra adventurousness" (181). Such opportunities to display one's courage and bravado further instilled the sense of nativeness and attachment to homeland in the "New Jew's" identity. Hence it is not surprising that Hareven, Oz, and Grossman provide compelling case studies of how contemporary Hebrew writers perceive the Israeli desert, with its sands and stark visual display of erosion, as the site wherein they explore the difference between national loyalty and diasporic dreaming in ways that institutions of the state, even the "family romance" of the kibbutz, cannot afford to sanction. They know that Zionism has had a charged and paradoxical relation with the Middle Eastern desert and its inhabitants. Hence, in their desert narratives, anxieties about the present precarious political situation are juxtaposed with the feelings of eternity and fatalism evoked by the archaic landscape. In part, this anxiety owes to what Rebecca Stein identifies as "the trope of emptiness" which has "a long discursive history" that may be traced to "that most freighted and classic of early Zionist narratives, and indeed of colonial narratives writ large: that of Palestine as 'empty land' (as rehearsed in the work of Herzl, Bialik, Mandelstamm, and others). 'Emptiness,' in this narrative, was the mark of the premodern—the sign of a place outside time and history, waiting, indeed beckoning, for Western intervention and development. The founding of Tel Aviv was enunciated through his story—that of a European city born out of sand, 'an outpost of civilization against barbarism,' in Herzl's troubling language."[32] Altogether, the desert setting enables writers to consider the indeterminacy of stable or enduring subject positions, particularly those identities fabricated by nation and ideology, in spaces that are also indeterminate.

I should pause to explain that the rationale behind the selection of literary works analyzed here owes to the combined factors of thematic comparisons; the prominent position of writers such as Hareven, Oz, and Grossman in Israeli intellectual and cultural life (and the presence of Jabès and Zelitch as important Diaspora voices); and finally the sheer artistry of their literary visions. These aspects, together with a desire to achieve the valuable comparative insights that gender balance often affords, have all played a vital role in my vision for the project. It should be noted as well that all the primary sources considered here are currently available in English translations.

Opposing the hyper-masculinity demanded by traditional Zionist narratives of the nation, the works considered in this study are often saturated with textual traces of powerlessness, dormancy, and a retreat from active forms of agency. For example, in Grossman's novella *Yani on the Mountain,* an ideologically and emotionally paralyzed army officer who "see[s] other people as shifting scenery, and nothing else" (62) is disturbingly entombed in a desolate outpost, a fossilized relic of Israel's youth. Here, the author opposes Israel's potent and lingering myth of the self-sufficient, virile, and productive "Sabra" with a fossilized, immobilized outcast. But in other instances, withdrawal leads to revelatory self-knowledge.

Both Shulamith Hareven and Simone Zelitch provide brilliantly imaginative feminist reconsiderations of the master/slave dialectic of their ancient sources. Similarly, both are interested in Moses' divided (Egyptian/Hebrew) nature as somehow prophetic of Jewish identity's future entanglements between worlds. If Hareven's return to the Bible is mapped against the imperfect social vision and political policies of modern Zionism, the Jewish American novelist's work is a profound return to the nagging questions of sacrifice, illusion vs. reality, and the true meaning of liberation with which the Torah still challenges contemporary readers. Told through an effective blend of lyrical magical realism and terse narrative, *Moses in Sinai* is a powerful investigation of the struggle of idiosyncratic wanderers' struggle to cast off their previous histories and selves to merge with the new nation being imposed on them in the wilderness. Zelitch's prose embellishes on the startlingly psychological ways that Numbers hints at Moses' own divided consciousness and burden as a leader, such as his plea to God: "Do you conceive me . . . a nursing father bearing the suckling child into the land?" (Num. 11:12–13). Readers familiar with the postmodern novelist Paul Auster's cautionary imperative that "the farther I go the more certain I am that the path towards my object does not exist. . . . Just because you wander in the desert, it does not mean there is a promised land" (*Invention* 32) will appreciate Zelitch's innovative attempt to probe deep under the essential myth of Jewish liberation, revealing its tyrannical potential, without surrendering its positive effects. *Moses in Sinai*'s exploration of nomadic ethics, as viewed through the subversive actions of Exodus's heretics and subversives, offers a deeply stirring counternarrative of liberated consciousness.

In this fourth chapter I also speculate on the aphoristic language of Edmond Jabès as one that reveals how, as a striking metaphor for writing, the desert is the most central trope of thought itself, the continuum that links one work to the next: "The unsayable settles us in those desert regions which are the home of dead languages" (*Book of Questions: Yael Elya Aely El, or the Last Book* 77). This discursive paradigm, in which presence and absence invade one another, did not seem to have entered his consciousness before his forced departure from Egypt after the Suez Canal crisis in 1957, which he acknowledges both as a personal rupture and a mere blip on the screen of Judaism's historical displacements. I see in the cultural works of Jabès a celebration of a unique spatial identity that is paradoxically also an "uprooting," in Levinas's sense of recoiling from the violence of nationalism and fetishization of place and origins: "Every word is an uprooting. Every rational institution is uprooting. The constitution of a true society is uprooting." This would mean an *outward* movement, whether from the egoistic self or from the insular society. Sharing common ground with the early-twentieth-century theologian Franz Rosenzweig's sense of exile as a desired state (in terms of both exterior ethics and interior consciousness), Jabès presents the desert to us as the place that permanently unmakes the kind of rootedness and complacency that Rosenzweig saw as the fatal seduction of the West.

My final chapter reaches well beyond the scope of these literary worlds, offering an assessment of the desert experience as a creative catalyst for new cultural forms of urban Jewish expression in the Diaspora, taking heed of such highly popular and influential phenomenon as Bruce Feiler's recent best-selling desert and biblical explorations. Here I also address cultural and political dimensions of the role of the desert in the lives of Israelis. In this regard, it bears mention that the desert is one of the few landscapes in the contemporary Middle East (save for a few rusting wrecks trapped in the Sinai sands) not visibly scarred by wars and displacements. Undoubtedly for that reason, the desert serves Israel's beleaguered tourism industry in strategic ways, wistfully selling the idealized landscape as if to create the illusion that in spite of the devastating toll of violence inflicted by Israelis and Palestinians on one another, innocence somehow remains. Hence, postcards from the "Holy Land" still display, as they did a century ago, images of palm trees, camels, Bedouin, perhaps an oasis, conjuring up the desert pastoral which is so central to Israel's national imagination, even as its potential as a contemporary site for Israeli life remains unfulfilled.

Perhaps it is as W. J. T. Mitchell argues: the "blinders" that "idealize the landscape" serve not only to artfully "erase all signs of violence" but nostalgically gesture to a distant moment "when the Israelites were merely another group of nomads among the Semitic tribes of Abraham" (27). The poetics of envisioning the landscape in an Israel under siege and embattled by ideological confusion suggests that there are political uses for integrating the desert landscape into the national story: "to make the desert bloom"—literally as well as metaphorically. As we will see, the desert lures writers into unpredictably mixing locales of past, present, and future, confounding the distance of geographic space. For the literary response to the desert provides a remarkable gateway into both the writer's geopolitical views as well as a more intimate perception of the deepest recesses of the self.

2 *Justice and the Old/New Jewish Nation*

> Like the moon, like death . . . the distant past is one of those things that can enrich ignorance. It is infinitely malleable and agreeable, far more obliging than the future and far less demanding of our efforts. It is the famous season favored by all mythologies. Who has not, at one point or another, played with thoughts of his ancestors, with the prehistory of his flesh and blood?
>
> —Jorge Luis Borges

> And then there were the Bedouin, whom the various hiking guides introduced to us both as noble savages living in a state of nature, and as remnants of our dignified Biblical forefathers who gained their freedom from Pharaoh's slavery and coalesced as a people in this very desert. I wanted to come back [to the Sinai] after my compulsory army service, despite the fact that I wholeheartedly opposed the transformation of Israel into the Israeli "Empire."
>
> —Smadar Lavie

Traversing Symbolic Geographies: "God as Bedouin Leader"

The desert experience of the ancient Hebrews was a temporal and spatial revolution that is still a catalyst for the modern literary imagination. Let us begin with the fact that the Hebrew scriptures, in their obdurate this-worldly orientation, do not lament the fall which permanently severs human beings from Eden. The exile from Eden ensures that the static harmony God provided for the earth-beings in the garden is permanently disrupted, as history replaces the graceful repetition of Adam and Eve's communion with the rhythms of nature. Unlike the aspirations that underwrote the European conquest of the New World, the biblical imagination does not foresee the return of history to a state of edenic grace. As William A. McClung astutely observes of the intrinsic progression of the Five Books of Moses: "The problems of transposing the model of Eden to the other end of history are many, and they turn principally upon memory; Eden cannot be new, and to regain it as it was is only to acknowledge the failure of history—the stasis that lies at the end of the progression must be paradise but not the same Paradise from which knowledge of good and evil was excluded" (18).

The desert is the antithesis of Eden's easeful abundance. And yet the Hebrew Bible does sanction a return of sorts, for its landscape of privation also affords a second chance unrivaled by any other biblical setting. The wilderness's meaning inherently resides in its return to sheer potentiality, a haven for the reinvigoration and reinvention of human community. The liberated Hebrews' startling experience in the landscape of sun, stone, and silence does not repeat edenic innocence or ease but rather is a momentum toward unprecedented consciousness—a new beginning promising radical transformation. It is revealing that at the very beginning of Exodus, Moses flees the chains of community (and his own act of murderous violence) into the remote desert expanses (which prove strangely hospitable) only to be summoned by a deity who sends him back to the folds of community.

In his poetic commentary on this unprecedented paradigm of leadership, the biblical scholar Gordon Brubacher comments that "taking the Israelites safely across this desert provided an extreme example of divine care and power, an image of God as Bedouin leader—the good shepherd of his people" (339). And as Bruce Feiler observes of the social dynamics of the individual Israelite's desert adventure, "it's that tension—between being with others and being alone, between reaching salvation within a sometimes unruly community and seeking enlightenment on your own—that lies at the heart of the story of Mount Sinai" (272). For both the individual and the collective, the desert of Exodus bestows a respite from history and the constraints of the static hegemony of empire, the vast stratified civilization that dwells under the shadows of the pyramids. This is the rejoinder to the divine sentence of mortality which fell on the naked couple in the garden. For most readers of the Bible, as especially those who walk its landscape invariably come to recognize, the desert is essential to understanding the world of all the Israelite patriarchs. Though sojourning in Ur, Shechem, Beersheba, and other settled locales, they maintained a culture closely aligned to the rhythms of pastoral nomadism. Indeed, the desert is the central condition of the lives of all the patriarchs (save for Joseph in Egypt), so much so that, as Brubacher relates "as a whole, this cycle created a symbolic salvation geography in which the desert fringes . . . rather than the great civilizations of the day (Mesopotamia and Egypt) functioned as the chosen place for training the nascent chosen people" (340). But besides playing the essential determining role in the destiny of the collective, the desert is often regarded as a compassionate space providing succor for the beleaguered and oppressed individual, as in the flight of Hagar from Sarai (Gen. 16:7), Moses from pharaoh (Exod. 2:15–3:31), David from Saul (1 Sam. 23–26) and later from Absalom (2 Sam. 15–17), and Elijah from Jezebel (1 Kings 19:1–4). These leave redolent traces in the modern Hebrew writer's imagination that we begin to explore in this chapter. Nevertheless, from the moment that Abraham departs from Ur, the Torah (Five Books of Moses) rapidly advances the story of how its people overcome the condition of homelessness—with the exception of the liminality of the forty years of wandering.

Though these years conform to the biblical paradigm of anticipating a new home (a variation on the promise made earlier to Abraham and later to David), Exodus contains too many moments of apostasy and backsliding to conform to the usual scheme of linear fulfillment. At such times, the desert plays a crucial political, cultural, and religious role. At Sinai, Moses receives the gift of the Law, with a special emphasis on a new way of observing time: the Shabbat is to be repetitively observed so that the people themselves will experience something of God's rest from creating the world as well as a permanent commemoration of their liberation by God's will. Moreover, the people receive the Sabbath in the sparsest of the earth's environments and indeed it seems as if no other landscape would be as conducive to truly becoming acquainted with the riches of undisturbed contemplation, to habituating the people to observing a day removed from mundane reality.

It is as though the sojourn of forty years, embodying cycles of wandering and settlement, returns the Israelites to the foundational desert wisdom of their forefathers, but only so they may eventually exceed the nascent ethics of that culture. The inevitability of the postlapsarian journey from garden to city is interrupted by the desert experience that follows deliverance from Egypt, which in turn ushers in a generation of quietude and communion. But if the weekly observance of Shabbat is itself a window onto eternity, as Abraham Joshua Heschel's *The Sabbath* suggests, an ascent out of the limits of temporality that promises to expand human consciousness in its rigorous observance, the nonlinear desert wanderings, which at times embody God's displeasure with his people, are poetically open-ended. As if these are experienced as an enduring Shabbat, a window out of conventional temporality. The people are held in limbo until God deems them matured for a return to the land and history. Perhaps Heschel's own poetic reading of Judaism's transcendence of space and materiality throughout *The Sabbath* owes its inspiration to the nomadic movement of the Mishkan (tabernacle or ark) itself.

It is particularly important to understand why the partnership established between God and the human community in the desert was immediately based on transcending fixed notions of material space. In this regard, the biblical scholar Harry Berger's reading of the wandering Israelites' peculiar relation to the sacred proves illuminating: "the traveling ark is a metaphoric embodiment, which is to say, it is portable. In the metaphoricity, the portability, of the text lies the seed of the one community that can gather around the holy of holies at its center, the circumference of which is nowhere, and that can bear it and birth it through time: the hermeneutical community, the community of textual desire" (136). Exodus recalls that whenever the hovering cloud came to rest, the Israelites understood that their journey too should pause: "The cloud covered the Tent of Meeting. When the cloud was raised up from the Tabernacle, the Children of Israel would embark on all their journeys. If the cloud did not rise up, they would not embark until the day it rose" (Exod. 40:34–37). The Mishkan itself was tirelessly disassembled and transported on each occasion, as if only by such repetitions would the people apprehend that "holiness" resides in the movement forward, the act, rather than material space. As Bonnie Roche observes, it was here in the indeterminate space between "dwelling" and "wandering" that the nascent community first learned what would develop as Judaism's chief metaphor of space and time:

> The "arrest" along a nomadic journey, was determined by a force outside the people. The Mishkan took on a life separate from human activity, a life choreographed by God, a pause, "so that he may dwell among them." What a wonderful theatrical device this was. Individuals in the infancy of forming a community are told when to stop, to organize in a collective effort that which they developed a growing passion to do, and which they repeated over and over, each time as for the first time. . . . By this living rhythm of anticipation, experience and memory, individual bonds grew to become a collective, made increasingly more real on the human plane and more palpable on the spiritual plane. (344)

Similarly, Roche concludes that within this ancient transformative mode of worship, "[h]orizontal time became vertical time. And vertical time became a people that knew no separation between the physical and sacred dimensions. The Mishkan was a metaphor for moving from motion to stillness, from measured time to timelessness, from the six days of the week to the Sabbath" (Roche 344). Finally, Diane T. Edwards finds that in this revolution in temporality, "the narrative pattern is henceforth firmly established as recuperative: work, slavery, and exile followed by deliverance, freedom, and a Sabbath rest. Delivery out of Egypt is equated with God's rest after the work of creation" (105). Of course Exodus is linked to Genesis in at least one other compelling way, for with the death of Jacob, his sons already worry about whether they will be one day oppressed by the nation that has offered them temporary shelter.

Joseph, whose deliverance from an Egyptian prison eventually provides redemption for the Israelites afflicted by famine, reassures his brothers. But their worry lingers, anticipating the dark reality that greets the reader in the opening chapter of the Book of Exodus. Here divine speech establishes the ephemeral nature of Moses' direct apprehension of God, shifting the spatial emphasis from mystical inwardness to external reality almost immediately. God's terms are precise: "Do not come closer. Remove your sandals from your feet, for the place on which you stand is holy ground" (Exod. 3:5). Curiously, the Hebrew phrase delineates the soon-to-be forgotten desert site as *admat kodesh,* "land of holiness." The *transitory* nature of the sacred encounter is essential to properly prepare Moses and the people for the long and slippery struggle to transcend idolatry's conventional fetishization of space. As Jean-Christophe Attias and Esther Benbassa evocatively state, of both Moses' encounter with the burning bush and the people's experience at Sinai:

> It is the visible presence of God in this corner of the desert that transforms it into a holy site. The sacralization is ephemeral, though, and lasts only during this presence, and in fact the place is never even mentioned in what follows, either as a holy site or a fortiori as a site of pilgrimage. . . . As a general rule, if the desert appears as the privileged site of the irruption of the sacred, the sacredness that this irruption confers on it is both localized and temporary. *Like the people who cross it, the holy site in the desert is an essentially nomadic site.* (18, italics mine)

The Jewish culture reborn of this experience must be seen as the joint product of nature—and divine nurture. Hence, the beckoning homeland portrayed in Exodus has to be evaded for four decades of circuitous wandering because, like other host lands, it is not empty but filled with social codes, values, gods, and other cultural norms that would have absorbed the people that were creating its own nascent story.

Attias and Benbassa further argue that the biblical desert serves as "liminary space, an in-between territory . . . simultaneously a site both of infidelity and revolt (the Golden Calf) and of revelation and submission, where Israel, by receiving the Law, is constituted as a free people and a holy nation" (18). Such a paradigm suggests that the desert is located between empty nostalgia and the migrant's indiscriminate worship of the symbols and institutions of the new land. As Judaism evolved, the religious/agricultural festivals that commemorate dwelling in the land are counterpart to Passover and Sukkot. Zali Gurevitch points out that these latter "commemorate the desert and stress wandering rather than settlement. The ritual text of Passover tells the story of deliverance in which the leaving of Egypt and the crossing of the desert are clearly depicted as formative events in the birth of the people, not the land of Canaan" (213). Even though Sukkot is an agricultural ritual ostensibly linked to "place," its proper observance requires that the Jewish family "reside for a week outside the permanent home in a temporary hut (*sukkha*) with a roof made of branches . . . to symbolize the possibility of leaving" (213). In his analysis of the cultural poetics of the *Sukkah* rite, Alexandre Safran concludes that "it is not enough to build an arbor and spend a day in it, for example, thus symbolically reproducing the ancestors' rough type of dwelling in the wilderness . . . the Jew is not to be satisfied with commemorating the historical events or reproducing the topographical conditions of the past; he must experience, effectively and existentially what his forbears experienced" (184). I will return to develop this point later in this chapter, but for now it suffices to note that, in the contemporary Jewish state, this imposed vulnerability, antithetical to possession and rootedness, has interesting implications for the literary uses of the desert experience. Without the writer's directly invoking Europe or other sites of Jewish exile, the Diaspora's presence haunts such works as a monumentally destabilizing signifier.

Longing and Arrival in Exodus and the Zionist Reclamation of Space

Among contemporary Israeli writers, scripture is not explored simply for its own sake but also for its continuing impact. David Jacobson insists that the Bible's ancient stories must be retold "to emphasize possible connections between what went wrong with political sovereignty in biblical times and what [is] going wrong in modern times" (154). It seems that every day one awakes to the news of another group's (Jewish, Muslim, Christianity) collective suffering over tensions rising out of the territorial possession of the "Holy" land. Because the impact of biblical materials on the contemporary condition of *all* of our lives has been made manifestly evident by the global repercussions of the conflict between Israel and Palestine, readers everywhere may be more interested than at any previous time in examining how such writers, working through a lens of constructive anachronism, are self-conscious about inhabiting a strange confluence of past and future, not to mention striking spatial congruencies. In this regard, the late Israeli novelist Shulamith Hareven's (1930–2003) *Thirst: The Desert Trilogy* (*Tsima'on: Shlishyat hamidbar* in Hebrew) offers readers an unprecedented exploration of ancient and contemporary understandings of justice and human liberation.

Though ostensibly set in the time of the Books of Exodus, Joshua, and Judges, the resolutely spare language of Hareven's three novellas offers a teasingly "timeless" perspective on the Middle East's history of conquests and displacements. Encompassing "The Miracle Hater," "Prophet," and "After Childhood," *The Desert Trilogy* interrogates the archetypal desert experience as a story of nationalism and authority—as well as an encounter with the sacred—in ways that creatively trouble the present moment wherever (ideologically or geographically) the reader might be located. Yet there is a certain inevitable logic to this retelling. As Israeli sociologist Oz Almog observes of the Zionist pedagogy with which Hareven's generation was raised: "Educators used the Bible as a guidebook and described the landscape to their pupils in the context of Biblical stories. The landscape was mythologized and turned into a stage for a national historical pageant before the eyes of enchanted pupils, bringing home to them the richness of the nation's past that endowed . . . its spirit on the present" (Almog 168). At the same time, the reborn Hebrew language would invariably carry with it the burden of ingrained palimpsests and archetypes of earlier conquests and victims.[1]

Taken as a whole, *The Desert Trilogy* offers an exciting gateway into the role of the biblical narrative in the immediate context of the troubling ideological debates that fragment contemporary Israeli life. In Hareven's narrative of transience, the comforts of home, unity, and dwelling are tested against the metaphoric spaciousness of a desert landscape with an endless horizon. Each of its three parts places solitary protagonists against the troubled backgrounds of violent sacrificial subtexts. Hareven writes out of an acute awareness that when it comes to imagining the austere wilderness, the Hebrew Bible's fraught relation to its disorderly wilderness offers the modern Israeli imagination a complex spatial poetics. In this regard, it is worth paying heed to Pardes's sense of the biblical desert as an indeterminate space of fissured identities, radical skepticism, and questioning of official narratives of the nation. Unlike their anointed patriarch, the desert wanderers of Exodus are "confused and fearful about homecoming," unsure about the binds of collective identity: "The wandering Israelites are skeptical about the very premise that Canaan is their homeland. The only land they wish to return to is Egypt. But they end up in the wilderness, between Egypt and the Promised Land, returning to neither" (Pardes 104). It is not that wilderness skepticism is sanctified or well-rewarded by God. The desert generation, doubting God, is "doomed to remain forever in the arid land of the desert" (Pardes 50). At times it seems as if both their God and the desert gleefully collaborate in an inexplicable plot to destroy them. The people's complaints earn them only the threat of utter annihilation and oblivion:

> Say to them, "As I live," says the Lord, "I will do to you just as you have urged Me. In this very wilderness shall your carcasses drop. Of all of you who were recorded in your various lists from the age of twenty years up, you who have muttered against Me, not one shall enter the land in which I swore to settle you—save Caleb son of Jephunneh and Joshua son of Nun. Your children who, you said, would be carried off—these will I allow to enter; they shall know the land that you have rejected. But your carcasses shall drop in this wilderness, while your children roam the wilderness for forty years, suffering for your faithlessness, until the last of your carcasses is down in the wilderness." (Num. 14:28–33)

Here is where, as Hareven's retelling itself underscores, the triumphal God of monotheism seems just as likely to exterminate the exiles as any other tyrant. In Exodus, Deuteronomy, and Numbers, the exilic sojourn in the desert is filled with death and tribal disorder but also blesses the people with God's undivided interest in their growth as a nation. Biblical scholar Athalya Brenner has noted that these books offer numerous variations on the related themes of liminality and "passage":

> A passage from loosely-defined population into ethnicity; a passage from a "religion of the fathers" . . . to a communal covenant bound, legally grounded, exclusive monotheism; a passage from the axis of space, from one country (Egypt) to the threshold of another (Canaan); a passage through the axis of time, represented by the typological forty years in the (mythic) wilderness; a passage from disorganization and confusion into institutionalization. (*A Feminist Companion to Exodus-Deuteronomy* 11)

Embracing this liminal space offered Hareven a way to write outside the Zionist metaplot of territorial redemption, even to mount a spirited critique of the nation—indeed of the very idea of "nation"—through two temporal continuities.

As if imagining each of Brenner's phases of flux and transformation, Hareven provides a refreshing return to the earliest Hebrew literary relation to the wilderness by reading "desert" as a geographic disjunction that urgently disrupts the clear continuity of national narratives in the Middle East even today, with its tensions between the unsettled and the settled, occupiers and occupied. Rather than repeat the conventional triumphalism of the pre-eminent biblical story of liberation, Hareven's bold intertexuality (containing traces of Exodus, Numbers, Deuteronomy, Joshua, Judges) reveals the diminished ethics of contemporary nationalist politics. In many ways, *Desert Trilogy* is the pre-eminent example of how employing a desert aesthetic allows a shift from nation building, Zionist heroics, and the collective cause to an exploration of alternative, inclusive, and accommodating visions. Throughout, the desert is strategically deployed to suggest that neither Palestinian nor Israeli can truly be "at home" in the land so long as racialized exclusions, violence, and dispossessions remain official policy. An eloquent humanist of the Israeli Left, Hareven casts her narratives on the side of the universal victims of conquest and war by invoking a new reading of one people's myth. As a cosmopolitan intellectual, her thought reveals a certain debt to the nature of the exilic intellectual delineated in the work of the German theorist Theodor Adorno, who, in *Minima Moralia,* asserts that "[d]welling, in the proper sense, is now impossible. The traditional residences we grew up in have grown intolerable. . . . The house is past . . . it is part of morality not to be at home in one's home" (87).

Alongside her critique of Zionism, Hareven presents a distinctly feminist intervention that provides a narrative focus that unmasks the women's and children's stories that are obscured by the patriarchal texts. Yael Feldman aptly portrays them as "these lean, poetic miniatures . . . nothing less than counterhistories" that present the biblical story of wandering "from a totally unfamiliar angle" (160).[2] Each of the three stories, revisiting some of the most charged dimensions of Hebraic myth, delineates different dimensions of a polytheistic desert tribe's struggle from murderous practices toward something resembling civilization. In Hareven's cultural imagination, this is by no means a triumphal or tidy evolution. Controversial aspects of nascent patriarchal leadership, the dangers of the core myths of monotheism, as well as treatment of cultural difference (just what to do with the Other?), are all part of Hareven's interpretive framework.

As numerous obituaries in the Hebrew and international press bore witness, Hareven was uniquely situated to address traumatic aspects of displacement. Though she rarely drew directly from her life experience as Holocaust survivor (she seemed reluctant to invoke her past as special status), it certainly bears noting her origins and subsequent political activities. Born in Poland, she arrived in Palestine in 1940 and remained in Jerusalem for the rest of her life. After serving in the Hagana underground, she was a combat medic in the 1947–48 siege of Jerusalem. During the fifties, Hareven worked with refugees from Arab countries in Israel's transit camps. The first female member elected to the Hebrew Language Academy, she seemed prouder of her longtime membership in the Israeli Peace Now movement. The French magazine *L'Express* included Hareven on its list of 100 women "who move the world." A passionate critic of Israel's military rule over the territories, the late novelist explored the lives and suffering of Palestinians during the first Intifada, and in her late career she remained committed to deconstructing the internal religious and ethnic divisions in Israeli life.

Accordingly, her trilogy, as it evolves, participates in the ancient Jewish midrashic tradition of retelling the sacred text in ways that creatively accommodate the shifting paradigms and perceptions of the present. In her rendering, the timeless desert becomes a fitting metaphor for human life, which is itself a hard land of exile. Hareven's richly meditative exploration of the dark and lingering power of ancient myth and language derives directly from her response to the urgent demands of the present. In the modern land of Israel/Palestine, the Hebrew Bible, much like the Qur'an, has been invoked not only to justify acts of murderous violence and dispossession, but also the dream of accommodation. Little wonder that when alluding to Abraham, the father of Middle Eastern monotheism and Jewish wandering as well as the pre-eminent refuser of idolatry, Sidra DeKoven Ezrahi, one of modern Hebrew literature's most innovative critics, cautions that "we dare not invest any place with absolute meaning or treat others' idols as targets for obliteration. Turning our iconoclastic hammers toward our own idols, as legend represents Abraham doing in his father's shop, may be the beginning of religious reformation; turning it towards the gods of others is the beginning of genocide" ("Sacred Space," 19–20). Hareven achieves that profoundly important reconsideration of the totems of myth and history with irony, compassion, and humor without resorting to arid didacticism.

Hareven's insistence that the sacred text serve the urgent moral dilemmas of the present offers a bold response to the material as well as psychological traumas of a reborn Jewish nation. In this regard, Israeli readers alert to the author's shifting temporal and cultural focus could appreciate the sensitive nuances of the full title, *Thirst: A Desert Trilogy*—with its stark emphasis on the deprivation of the Jews' wilderness experience—insinuating that Hareven's ancient Hebrews/Israelis/Palestinians live in a constant state of both literal and existential thirst. A disturbing exploration of the ever-elusive, insatiable conundrum of achieving "justice," *Desert Trilogy* is one of the most provocative examples of the modern Hebrew literary community's response to the troubling weight of the Bible as a living part of both the individual psyche and a collective sense of national belonging. As both Brenner and Pardes remind us, the desert of Exodus is often envisioned as the site of the Jewish people's birth as a national collective. Hareven's novel, however, considers that fraught origin as a sentient landscape that wisely "teaches" a refusal of stasis, a strange realm shaping Judaism's future as a constant unfolding and adaptation to the new.

Examining her culture's conscience in "God Is the Other Language," an essay of the 1990s, Hareven asserts that "[t]here are people in this generation who have decided for some reason that the values of the Book of Joshua take precedence over the morals of Isaiah and the prophets; this is their order of primacy in keeping the commandments, and it is far from mine. In other words, their God is far from my God. According to their model, God is cruel and human beings even crueler. According to my model, very often human beings are better and have a greater sense of justice than does the God that people fashioned for themselves in ancient times" (*Vocabulary of Peace* 59). For Hareven, the Book of Joshua's grisly slaughters and conquests form the cynical palimpsest for present-day violence and the problem of the ever-threatening Other. Interestingly, Yerach Gover tells of an investigation by a social psychologist who determined that Israeli youth were so impacted by "uncritical" teachings of the Bible that they came to regard Joshua's destruction of the peoples of Jericho and Makkedah as "rationales" for the contemporary Israeli army to act vengefully against Arab villages in the aftermath of war.[3] Perhaps this is why Hareven is drawn to the open potentiality of the desert—as a space ethically charged by the human imagination—ideal for meditating on the current plight of her society and indeed all "tribal" aspirations.

Hardly comfortable with the Bible's official version of events with its strong paternal images, Hareven's trilogy offers an elaborate counterhistory that nevertheless resonates with the sacred text's own representation of the friction between faith and doubt—an existential tale of the wilderness gesturing beyond temporal confines toward suppressed stories and repressed identities. Thus, far from adapting the reductive tendency of some feminist scholars—which first began to emerge in the late 1980s—to condemn the Hebrew Bible for everything from the invention of genocide to the "slaying of the goddess," Hareven proves at times a surprisingly conservative redactor, underscoring the universality of the text, especially insofar as the latter implicates injustices in the present.[4] For here, in a highly suggestive passage from the introductory paragraphs of "The Miracle Hater," the situation presented is an unavoidable challenge to the Israeli reader:

> The Hebrews had multiplied greatly and not all of them could find work in and around Raamses. They descended on the province, innumerable flocks of men and women who stood long hours in the sun, or sat in the shade of the baked-brick walls, looking for work. The Egyptians would come, take the five or ten of them that they needed, and drive the rest off. For a while they would vanish; yet soon they were back again, mute in the fly-ridden sunlight, waiting, more of them every year. There was no getting rid of them. (*Desert Trilogy* 7)

In this passage, Hareven's ancient Hebrews rapidly acquire a certain resemblance to the masses of the Palestinian day-workers who, in the pre-Intifada days of the trilogy's composition, would cross the Green Line daily in search of meager employment opportunities in Israel's building trades, constructing its modern pyramids in place of the Jewish labor that was no longer attracted to literally building the state. Invoking the archaic conflict over Canaan between colonizers from the desert and the colonized, Hareven reveals a pattern of disruption that hasn't changed over the centuries. Her historical perspective suggests that Zionism, whatever its moral strength and historical necessity, must be viewed as the blind reiteration of this conflict.

In her account of the functions of biblical allusions in modern Hebrew literature, Smadar Shiffman argues for a hierarchy of intertextual achievement worthy of consideration here. Least of all in her rankings is the presence of biblical allusion in a way that grants "depth" but somehow diminishes the contemporary scene of the novel, "as if we and our deeds can hardly be of much significance when compared with our forefathers." Shiffman's next level of achievement identifies instances where the allusion not only "grants the novel depth and enriches it [but also] may shed a new or unexpected light upon the biblical origin." Finally, Shiffman extols those narratives in which "the biblical story could be read both as the original myth . . . and as a quite mundane human story, the regaining of which is not especially tempting" (86). Hareven provides us with a rich exemplar of this model. In *Thirst: The Desert Trilogy* she illuminates the alluding narrative, allowing this doubling to expose our own contradictory responses, whether as Israelis or others, to the pressing exiles and homelands, totalitarian deities and false prophets, which form the interwoven strata of the ancient past and our grim contemporary reality.

Hareven long perceived her culture's reliance on the reassuring category of eternal victimhood as profoundly inhibiting when it comes to cultivating empathy for Others. If one is "the sole and eternal victim," one invariably inhibits one's children from seeing "anyone who is not me" (*Vocabulary of Peace* 151). This perspective would explain her intentional ambivalence in the critical early passage of "The Miracle Hater" cited earlier. Inevitably, Hareven inhabits the unenviable position of the modern Hebrew writer who, as Eliezer Schweid contends, necessarily possesses "a double identity: identification with the Zionist realization and identification with its victims. The realization of Zionism was the hope, the salvation . . . the field of activity and creativity and self-realization. At the same time it was the source of injustice to the defeated-undefeated enemy, which continued to confront it" (39). The rift between divine law, the law of nature, the law of the state, and the law of the individual (conscience) has of course served as an enduring provocation in world literature since at least the moment that Sophocles' *Antigone* first erupted on stage. Certainly the strain between law and justice has been a major modernist theme in Jewish literature, building on the foundations of Abraham's arguments with a wrathful God in Genesis: one thinks immediately of Franz Kafka's "The Penal Colony" and *The Trial* as well as recent works such as Philip Roth's provocative "American Trilogy." And with increasing emphasis, Israeli fiction (arguably more than any other recent national literature) has evolved as a corpus focused on the plight of the individual, caught between a dream of justice and the often draconian consequences of state law. For Hareven, even the triumph of Mosaic law over persecution is liable to succumb to a tyrannical dictatorship. Therefore, her feminist retelling of scripture affirms its universal dimensions of human liberation while, at the same time, "the law" itself is unsparingly depicted as a rigid bureaucratic system, insensitive, arbitrary, often engendering injustice. The individual's conscience is trampled and ground to bits in the hands of external justice.

Throughout Hareven's three stories, the hapless individual gets into terrible trouble in the name of an established system's rules, power, and authority. In this regard her readers are always confronted with something even more universal and enduring than a veiled allegory of the contemporary Middle East would otherwise afford. Attentive to this far-reaching dimension of Hareven's vision, Feldman declares that "the damaging potential of myth had preoccupied Hareven" for many years (165). Indeed, the late novelist wrote as if set on unraveling the Torah's own repressed unconscious. Moreover, if the *Trilogy* sets forth a rewriting of the Bible, it must therefore critique some of the most central myths upon which Western culture, with all its attendant forms of cruelty and insanity, is founded. As Feldman emphasizes, readers should be aware that a short time following the appearance of "After Childhood," the conclusion to the trilogy, Hareven published an innovative critique of Freudian therapy, charging that Freud ignored a crucial patriarchal myth at the core of both culture and the individual's psyche (Feldman 175). This of course is the *akedah,* the Hebrew term for the near-sacrifice (and in some rabbinical sources even murder) of Isaac by Abraham.[5] Feldman refers to this as one of the central myths that "repeatedly preoccupied Hareven in her essays" (171). Considering such a forceful conviction that this is the fatal repetition of Western culture that extends into our own uncertain times, it does not seem a stretch to read Hareven's trilogy in the spirit of a challenge to that pernicious presence.[6] In his powerful investigation of the return to myth in literary modernism, William Johnsen considers such attempts nothing less than "an archeological dis-covery of the roots of all human societies in violent sacrifice" (quoted in Cousineau 16). Correspondingly, a key mode of intervention Hareven's own narratives share operates as a rigorous interrogation of the insidious ways that righteous myths that rationalize violence serve contemporary political realities. In this sense, Hareven is a "traditional" modern Hebrew writer, for the metaphor of the *akedah* is a prominent feature of secularist Israeli literary culture. Indeed, Ruth Kartun-Blum claims that this motif "remains indisputably the most prominent and most powerful biblical intertext of modern Hebrew literature" (20). Each generation of twentieth-century Hebrew writers has told it anew. For instance, we have the Mandate-era poet Zelda (1914–1984), whose work appeals to messianic, nationalist, and liberal secular audiences alike, darkly juxtaposing the biblical nomad with her memories of a familial patriarch in "With My Grandfather": "Like our father Abraham / who counted stars at night / who called out to his Creator / from the furnace. / who bound his own son / on the altar— / so was my grandfather" (Schwartz 230). The poet Haim Gouri (b. 1923), another foundation figure in the early years of Israeli poetry, penned a lyric "Isaac" (1960) describing Abraham's modern descendants as individuals "born with a slaughterer's knife in their heart."[7] And Aryeh Ben-Gurion, editor of a recent collection of poetry and essays on the binding of Isaac, writes, "Our soul has been wearied by all those who have been killed."[8] As a whole, Hareven's work underscores that this inherent violence is the most promising—and threatening—feature of all three monotheistic religions: the father sacrificing his son (which of course includes the murder of Jesus by *his* father, God).[9]

In "The Miracle Hater," the first story of the series, we encounter the events of Exodus from the distant vantage of Eshkhar, a marginal shepherd who prefers the farthest outskirts of the wandering Israelites because of a fixed distrust of prophets and elders. Joining him, the reader meanders among the camps of the lesser families, suffering women, disconsolate worshippers of lost gods in the form of molten idols, and a variety of other transgressors. In Hareven's retelling, their story (the unofficial one) is central; the biblical focus on the collective details of "frustration and death, thirst and hunger" (Pardes 57) is shifted to accommodate the individual's direct experience of the consequences of nation building. It takes a while to get used to the fact that "The Miracle Hater" offers a rather carnivalesque view of the Exodus, especially of Moses and the inner circle of elders, from the eyes of the skeptical shepherd. Readers anticipating a loftier approach to nation building and Moses' leadership will be surprised. As a leader of the lowest classes of wanderers, Eshkhar is a socially diminished, unhappy version of Moses (the latter is barely visible in this narrative). He even shares Moses' concern with justice. But here is the pivotal difference that Feldman observes: "Like Moses, Eshkhar is motivated by a quest for justice, except that in his case it is individual rather than national" (161).

Believing the woman he was destined to marry has been taken from him unjustly, Eshkhar beseeches Joshua to overrule the calculating logic of arranged marriages and bride-prices.[10] But he is dismissed by the haughty leader, who remarks, "We work miracles. Justice is not our concern" (23). And that stands as a succinct enough summary of the novel's own concerns. For apparently, the newly established code of abstract law is not equipped to take care of the existential fate of the alienated individual. So, not unlike a disaffected Jew of modernity, Eshkhar's radically alienated wanderings take him "far" from the miraculous pillars of smoke and fire (negatively echoed and bitterly parodied as "from God there came no accounting, neither by day, nor by night, when the huge stars hung in their orbits overhead" [52]). Wandering in solitude, his self-emancipation is slyly set against both the collective emancipatory rhetoric and the strangely prolonged epic of Exodus, Numbers, and Deuteronomy: "he knew things that they did not: that the desert was inhabited, that it had limits, that it could be crossed from end to end in a matter of weeks. The deception of miracles was keeping them purblind and lost" (51). Thinking about Eshkhar, it helps to remember that in the Jewish scriptures, the desert is a place of severe deprivation, but also a landscape of flux producing radical clarity and revelation. It is a formless but sublime expanse wherein the bold human imagination first conceives of divine intelligence, a revolutionary conception of a bodiless God that is without form, as this passage dating to the late seventh century B.C.E. asserts: "The Lord spoke to you out of the fire; you heard the sound of words but perceived no shape—nothing but a voice. . . . Take care, then, not to forget the covenant that the Lord your God concluded with you and not to make for yourselves a sculptured image in any likeness, against which the Lord your God has enjoined you. For the Lord your God is a consuming fire, an impassioned God" (Deut. 4:12–24). In the penetratingly poetic language that has challenged the reach of centuries of Jewish imagination, the writer of Deuteronomy seems to proclaim that the unknowable is the realization of what can be. For Hareven too, the desert is a site critical to perception, distance, and imaginative change. The novelist's skepticism toward the viability of the nation-state simultaneously embraces the desert as a place where the lack of static demarcation engenders exciting readjustments and new interpretations of reality. To put it simply, her desert is where individual consciousness emerges.[11]

At times, Hareven's focus on her ancient characters is complicated by her sense of the tragic dimensions of Jewish wandering in ensuing centuries. Throughout *Desert Trilogy,* the specter of contingency and the acute vulnerability of human communities are underscored, particularly when urban space threatens to crumble into desert space. In her long unsparing view of human history, the present's complacent urban dwellers are the future's humiliated refugees: "The whole city became one great hunger of goats. . . . Soon the whole city will be a desert, cried the women. Soon it will be a wilderness. Come see the mighty citadel of Gibeon turn into a land of jackals" (77). The fated dissolution of a people in the maw of a surrounding wilderness is a tangible threat. Eventually, adding to Eshkhar's own doubling of Moses, the shepherd and his fellows form what Feldman insightfully identifies as a parallel universe on the outskirts of the main camp: "complete with a popular leadership" and a sort of "mock shadow government" whose guiding principle seems to be the "avoidance of miracles" (161). At such moments, in imagining the existential exile of Eshkhar and his confederates, Hareven transports the reader via rueful, often darkly comic, reverberations of the biblical text, though as if through a distorted lens: "Eshkhar asked what they would do if the people did not let them go. We shall have to wait and see what we do then, said Aviel uncertainly. Though Yakhin says that we will smite them. . . . If the people do not let us go, said his perfectly still eyes to Eshkhar, then they are a people of slaves and will be cut down just as he was. Did you not see for yourself how easy it was to kill?" (45). In her sly reversals and inversions of the Bible's liberatory rhetoric, Hareven casts the problem of the individual's role in a new light. The problem with divine miracles is always that, for the sake of epic destiny, they apparently ignore the lived experience of the first generation doomed to be killed off in the wilderness, particularly the quotidian plight of women.

In the original text, though a variety of women (midwives, wives, mothers, daughters) prove to be wise and resourceful agents whose humane interventions (e.g., disobeying pharaoh's edict to slay all male babies) ensure that Moses will survive to liberate his people—these women's voices are almost obliterated from the text. In this regard, it is important to appreciate how, while re-examining the biblical text's ethical potential and bringing it to bear on present realities, Hareven's trilogy constitutes one of the boldest exemplars of a feminist critique of the Hebrew Bible's silencing of women. For example, as Brenner argues, even though the ancient text's androcentric ideology works "through the rationale that female nurturing capacities are indispensable to individuals, society and nation" after the domestic/reproductive agenda is fulfilled, the accompanying gender politics "wisk them off [the stage] at once in order to make place for the 'real' figures of *history*—the fathers" (13). Perhaps for that reason, Hareven's female characters have no consciousness of dwelling in an incomplete present, nor is the awaiting land their exclusive orientation.

An investigation of how Hareven's gender politics is formulated in relation to the biblical text may be further strengthened by considering Judith Butler's notion of the male body configured through its exclusions, which, not surprisingly, Butler derives from a similarly ancient Western discourse: "Plato's scenography of intelligibility depends upon the exclusion of women, slaves, children. . . . This domain of the less than rational human bounds the figure of human reason, producing that 'man'. . . . This is a figure of disembodiment, but one which is nevertheless a figure of a body, a bodying forth of a masculinized rationality, the figure of a male body which is not a body. . . . This figuration of masculine reason as disembodied body is one whose imaginary morphology is crafted through the exclusion of other possible bodies" (*Bodies That Matter* 48–49). When considering this ancient Greek/Hebraic topography of exclusions, one appreciates just what is gained by Hareven's dark recasting of the miraculous bringing forth of waters in Numbers 20:10. "In all this commotion the two women were unable to reach it. Duress had overcome them and left them too weak to fight. In any case, their babies were no longer alive. Moses and his escort passed by without seeing them. Hopelessly, they stood staring at the wall of flowing water and at the hideous, fatal fracas taking place there. The infants' arms dangled earthward, obviously dead" (38).

Eventually, the two women join a nomadic group of those who feel their interests are neglected by the priestly officials, headed by Eshkhar and his friend Aviel and accompanied by Aviel's sister Yona, whose leadership mirrors the official "Moses-Aharon-Miriam triad," which Feldman calls a "kind of mock shadow government."[12] In discerning an alternative story beneath the surface of the text, Hareven joins her characters' refusal to align themselves with the narratorial "we"—as if to provide a secure existential dwelling place for the disloyal and the "unfaithful" secular reader more at home with the unprecedented autonomy of the postmodern world than with traditional obedience. Deeply mindful of having left the Egyptian "House of Bondage," the trio's mundane struggle toward independence from both the collective fate decreed by a vengeful desert deity and the cattlelike collectivity of "the people" ruefully echoes Moses' fiery rhetoric before pharaoh: "Eshkhar asked what they would do if the people did not let them go. . . . Yakhin says that we will smite them. . . . If the people do not let us go" (45). And so on.

Growing up in Israel, fully acquainted with the traditional Jewish canon, Hareven composed her narratives out of an acute awareness that Moses is not mentioned—except once in a very modest way—in the *Haggadah* that Jews read at the Passover celebration of the Exodus. Some rabbis have speculated that this omission discouraged hero worship. In this light it is significant that rather than offer a legendary figure who would conform to a model of a Spielberg or De Mille epic-heroic scale, Hareven consciously strives to keep her Jewish hero within these perversely diminished proportions. It is exciting to explore how Hareven's distrust of the power guiding the patriarchal staff—quite congruent with Judaism's refusal to lionize Moses or any other human being—attains even greater significance when set against a feminist critique of Zionism she voiced elsewhere. Feldman describes how in Hareven's 1974 essay "Fraternal or Filial Society?" the author already expressed concern over the paternalistic role and greatly magnified status of Israel's political leaders, such as David Ben-Gurion and Moshe Dayan (perhaps today one might add Ariel Sharon), claiming that their "big daddy image" conditions the "sons" to be dependent, to be thoughtless, and to shirk personal responsibility.[13] From the early pages of "The Miracle Hater," and throughout her *Trilogy,* Hareven strategically distances the reader from the consolation of fascism's "great leader" paradigm—insinuating an ominous equation between the childlike people's reliance on the miraculous and the contemporary Israeli acquiescence to the violence of the state.[14] Though she never dwelled on it, the fact that the author arrived in Palestine as a child refugee from Poland sheds additional light on the issues of power and vulnerability that resonate in such a sustained way throughout her essays and fiction.

In spite of its trajectory of dissent, Hareven's reading of the biblical source is neither reductive nor consistently antagonistic. For in yet another essay, "Against Charisma," she warns that "the first things that get lost in charismatic leadership are facts," since the people are not interested in assessing reality but rather in achieving a "giddy symbiosis with their leader" such as occurred in Hitler's Germany (which created her own displacement as a child). Here she pays affectionate tribute to the biblical Moses as the archetypal anticharismatic personality, "the most humble of men, a stutterer, inelegant of speech, who needed an interpreter; a man with whom the people were most certainly not enthralled, calling him 'that man Moses,' barely accepting his rule over them" (*Vocabulary of Peace* 201). Hareven notices that Moses' thankless task is to wean the people away from their yearnings for the idolatrous past to embrace historically revolutionary ethics. As biblical scholars such as Pardes aptly observe of Deuteronomy, "the entire period of wandering" is "an initiatory voyage" into true individualism. The latter is a condition that transforms slaves into "active participants who . . . may fashion new social models while questioning the validity of the sacred corpus that is passed down to them" (Pardes 68–69). In a highly compatible spirit, Hareven asserts that "the charismatic leader destroys the boundaries of the ego in his mythic relationship with the public: I am you and you are me" until "norms vanish and obedience to the law becomes unimportant . . . the charismatic leader trades in amorphous myths, before the existence of law and democratic organization" (*Vocabulary of Peace* 204). The lesson to be gleaned for all societies in crisis is that "mythology prevents real confrontation with the regime because it creates a situation of no doubts." And, since left alone, "myths inhibit change" (204), the artist's vigilant re-creation and retelling are required in each generation.

In his innovative study of the controversial "Post-Zionist" debates that have flared in Israel in recent years (its voices have subsided somewhat since the outbreak of the Al-Aqsa Intifada), Laurence Silberstein observes that "the binarism of homeland/exile is central to Zionism" (20). He argues that this stark opposition has engendered further ostensibly irreconcilable (and stagnating) polarities:

> Homeland as a source of security, stability, refuge, nurturing, safety/exile as site of danger, insecurity, instability, threat, anxiety; *heimlich/unheimlich;* homeland is good/exile is bad; homeland is productive/exile is parasitic; homeland is conducive/exile is not conducive to redemption through labor; homeland is welcoming/exile is hostile; homeland is life-giving/exile is life-threatening; homeland is creative/exile is stultifying; homeland is nurturing to Jewish national culture/exile is destructive; homeland is unifying/exile is fragmenting. (22–23)

Well aware of the intrinsic contribution this series makes to her nation's myths and identity, Hareven writes as if the desert, as both Diaspora space and corridor toward reterritorialization, fatally scrambles and disrupts the certitude of the binary oppositions Silberstein describes. Even her Moses embodies the author's paradigmatic indifference to national coherence, inhabiting a divided consciousness, a torn ego haplessly divided against itself: "Some said that he had two hearts in his breast, one Hebrew and one Egyptian, and that he had murdered the Egyptian one so as to leave no trace of it" (11).[15] And for his pragmatic followers, it is telling that they know *nothing* of a divinely sanctioned "Promised Land," and strive only to return to an "ancestral" haven or refuge. One of the most provocative of her polemics, which addresses the contemporary resonance of the Mosaic laws, asks rhetorically:

> To which commandments would I give primacy today? What oppressed us in previous generations and threatens to oppress us today is the patriarchal establishment, which contains hierarchies, holds ceremonies, and sanctifies the past. Like every patriarchal establishment, it foments feelings of ownership, of nationalism, of condescension toward anyone who is not like me, as well as fanaticism. I prefer the commandments that are based on personal righteousness and doing justice—that is, everything concerning the dynamic between people—over every commandment

> dealing with place and land and ownership. Every time the group that calls itself "The Temple Mount Faithful"—the very designation smacks of idol worship—goes up to rant and rave on the mount, to pray there and to fan the flames of hostility and discord and hatred, I want to shout in their ears: "When ye come to appear in my presence—who hath required this of ye, to tread down my courts? . . . incense of abomination it is unto me. . . . Yea, when ye make many prayers, I will not hear; your hands are full of blood. . . . Cease to do evil; learn to do well; seek justice, relieve the oppressed, do justice for the fatherless, plead for the widow." Are any words clearer than these? "Do justice for the fatherless and plead for the widow," even if they are not of the people of Israel. One justice for the stranger and the dweller. (*Vocabulary of Peace* 59)

Outraged by Jewish fundamentalism's failure to understand the revolutionary spirit of the prophetic text, Hareven's insistence on a just Middle East has a rich corollary in her backward glance at the ancient Hebrews.

"Prophet," the second novella, revisits the sanctified violence of Joshua 9. Hareven craftily places readers this time in the walled city of Gibeon (rather than the camps of the Hebrews), where they experience events through the woeful perspective of Hivai, a Gibeonite seer staggered by the apocalyptic events that engulf him and his society. In a sense what is at stake throughout this narrative is the human imagination as a conduit for empathy and proper understanding of the Other's plight. It is useful in this respect to think of Baruch Spinoza's observation in his *Theological-Political Treatise* that "the prophets were endowed, not with a more perfect mind, but instead, with a power of imagining unusually vividly" (313). Aptly, Feldman declares that "[f]or the Hebrew, or any biblically literate reader, the crucial reversal of narrative perspective is signaled by the mournful Gibeonites' dire phrase 'It was from the east, from the desert, that evil would come'"(Feldman 163; Hareven 66), which reads as a direct inversion of Jeremiah's famous prophetic dictum in Jeremiah 1:14: "From north evil shall come." In this regard, Stanley Nash's view is also useful: Hareven consistently "stresses the need for anthropological breadth to endow . . . Israeli[s] with 'the primary capability of accepting [that] which is different from [them] as a fundamental equal'" (223).[16] Even more to the point, Feldman asserts that, beyond merely thinking about the Semitic Other in the abstract, Hareven effectively places the Israeli reader "in the uncomfortable position of reading about *themselves* (at least in the generic sense—biblical ancestry being an integral part of Israeli identity) as the *Other*" (164). Apparently it is intrinsic to Hareven's narrative strategy of destabilization that readers must "constantly shift perspectives if they want to 'get into' the narrative. This is especially true of the second novella. While in the first we are still within the Israelite camp . . . in ["Prophet"] we are asked to step into the shoes of an utterly other" (161). Moreover, readers inhabit the position of a people facing a particularly menacing, threatening entity, the very rumor of whose approach is capable of annihilating everything sacred to a once-complacent people, whose city has not seen war "since the days of their great-grandfathers" (73). The narrative's tone grows ominous in just a few deft phrases: "the ways of the world began to turn upside down about one hour after sunrise," and the "whole apprehensively lowing swarm of life" flees its proper dwelling place in the countryside for the habitation of humans. This was once a haughty site of security: "No one had threatened Gibeon for ages. It was a city as large as a royal capital and it had forgotten what fear was like" (66–67). But now it is stricken by dread. Hareven's apocalyptic imagery of the material privations and cultural decline endured by the Gibeonites dexterously draws the reader into a scene of desolation whose timeless and melancholy resonance rings all too universally:

> Longingly they watched the fruit in the valley rot on the trees, dropping to be eaten by great clouds of raucous birds that arrived with the eastward-racing clouds. . . . With the autumn breeze came the smell of rotted grapes, as heady as wine, and the fierce, sweet, cloying odor of ripe figs. Summer was over. The city was barricaded tight. Large jars of olive oil stood against the walls and all the storerooms were full of lentils and beans. And yet people stared at the full jars and sacks as if looking right through them. There will be hunger, they said, it isn't far off. (76)

Provoked by fear of a future that Hivai can no longer prophesy, the community's widening existential crisis ironically resembles the condition, and self-perpetuating rationales, of a certain embattled Middle Eastern state: "Of course there was no justice in the city. How could justice be dispensed when the enemy was at the gate?" (79).

With much justification, Israelis and other readers attuned to the problem of nationalist violence are likely to read the Book of Joshua as a disturbingly affirmative representation of the execution of an ancient program of ethnic cleansing, which appears to be prescribed by divine agency. The program is accomplished through a war of conquest, in which difference of religion and ethnicity constitute a sanction for annihilation. For many readers after a century of violence sanctified by state, ethnicity, or religion, Joshua is a grim tale that has little consolation to offer the present (excepting for the messianic politics of the Right). It might profitably be read as a mirror of our own atrocities. The story reads as relentlessly ugly and violent as the latest headlines from the Palestinian-Israeli conflagration. Yet as Hareven is clearly aware, Joshua is also a text configured by contradiction and ambivalence in ways that might just as easily inspire the writer's ethical response to contemporary crisis. "Prophet" gestures especially to the campaigns conducted in Jericho, Ai, and against the five kings at Gibeon. In the stories of Rahab and the Gibeonites, Israel not only accommodates outsiders but punishes an insider for the crime of appropriating Canaanite plunder. What Hareven undoubtedly noticed about these transformations is that they undermine or blur the boundaries articulated by the Deuteronomic code: the stories of Rahab and the Gibeonites argue for flexibility in the determination of Israel's internal boundaries. "Prophet" imaginatively draws from the scripture's commemoration of singular moments in which the inhabitants of Canaan approach Israelites and succeed in securing an exemption from destruction.

Ostensibly, the scriptural text is preoccupied with group survival, which requires the coherence and maintenance of internal boundaries at any cost. A careful reading reveals another current, one that seems to argue for moderation, seeing Israel as only one of several disparate peoples who inhabit the land ostensibly reserved for them. It is as if the ancient narrative energy of the biblical text itself resists the imposition of inflexible idealism, so that we are left not only with a certain ambivalence regarding Israel's identity and relationship to other peoples of Canaan but also what we might call a resistance to the official narrative of Deuteronomy. Perhaps the most representative example of the latter's teleological thrust is articulated in these stark terms: *when you have driven them out and settled in their land, and after they have been destroyed before you, be careful not to be ensnared by inquiring about their gods* (Deut. 12:29–31).

In various ways, the Deuteronomic code prescribes the preservation of the boundaries that distinguish Israel from the other peoples of Canaan. The social environment encoded in Deuteronomy clearly reflects a great deal of internal anxiety and vulnerability. The *b'nei Yisrael* will certainly enter a land inhabited by others more numerous and powerful than themselves. However, the true threat posed by the indigenous inhabitants is not their imposing cities or great stature (which can be neutralized by divine might) but rather through their *difference.* Israel's perceived vulnerability to the power of difference finds expression in Moses' directives: the people of Israel must vanquish and overcome the "seven nations," while ensuring that they do not associate or intermarry with them in the process.

So if the Book of Joshua may be read as Israel's evolving confrontation with difference, it is interesting that one of the key retellings in Hareven's narrative concerns the *b'nei Yisrael's* encounter with the Gibeonites, no doubt because it *reverses* certain aspects of the conventional scheme I just outlined. Now in his mid-forties, Hivai, the failed prophet (or rather seer in the Hebraic sense, since he merely predicts the future rather than critiques society [Feldman 159]), enjoys a few brilliant but ultimately ephemeral flashes of insight. Ruefully pondering his four misspent decades, he finds that "his life had the plodding gait of an ox that walks the straight furrow of time from the Was to the Will-be" (69) and sees in his waning powers of prophecy and his culture's impending catastrophe an opportunity for self-liberation. After making one final futile gesture to his old belief system, the sacrifice of "a small slave child," Hivai fatally misreads the future in the child's entrails, later discovering to his horror that he has inadvertently caused the destruction of his own beloved daughter as well. Intriguingly, Feldman considers the grotesque consequences of Hivai's "prophet's block" (163) as a likely reverberation of the novelist's indictment of the moral paralysis of her own culture. Through such devices Hareven boldly underscores her timeless message that the mythic template that still underlies human belief systems remains a dangerously pernicious presence.

Weary of failure, the hapless seer abandons his people to dwell among the Hebrews. Newly arrived from the desert flatlands, the latter are a strangely uncultivated people who seem to dwell in the future, so ill-equipped to cope with their new surroundings that at first Hivai is persuaded that they will soon disappear from the landscape:

> Why, they were like newborn babes in this mountain land, they and their god together. . . . Their god was not of this country, neither bone of its bone nor flesh of its flesh . . . soon the Hebrew god would flee back to the desert he had come from and show his face no more in the land of men. And the invaders would flee with him, like chaff before the wind: from the desert they had come and to the desert they would return. No one would remember them or their god. (96)

But as time passes, the strangers remain an obdurate presence, and Hivai reluctantly elects to sojourn among them: "He knew he could not stay in this place, yet he had nowhere to go. He was neither Gibeonite nor Hebrew . . . an outcast in the mountains, with nowhere to return to, no people, no city, no god" (119). For their part, the Hebrews are troubled by Hivai's acquired hybridity. Is the seer a "convert" or is he merely Other, and hence a polluting presence? Hareven is clearly fascinated by the Torah's infatuation with the fraught relation between the unassimilated Other and the threshold of national adulthood as the Hebrews inherit Canaan. Is it possible to accommodate the alien and still serve God by "dwelling apart"?

Besides succeeding as a profoundly moving meditation on the nature of insider-outsider consciousness as an ancient, rather than exclusively modern, phenomenon, "Prophet" responds to another pressing dynamic that, though unspoken, nevertheless haunts the original text. It is as though as long as the people of the land remain faceless or voiceless, the ethic of extermination may be fulfilled without compunction. The Book of Joshua, though, underscores the danger involved in intimate, quotidian contact with the people of the land, for recognizing the humanity of others would appear to make killing them a more dismal prospect. Hareven reads her desert sojourners through Exodus and Deuteronomy's representations of the unsettling transformation of Canaanites from Others into marginal Israelites in ways that trouble the present. "Prophet" challenges the exclusivist boundaries set out in Deuteronomy, ultimately expanding those boundaries to address the current tensions between contemporary claimants to the land of Israel/Palestine as well as such ambivalences as the "Arab-Israeli" vs. the "Palestinian" or the Jewish Arab vs. the dominant culture. As a whole, her project provokes a reexamination of Zionist ethics. For instance, though the Hebrews tolerate Hivai, who labors tirelessly for the strangers from the eastern deserts, it is a utilitarian relation at best: "They thanked him with a rough pat on the shoulder and forgot him the moment they left him, as though he himself were but another of their tools. . . . Not once had he failed them, not for a moment had he left the camp or stopped cutting wood, fetching water, and faithfully doing his chores. And still he was as much an outsider as ever" (109).

At such temporally ambiguous moments as this, it is clear that the wilderness, the most liminal geography on the Jewish map of the world, remains the most apt landscape for a Hebrew writer to plead for the rights of minorities without altogether repudiating the justice of the Zionist cause.[17] The desert serves as a subterranean conduit for smuggling in the values of Diaspora and heterogeneous coexistence. Perhaps it may *also* be the best way of addressing the exilic or liminal condition of being a Jewish woman in a martial state. In the end it is perhaps less ironic than fitting that Hareven employs the Exodus narrative, the Bible's greatest argument for freedom and liberation, to question the modern assumption of the power of territorial redemption. Hareven's ambivalence in relation to Exodus's official narrative of homecomings, indeed the prospects for reading *Trilogy* as an allegorical commentary on contemporary Israeli society, is clearly linked to her sober awareness of her culture's deep melancholy: "A recent study that examined the causes of emigration came up with a finding that surprised many Israelis, particularly those who perfunctorily cite 'security, army, reserve duty' as the prime causes of tension. It emerged that so-called security tension was very low on the scale of the causes of emigration. The highest places were occupied by feelings of disappointment and frustration, defined as dissatisfaction with and a sense of not belonging to Israeli society, a feeling that they had not found their place, an inability to influence events—all social causes par excellence" (*Vocabulary of Peace* 123). Throughout her writings, Hareven is mindful of the unfortunate divide that often prevents the individual from identifying with the wish fulfillment of the mythic collective.

Hareven's bold narrative focus on the marginal affairs of women or the otherwise powerless within the grand design of a mass movement orchestrated by a remote God epitomizes an acute questioning of the prospect of a genuine homecoming for those forced to linger on the margins of the official story. Moreover, the very prospect of arrival is greeted with a marked degree of ambivalence by Hareven's Hebrews: "Some said it was foolish to work the land. They were a people of shepherds, and shepherds they would always be, wandering untrammeled from place to place with their flocks. . . . Their birthplace was the desert, stone houses were not for them; they and their children were meant for mats and booths, free to come and go as they pleased" (107). Hareven's portrayal of the lingering traces of a desert zeitgeist in her characters is comparable to Berger's speculation that, in encountering permanent (which he calls "customary") nomads, the Israelites might have seen the "ideal condition" strived for by those "who wish to avoid being taken over by the land they take over" (135). For Hareven, Mosaic wandering inhabits a liminal space between the triumphal fulfillment of conquest and the painful deferment of a dream.

Perhaps such precarious habitation is as William Pinar suggests: "Living on the margins may be dangerous but at least you can breathe there" (28). For in "Prophet," though years after their arrival in the destined homeland, having reluctantly begun to move into crude stone shelters and perhaps somewhat saddened to find themselves suddenly bound to agricultural and natural cycles, the people remain as existentially unsettled as dry leaves, for "sometimes hot and fierce, a desert wind blew through the camp, they would stand for a moment gazing silently eastward, breathing the wind in deeply, with endless longing" (108). At such moments, one senses an unsettled undercurrent of melancholy diasporism in *Des-*

ert Trilogy, a nostalgia for a morally unblemished exile that resists the triumphal Zionist assumptions about destined homeland and territory that continue to underscore the works of many of her literary peers even on the Zionist Left.

Hivai, now an old man with a hard-won share of modest wisdom who no longer bears the burden of prognosticating the national destiny of the Gibeonites, remains content that his prophetic powers, though rejuvenated, are limited to the quotidian and daily practical exigency rather than the collective, or epic: "He knew when it would rain on the mountains . . . he knew which date palm would would bear the first fruit, and what he would find when he opened his traps, a lizard, mouse, or jackal cub. They pleased him, these prophecies, like small, humble blessings" (126). In a similar spirit, both the title and spare plot of "After Childhood," the conclusion to the trilogy, suggests a plea for a transcendence of the violent biblical reality, urgently underscoring the need to discover post-exilic arts of living in the present that transcend all forms of violent martyrdom.

Both textually and geographically, Hareven's vision embodies Trinh Minh-ha's evocative call for a postcolonial feminism that serves as "a permanent sojourner walking bare-footed on multiply de/re-territorialized land" (334). The quiet community depicted in "Prophet" behaves as though committed to remain on the outskirts of the violent nationalist conquest of the land which Joshua undertakes, content to eke out a quiet existence in the dry lands of the Negev, a quotidian preoccupation with goats and desert wells, as if yearning to preserve something of the pristine wilderness experience.

In the final story, "After Childhood," Salu, a youth from the remote settlement, grows up with the grim knowledge that his father tried to sacrifice him to settle accounts with God: "ever since then his eyes blinked rapidly, as if fending off a strong light" (131). Again Hareven riffs on the persistent mythic wound of the *akedah* to great effect. The villagers are embarrassed by the atavistic presence among them, by the living parody of the old stories: "A mad dog, a dreamer, they said about Salu's father, today every flea says I'm Abraham. . . . They spat as if to get rid of an unclean taste" (134). Eventually, Salu's narrative reverses that of Hivai's position in "Prophet," for, as an adult, his father's madness causes his tribe to shun him.

A wayfarer for many years, Salu eventually settles among a community of other Semites, the Hittites, who, as he learns their language and ways, tolerate his alterity: "The blinkard, they called him. As if his twitch had made him tribeless, they had long ago stopped thinking of him as a Hebrew" (158). Thus, *Trilogy* concludes much as it began, with a peripatetic character lingering just outside of the nation, on the margins of the official story of homecoming. As an adult (embodying Hareven's sense of these recalcitrant Hebrews' enlarged consciousness), the desert dweller marries Moran, a visionary woman from the mountains, who insists that they live out their lives on the fringes of the power struggles of premonarchical Israel. Consoled by the enigmatic but inveterate voice of the desert, Moran savors "the warm air stroking her face as if the whole strong wilderness were breathing close to her, quiet and warm" (186). Hareven's desert, not unlike her sense of the Bible itself, always teases the individual toward eternal paradigms beyond the false gods of their cultures, though sometimes that beckoning leaves them stranded in cultural isolation.

Unfortunately, after many years, Salu makes the fatal choice often exhibited in Hareven's critique of the masculine imagination. Upon discovering an abandoned Egyptian fortress, Salu returns to fantasies of conquest. The "empty fort . . . captivated him. This was a strong place, he thought, with a commander and a god to bow to. A place well-protected. From day to day the fort fitted him more, like a second skin" (177). For her part, Moran refuses to visit the site of her husband's ritualistic devotion, preventing her four small children from exposure to the site of male fantasies and adventure where Salu begins to imagine himself "king of the fort" (179). When the Egyptians return to the place, Salu and his friends are swiftly slaughtered. Moran is left alone, tormented by dreams in which Salu appears as a child, still fearful of a father set on butchering him. Readers learn that with the passing of time, "the old, impassable distance between village and fort was back again," as if the surviving community remains committed against a remystification of violent sacrifice. Suggesting the (temporary) disruption of old patterns, this terse phrase amounts to the trilogy's most resounding gesture toward the need to create a non-sacrificial human community that does not cling to such totems. In a similar mode of resistance, the conclusion to "After Childhood" leaves us with a heroine whose many years in the wilderness have taught her to look beyond the patriarchal religion for her sense of reality. Rejecting the tribal blessing offered by an old man, that the God of the Hebrews "should always be with her," she wills the deity to stay far from her: "Let him ignore her in his heaven, because the gods burned all when they came. They brought death and sickness and madness and drought. It's all we can do to make good what they ruin. Spare us both their honey and their sting" (183). This moment characterizes a shrewd intervention on Hareven's part, at once completing the journey of her psychologically complex heroine in a manner that seems fully justified while offering a sly wink to readers accustomed to the distrust toward all master narratives often exhibited in the literature of postmodernity. Like other gods, Moran's experience with the Hebrew God leaves little room for confidence in the compassion or wisdom of a divine plan, or even in its existence.

In light of such a skeptical conclusion, the question may linger for many readers: just how does Hareven read the ancient story of liberation and chosenness in the age of a Jewish state? Perhaps Hareven's motives become clearest when juxtaposed with a striking statement made in the conclusion of a lecture she delivered to graduates of the Hebrew University in June of 1990:

> All of us in all generations were, are, and will be present at Mount Sinai—not Sinai as a sound-and-light production or a single pyrotechnical happening, a spiritual stock exchange in which those who were present gained and those who were absent, or not yet born, lost. Not even Sinai as territory, which may be ours today and under the rule of others tomorrow. In the Sinai of knowledge there is room for all of us, friends and enemies, opponents and admirers, all of us who populate the earth, without any limitation at all, in a different ecology yet unknown to us in most other fields. Perhaps, very slowly, we shall come to know it. (*Vocabulary of Peace* 78)

Inhabiting the fraught contemporary world of identity politics—rightly recognizing that we define ourselves not only by virtue of who we are, but by who we are not—biblical scholars and readers have been forced to grapple in recent years with the troubling dimensions (with their contemporary resonances) of becoming Hebrews and not Egyptians; Israelites and not Canaanites; the destiny of *am-segulah,* the "chosen people," vs. the *goyim asher lo-y'da-ucha,* "those people who do not know you," the one, true God. In our age of unredeemed territorial conflict, many somberly conclude that this postdesert legacy has led to exclusive claims to land, to boundaries drawn in blood, and even to sanctioned acts of violence, including genocide, against the Other. In her controversial study *The Curse of Cain,* Regina Schwartz bleakly concludes that the ideology that predominates in the ancient text is "agonistic," one in which a sense of unique identity or social memory is consistently developed against or antagonistic to another person or religion or nation.[18]

Hareven's retelling embraces this troubled reading while at the same time manages to offer a more nuanced view. Her stories affirm that few paradigms are ever exclusively or intrinsically adhered to in the Hebrew

Bible, a corpus woven from many different sources and periods.[19] Too, it is worth remembering that Hareven's trilogy is creatively bound up as much with the biblical language of origins as it is with a daily language increasingly inflected by violent realities. For if *Thirst: The Desert Trilogy* is a cautionary tale of the dangers present when we create identities agonistically, by violently stressing the difference between ourselves and those we label as the "other," the narratives also succeed by offering a generous reading of the Hebrew Bible's own complex ethical currents. Hareven demands that contemporary readers recognize that postmodern ambivalences over identity, the coherence of the nation, the sanctity of territory vs. human life, are already woven into the strangely rich fabric of the ancient Bible. As Pardes cogently argues, while patriarchy reigns in many of its individual texts, the Hebrew Bible also contains significant countertraditions that do not support the "monotheistic repression of femininity" (Reinhartz 47). Knowing that she inherits the Bible's weighty burden of language, Hareven is never free "intertextually"—she can never invent a new liberatory language out of nothing. Instead, she toils, patching together fragments of the Bible's contradictory and multiple strands to respond to the urgent needs of the present. In developing these stories, Hareven strives to ameliorate the encoded tribalism of liberation, to ensure that the prophetic message of the sacred texts was restated in the most inclusive terms possible. Ultimately however, it is the desert vision of Numbers itself, promising a just allocation of territory for the land's inhabitants, that provides the foundation for her own vision: "Unto these the land shall be divided for an inheritance according to the number of names. To many thou shalt give the less inheritance: to every one shall his inheritance be given according to those that were numbered of him" (Num. 26:53–54). A peaceful and just dwelling is prescribed here. Yet, embracing a skeptical perspective on the national narrative, embracing transience over stasis, Hareven participates in a global feminist literary paradigm of doubt.

Kerstin Shands evocatively describes such an ethos as a "hypertransgressive contemporary feminism" in which "stillness, home, rest, and refuge . . . are left behind by impatient and incessant movement" (10). Dispersal from the linear absolutes of the male canon of conquest into the nude and forlorn landscape reveals more fully both contemporary reality and what we might still aspire to become. Demonstrating how an Israeli novelist might combine an unequivocal commitment to the Jewish state with a prophetic zeal for peace and social justice, Hareven, like many of Israel's writers of conscience, occupied a challenging position in a deeply threatening Middle East beset by dangerous fundamentalisms on all sides. Throughout her life, her work expressed the spirit of the renowned cultural historian Yael Zerubavel's view that "the collapse of historical time into a mythical temporal framework . . . poses its own danger of obscuring historical distinctions and the need for a more critical attitude toward the examination of current historical developments" ("The 'Mythological Sabra' and Jewish Past" 128). For the Israeli concerned with the ethically fraught nexus of national space and peoplehood, the Hebrew Bible, particularly Exodus with its epic narrative of exile and homecoming, will always cast its shadow over the present conflict. But the sacred text also offers a rich language for narrating the dilemmas and uncertainties of dwelling in a contemporary space that is also an ancient site of painfully similar conflicts.

Hareven's three desert meditations, bridging past and present, remind us that those who wandered out of Egypt, including Moses, perished in the desert ("For the Lord had said of them, They shall surely die in the wilderness" [Num. 26:65]) and it was a new generation born in the wilderness whom God deemed worthy to enter the land. Each story offers a synecdochic portrait of the national scene, and the news is in many ways grim. One can only hope that those of us shattered by the despair of appalling violence, the desolate wilderness of inhumane relations between Israelis and Palestinians, will somehow endure long enough to emerge blinking from our age's idolatrous territorial fantasies and witness a new generation come forth to deliver a fresh beginning and open up all of our horizons once again. I suspect that for many readers, Hareven's indirect biblical commentary—juxtaposing exilic ambivalence with a feminist reading strategy—will emerge as a benevolent alternative to losses incurred by Zionist "security" on Jews and Palestinians alike.

In the contemporary situation of Israel and Palestine, one might wonder about a modern Hebrew text that so stresses the desert experience as the necessary narrative of the moment, antithetical to myths of territorial possessiveness. Still, while Hareven's novel clearly appeals directly to contemporary Israelis, who may still be "purblind and lost"—whether haplessly intoxicated with the imperative of regained soil and place or simply benumbed after the centuries of wandering that culminated in the European Holocaust—her work may be profitably read by all readers not to endow any place or "truth" with a value that obscures the sanctity of human life.

3 *Desert Space and National Consciousness*

> Each city receives its form from the desert it opposes.
> —Italo Calvino

> The act of departure is the bravest and most beautiful of all. A selfish happiness perhaps, but it is happiness—for him who knows how to appreciate it. To be alone, to have no needs, to be unknown, a stranger and at home everywhere and to march, solitary and great, to the conquest of the world.
> —Isabelle Eberhardt

Any analysis of the vital cultural role played by the disruptive signifier of "desert" in the Israeli literary setting, or the Jewish canon itself, would hardly be complete without considering the rich fictional universe of Amos Oz (b. 1939). One of the most widely read Israeli novelists of his or any generation, Oz always proves a highly rewarding writer to examine in relation to the pervasive and permanent antagonism of the settled and unsettled, the occupied and the occupier. He is, after all, the writer the *Guardian* once hailed as "the desert conscience of Israel." With the possible exception of A. B. Yehoshua, Oz, who calls the small Negev town of Arad home, is the most translated and critically esteemed Israeli novelist. A favorite target of attack by Israel's ultranationalist Right during the years of Israel's occupation of Lebanon and more recently during the Intifada that has raged in the Palestinian territories, at such moments Oz has often stood in the international community as Israel's moral conscience. American and European newspapers often highlight his response to tumultuous events such as the assassination of Israel's Prime Minister Yitzhak Rabin, and he has won prestigious literary prizes both at home and abroad.

Wherever one might look throughout his far-ranging oeuvre, Oz offers highly inventive responses to Israel's existential difficulties. Whether in his political essays or fiction, one finds a penetrating iteration of the quotidian aspects of Israeli life—as well as its intractable violent conflicts and historical upheavals. Oz exemplifies a generation that consciously distanced itself from an earlier generation's solidarity with the prevailing public line (a struggle that serves as a classical confirmation of Harold Bloom's idea concerning the writer's Oedipal revolt against writers of preceding generations) and collectively sanctioned ideas.[1] A formidable influence among the New Wave Hebrew literature (1960s–70s) and still a vital presence in Israel's literary scene, Oz spent his childhood in Jerusalem, his formative years in Kibbutz Hulda, and has resided since 1982 in the desert development town of Arad. This trajectory has made him into a kind of Israeli everyman. Moreover, having experienced Jerusalem as a divided city and serving in a tank unit in the Six-Day War and the Yom Kippur War, Oz displays an intimate understanding of the movement of Israeli society during critical times of transition. In his works readers encounter the social transition of the Jewish state from a collectivist organism to a socially critical democracy and finally to an increasingly Americanized and, hence, individualistic capitalist state troubled by deep ethnic, religious, and ideological fissures. Indeed, the novelist's rebellion against his father's religious Jerusalem household when he was only fifteen mirrors the path taken by many of his alienated characters and reflects the tension between the individual and the collective which has informed his oeuvre ever since. As he wrote in his autobiographical epic, *A Tale of Love and Darkness:* "I stood up and killed my father, and killed the whole of Jerusalem, changed my name and went on my own to Kibbutz Hulda, to live there above the ruins" (464).

A number of critics have offered interesting perspectives on Oz's dialogic encounters with the Hebrew Bible and its bearing on the contemporary Israeli reality. Joseph Cohen asserts that Oz's singular achievement resides "in his bypassing polemicism to move upward to a substantially higher plateau of metapolitical writing. . . . Oz is nothing less than a modern mythmaker who has been highly successful in taking the exoticism of Israel's location in the desert and Mediterranean Sea, a country already saturated with a biblical, mystical, apocalyptic and miraculous history, and combining it with the myriad realities of contemporary life"

(179). To this I would add that above all the diverse features that link the modern state of Israel to its ancient roots, the desert seems to have been most intrinsic to this mythopoetic dimension of Oz's imagination.[2] For years he has been a keen observer of this environment, beginning each day with a predawn walk in the wadis and slopes that surround Arad (Negev 104).

Throughout Oz's novels, the desert expanses, far from serving as transformative or heroic space, often raise the troubling specter of cracks in the individual's loyal commitment to the chain of national identity. As Nehama Aschkenasy declares, "a reader who revisits Amos Oz's works in the current postmodern climate is inevitably attuned to the writer's treatment of his national metanarrative" (124). Some of the novelist's most memorable characters flee homogenous insularity—even the classic kibbutz ideology that Zionism often touted as one of its proudest achievements—longing for a distinct sense of self, unreconciled to their surroundings. However, in *A Perfect Peace,*[3] that quest seems so compromised by the hero's narcissism and selfishness that the novel ultimately affirms the collective national identity as the steadfast antidote to the indulgence of the self-interested individual. Set between 1965 and 1967, when Israel's Prime Minister David Ben-Gurion was already seventy-nine years old, there is a distinct schism between the founding ideals of the parents and their successors, who find themselves weary of what appears to be an endless state of war and its high costs of survival. By the time of its writing, the solidarity with the collective that had characterized the Palmach generation of the late forties and early fifties was far from a sacrosanct assumption.

Early in his career, Oz discovered that the desert offered a unique environment for posing critical questions about the individual and society that emerged in this period of doubt, for expressing a tangible unease with ideologies that were willfully blind to human realities.[4] An intimate relation to the desert landscape has proved decisive for the nourishment of Oz's artistic consciousness to a degree unsurpassed by any other Israeli writer. But I am not suggesting that any form of mystical retreat or withdrawal is prescribed. In this regard, Oz shares a strong affinity with the late poet Yehuda Amichai's view of the desert as a source for deep reflection about the bloody wages of regained Jewish sovereignty that is worth pausing to explore. Amichai once declared that his "two years of war in the Negev" were a revelatory experience. Like Oz's prose, his poetry resonates with the embattled nation's most pressing cultural themes (love and war, the tension between secular and religious imaginations, ideological tensions between fathers and sons). Amichai's verse also happens to be filled with references to the desert. Admitting the attraction of "the white sands of the desert [where] everything is whiteness and shadows," Amichai emphatically denied that the desert was conducive only to a "mystical" or otherwise solipsistic experience of the solitary individual: "it is anything but a mystical experience. Everything in the desert is clear-cut. Where you have trees, streams, mist, there you have mysticism. The desert doesn't allow you anything, everything is clear-cut. . . . Everything is outside, just as it is in Greek mythology that allows no mystery because it is bathed in the clear light and color of the Mediterranean. It is an illumination that is unlike any other in the world." In this late interview, Amichai added simply that "I need the desert as a part of my life. It is an intrinsic part of my experience, like day and night. . . . I use it. It keeps me going. . . . In the desert . . . experiences stay with you but they are translated into something larger, something more memorable. It provides a wonderful dimension of consciousness" ("Interview" 41–42). For his part, Oz, who as mentioned has for many years lived in a small town in the Negev, seems to embrace Amichai's sense of the desert as a site of "translation" and has proved equally resistant to notions of the desert as a consolatory haven of inner mystical retreat. Instead, his work expresses desert as a liminal site in which characters struggle to come to terms with the pressing social realities of Zionist sovereignty.

This paradigm already emerged vividly in his 1963 short story "Nomad and Viper" (*Where the Jackals Howl and Other Stories*), where Oz represented the desert as the site of the clash of civilizations between "cultured and rational" kibbutzniks—whose community is set on the borders of the uncultivated wilderness—and "barbaric" Others. In his early narratives, the kibbutz frequently served as a stage for Oz's dim view of the utopian imagination. For instance, Oz's first novel, *Elsewhere, Perhaps* (1966), written while he was still a member of Kibbutz Hulda, explored the kibbutz as a troubling realm of thwarted individual aspirations and raging sexual desire. Robert Alter argues that "the most crucial motif . . . in all of Oz's fiction of kibbutz life is that of enclosure. The kibbutz enterprise is seen as a dream of overweening rationality, an attempt to impose a neat geometric order on the seething chaos of the natural world . . . a reflex of turning away from the unsettling darkness of reality to an illusory light" (*Modern Hebrew Literature* 331).

In "Nomad and Viper" Oz essentially recast the biblical tale of Dinah, whose rape leads to the massacre of the male inhabitants of Shechem, one of the most horrific of the atrocities Genesis relates. Geula, a young woman living with other pioneers on a new Negev kibbutz, falsely accuses a desert nomad of rape. Juxtaposing the putative values (liberalism, egalitarianism, and democracy) of the "civilized" rational society of the kibbutz members with the "savage" Bedouins, Oz's story brilliantly deconstructs the Zionist metadiscourse of enlightening and uplifting the indigenous population through a number of devices beyond the essential deceit at the heart of the conflict.[5] In the *sulha* (ceremonial reconciliation) arranged to resolve tensions between the two groups, Oz unsparingly portrays the Israelis' Orientalist condescension toward their desert cousins. In his analysis of Oz's subversion of his culture's assumptions, Aschkenasy observes that "Lévi-Strauss's binary opposition between 'savage' and 'cultured' collapses when the Bedouin elder phrases his elaborate, courteous remarks 'in careful, formal Hebrew' while the kibbutz secretary insists on replying in 'broken Arabic.'" Moreover, Oz's story emphasizes that "the Arab's knowledge of Hebrew is a tactic for survival, not an admission of defeat or inferiority. His insistence on using Hebrew rather than Arabic may be understood as his exclusion of the Israeli from his own linguistic territory . . . the Bedouin will neither be suppressed nor assimilated nor integrated into the inevitable march of history" (Aschkenasy 127). In this powerful early desert narrative, Oz was already raising increasingly provocative questions in which the nation's sacred assumptions—its very sense of "at-homeness"—were evocatively unsettled and challenged. Elsewhere, in *Black Box* (1988), a troubled juvenile delinquent who is the product of a broken marriage emerges like a postmodern prophet from his sojourn among the Bedouin and hippies of the Sinai Peninsula with a new vision bestowing unexpected grace on the fragmented lives that surround him. In these and numerous works, Oz helped inaugurate a discursive tradition in contemporary Hebrew letters of artistically engaging not only with biblical precedents and archetypes but with the landscape itself. At the same time, his long-standing critical examination of the enduring conflicts and paradoxes that beset Israeli society link his practice to writers such as Shulamith Hareven and David Grossman, whose subtle narratives, while frequently committed to social justice, avoid the taint of didacticism.

As suggested by the narratives briefly outlined above, many of Oz's younger characters dwell on the cusp of a certain exhaustion of solidarity with the official story, and over the years, this distance continues to be one of the most enduring themes of Oz's oeuvre. For instance, in Oz's memorable young adult novel *Panther in the Basement* (*Panter Ba'martef*), set in Palestine of 1947, Proffi, a precocious twelve-year-old, though thoroughly indoctrinated by staunchly Zionist parents, eventually abandons his sweet dreams of proving himself to the tribe by fighting in the Underground to hasten the collapse of the British Mandate. A growing friendship with a friendly British soldier, whose scatterbrained earnestness endears him to the Sabra youngster, severely tests Proffi's nascent apprehension of the shifting values of slippery concepts such as "loyalty" and "betrayal." This bitter knowledge effectively isolates him from his peers. Like Proffi, Oz's restless adult characters struggle, and often fail, to practice a morality that sometimes exceeds the comprehension of those surrounding them, by coalescing seemingly mutually exclusive qualities such as egoism and altruism, self-realization and compassion. Ultimately of course, this amounts to questioning the official custodians who monopolize and define the public interest. That these austere and authoritarian figures are, incidentally, frequently their fathers, only intensifies the dramatic conflicts that enliven Oz's novels.

Long identified with a succession of political groups within the Israeli Peace Movement, Oz's efforts to promote coexistence with the Palestinians have been unwavering, at least until the horrific carnage of the *Al Aqsa Intifada,* which so successfully shattered the Israeli left. And even in its vicious aftermath, in the virtual state of war that has become the quotidian Israeli reality as of this writing, Oz doggedly champions a two-state solution. Regarding the need for both sides to come to terms with compromised versions of their ideal borders, the novelist has chosen to delineate his pragmatic view of the future in distinctly literary terms, distinguishing between a "Shakespearean" and a "Chekovian" resolution of the tragedy that engulfs Palestinians and Israelis alike:

> My definition of a tragedy is a clash between right and right. And in this respect, the Israeli-Palestinian conflict has been a tragedy, a clash between one very powerful, very convincing, very painful claim over this land and another no less powerful, no less convincing claim. Now such a clash between right claims can be revolved in one of two manners. There's the Shakespeare tradition of resolving a tragedy with the stage hewed with dead bodies. . . . But there is also the Chekov tradition. In the conclusion of the tragedy by Chekov, everyone is disappointed, disillusioned, embittered, heartbroken, but alive. And my colleagues and I have been working . . . not to find the sentimental happy ending, a brotherly love, a sudden honeymoon to the Israeli-Palestinian tragedy, but a Chekovian ending, which means clenched teeth compromise.[6]

In *A Perfect Peace,* the festering seeds of the present Israeli-Arab crisis (as well as a strong hint of Oz's insistence on a "clenched teeth compromise" of moderation) are present in the ideological soil of Oz's troubling fictional portrayal of claustrophobic kibbutz life and expansive but ultimately sterile desert space. Traversing these terrains, he candidly lays bare a microcosm of Israel's fears, dreams, and anxieties. In the course of the novel, Oz portrays the insular defensiveness of the modern Jewish state as smothering the lonely individual whose flight from national space toward desert space is seen as a cultural and political relapse.

Yosefa Loshitzky, while hailing Oz as one of Israel's greatest "advocates of nonfanaticism" or "sane Zionism," nevertheless sees a paradox at the heart of his oeuvre: "Both in his fiction as well as in his polemical essays, Oz . . . indirectly celebrates madness (both personal and political) mainly through his use of poetically charged and excessive language that makes madness look more 'interesting' than sanity. One may gauge the evolving sense of Israeli personal and political identity in this tension between madness and normalcy" (111).

The struggle between madness and equilibrium, whether that of the society or the individual, is surely one of the most compelling features of Oz's work. He often presents characters vividly caught in this tension, engulfed by crisis, often struggling with a sinking awareness that meaning, morality, and justice are not preordained in the modern Middle East. The individual's moral resources are severely taxed by a society whose transcendental values of communalism, solidarity, justice, and ultimately democracy are themselves rapidly decaying. Hence, the open-ended desert beckons as an apt space for the resolution of crisis faced by characters that face a claustrophobic Jewish society which has lost its own way in a perilous realm of fault lines, cracks, and gaps, a geography in which no one really knows the way.

Nobody writing in Israel today has a more intimate understanding of the fraught intimacy of the bold social revolution of the kibbutz, so often portrayed in the Hebrew novel as "Israel's quintessential social structure and the Zionist ideal in microcosm" (Rachel Brenner, "'Hidden Transcripts' Made Public," 85). After a hiatus of more than a decade in which Oz experimented with a variety of shorter forms including political essays, novellas, and even a well-received children's book, *A Perfect Peace* marked a significant development in his oeuvre. Set between the winter of 1965 and the eve and aftermath of the 1967 Six-Day War, *A Perfect Peace* is Oz's far-reaching exploration of the dangerous ideological and political divide between kibbutz generations as experienced by an unhappy young man for whom, smothered by the communal responsibilities and ego-suppressing nature of kibbutz life, "madness" (to borrow Loshitzky's formulation) indeed begins to appear more enticing than "sanity."

The novel asks important questions about identity and self-consciousness by centering on the internal crisis of Yonatan Lifshitz, raised in a kibbutz situated near the ruins of Sheikh Dahr, an Arab village destroyed during Israel's 1948 war for independence. As we will see, the stark fact of that destruction is a quiet but increasingly urgent motif throughout the novel. As the story begins, Yonatan's crisis is ironically foreshadowed in the imagery invoked by a religious broadcaster: "One evening, on the radio news, a certain Rabbi Nachtigall . . . used the phrase 'a desert wasteland and a wilderness.' For the rest of that night . . . through the next day, Yonatan absentmindedly recited these words as if they were a mantra: the magic of wilderness . . . the magic of wasteland" (15). Here and elsewhere, Yonatan imagines that he is being summoned by the voice of the desert, but to what purpose he is unsure. Perhaps this hesitation is due to the fact that in *A Perfect Peace,* as with Oz's earlier "Nomad and Viper," the kibbutz and the wilderness embody the Apollonian and Dionysian polarities of culture which often course through many of Oz's characters. Building on the logic of Loshitzky's critical terms of "madness" and "sanity," Yair Mazor's lofty but apt distinctions between the essential tensions of Oz's creative universe offer a useful interpretive framework:

> On the one hand, Oz's world is founded on logic, discipline, pure reason and solid, cogent rationality; on the other hand, it is a dark, demonic world of unbridled desire, echoing with the hoarse shrill shrieks of passion and lust. The turbulent, murky world of gushing, untamed emotions threatens to invade the sober, well-lighted world of rationality and spread its deadly venom there. It seeks to undermine and destroy its order, balance, and serenity; to instill a sinister and evil spirit of malignancy and nightmare that will rob the other domain of its happiness and tranquility. (2)[7]

Such uneasy tensions are indelibly evident from the novel's first page, where we learn that Yonatan—kibbutz mechanic, army reserves captain, and specialist in reconnaissance who, after being wounded in war embodies the virtues of Zionist soldiering, has been decorated with a medal for his bravery under fire—is inexplicably determined "to leave his wife and the kibbutz on which he had been born and raised" (3).

In deft strokes, Oz insinuates Yonatan's conformity to the popular notion of the brash and ever-youthful Sabra, the "authentic" representative of the native-born Israeli often portrayed in the nation's literature and civil rhetoric as "wild and untamed, yet innocent and sincere" (Weiss 25–26). And as Yael Zerubavel observes, this figure was but one part of a deterministically scripted binary opposition: "the Jew of exile was portrayed as uprooted, cowardly and manipulative, old and sickly, helpless and defenseless in face of persecution, interested in materialistic gains or conversely, excessively immersed in religion. . . . In contrast, the New Hebrew . . . was characterized as young and robust, daring and resourceful, direct and down-to-earth, honest and loyal, ideologically committed and ready to defend his people to the bitter end" ("The 'Mythological Sabra' and Jewish Past" 115). Ironically, though often perceived as ruggedly "individualistic," this figure actually embodies Zionist collectivism, raised under cultural imperatives that link self-fulfillment to the successful pursuit of national goals often requiring violent sacrifice. Little wonder that (like Hareven's ancient/modern dissidents), the unsettled desert eventually tempts Oz's contemporary paragon of these civic and martial virtues as a refuge from the stifling demands of socialist conformity.

Yonatan's urge to liberate himself from the monotony of the provincial kibbutz (that is the nation's idealized embodiment of itself) casts deep shadows of discontent over his surroundings. Intimations of the psychological torment that culminates in his flight toward transcendence are hauntingly projected into the details of a landscape displayed in the young man's home in which "[a] dark bird perched on a red brick fence. Shamelessly piercing the surrounding murk like a golden spear was a diagonal shaft of sunlight. Lancing a brick at the bottom of the picture, it caused it to blossom into a nimbus of blinding light. The bird looked weary; its bill was slightly, thirstily agape, its eyes closed" (92).

There seems little danger of exaggerating Oz's hint that the "weary" bird connotes Yonatan's own dream of flight and wandering, distances, and the faraway. Yet the fact that for 170 pages the young man doesn't act on this displaced yearning seems indicative of Oz's greater interest in fully elaborating the complex psychological and political issues that culminate in his character's crisis. Trapped in the smothering mechanistic routine of kibbutz life and an unsatisfactory marriage, Yonatan resents his father Yolek (one of Oz's most memorable characters), the aging but still potent kibbutz secretary who was a member of Ben-Gurion's cabinet, a famous member of a generation of political giants that overshadow their disaffected sons. Little wonder that the son has uneasy dreams of his father, whose role in the novel resembles the medieval legend of the wounded fisher-king (particularly insofar as his realm is unstable), commanding him "on behalf of the secret service . . . to undertake a dangerous journey to some northern land and lay the serpent low in its lair with an ax stroke from behind" (21). Oz shares Hareven's interest in the lingering cultural traces of ancient stories, suggestively intermingling biblical with European myths throughout his portrayals of both the father and son's restless imaginations.[8] For instance, Yolek has a disturbing nightmare in which "Ben-Gurion, red-faced and terrible, had sprung at him from a nearby Arab well and roared 'I don't want to hear another word about it! You'll shut up and kill if you have to . . . just as King Saul killed his own son!'" (119).[9] And later during his sojourn in the desert, Oz's tightly interwoven portrait of father and son has the exasperated and biblically literate young man drawing illumination on his situation from the same scriptural source, albeit from a reverse perspective: "Just like that shitass son of King Saul in the Bible who wasn't good enough to be king or good enough for anything except to get himself killed in a war. . . . Hats off to you, Little John, slain upon the high places" (267).

The conflict here presents one of numerous echoes of one of Oz's earliest stories, "The Way of the Wind," where another kibbutz father sternly cleaves to the paradigm of a new genealogical line of the "new Jew" who is "free of deformities," or exilic neurosis. His son (who like Yonatan bears the burden of being named for a biblical hero) is a gentle intellectual who struggles to please his father by enlisting in the paratroops. In the somewhat heavy-handed allegorical denouement, the youth joins a celebratory jump on Independence Day above the kibbutz only to be fatally electrocuted when his parachute catches on high-tension wires. His corpse is transformed into a grotesque exhibit of non-belonging when he is left dangling "like a slaughtered goat on a hook" (39). The momentous role of this visceral image aligns Oz with Hareven and numerous Israeli writers imaginatively preoccupied with the *akedah*'s enduring cultural relevance.

In *A Perfect Peace,* the psychologically fraught dreams of both father and son underscore the sense that the founding generation, whose authoritarianism reaches mythic proportions, has only a legacy of violence and self-destruction to pass on to their sons. Hence, it seems fitting that Yonatan's wife Rimona perceives her husband and all men of his generation as predatory beasts: "Just a rumor or whiff of war is enough to make them both more dangerous, more handsome, more passionate . . . the sex part is simple. It's over with the minute they come, like a wound you heal with saliva. But this other thing is cruel. The smell of death makes up for what they're missing" (164, 166). Though there is evidence that Yonatan too has grown weary of the martial identity that has produced her unflattering perception, he is at a loss to transcend his training and environment. Even his fantasy life retains the aggressive imprint of this masculinist ideology. Well aware that his actual paternity has been a dark scandal whispered on the kibbutz for years (his "real" father may be "Trotsky," a millionaire living off his hotel profits in Florida), Yonatan feverishly dreams of going to "[a] faraway place where anything is possible—love, danger, arcane encounters, sudden conquests" (6). Perhaps because he intuits that his patrimony is so heatedly disputed by these competing Zionist and diasporic fathers, he is fated to be torn between rootedness in national space and the allure of forbidden territories and identities.

Yet before he renounces Zionist masculinity, fleeing heedlessly into the desert that lies beyond Israel's southern borders, Oz ensures that we first learn a great deal about the moral cost of building a state, the existential toll exacted on both its founders and sons. How can the longing for self-determination be brought into harmony with the longing for shared community, particularly when the latter demands rigorous conformity? Through Oz's rich delineation of the hero's crisis of entrapment, these questions are put to the test. For an individual subject to a utopian upbringing intended to create the ultimate socialized, contented subject, Yonatan's soul-sick musings exhibit distinctly dystopian tendencies: "I was thinking of a dirty little book I once read in English about what the seven dwarfs really did to Snow White while she was sleeping off the poisoned apple. It was all a fraud . . . That, and Hansel and Gretel, and Little Red Riding Hood, and The Emperor's New Clothes, and all those sweet stories where everybody lived happily ever after. It was all a fraud" (11).

This rueful memorial pastiche of fairy tales and lost innocence offers a significant clue to Yonatan's bitter sense of entrapment, the failure of kibbutz ideology to meet the individual's deepest longings. This flood of memories also signals his need to set off on his own quest of self-discovery, ironically an impulse that will unconsciously substitute hot desert sands for the cold and dark European forests of the Brothers Grimm. Yet another vital clue is offered by Oz's portrayal of Rimona, Yonatan's beautiful but disturbingly vacuous wife, as a dormant Snow White.

Yonatan perceives her as a "barren desert" and their sterile bedroom appears "[a]t three in the morning on a wide, arid sheet beneath a wide, arid ceiling with everything gleaming like the bones of a cadaver in the light of the full dead moon in the window, wide awake yet abducted by some white nightmare in a . . . wasteland, wide awake but alone with a corpse" (60). Oz's charged imagery insinuates that, when at last Yonatan melts into the sparsely settled south of Israel and exchanges the disappointing illusions of a marital wasteland for the bedrock truths of the real thing, it is as if to exorcize the internal desert within his soul.[10] For her part, Rimona distrusts the very basis of her husband's restless wanderlust and eagerness to transcend a life that adequately satisfies their mundane needs: "Maybe you think new things should happen all the time, but that isn't so. . . . What should happen, Yoni? You're a grown man. I'm your wife. This is home. All this is us. And it's the middle of the winter" (65). Some readers may cringe at Oz's overdetermined depiction of her simple-minded, maternal nature. Rimona's instinctive, nondiscriminating nurturing is perhaps too readily available to everyone. But Yonatan's rebellion against this admirable but heatless love (he sees her as a "cold, exquisite slab of marble" [60]), further signals the true source of his dissatisfaction, for like the kibbutz itself, Rimona seems unable to assign special meaning to any individual (in equal shares, whether stray animals or lonely, single men). And yet corroboration of his individuality is what Yonatan most sorely needs.

Rimona's uncomplicated description of the harmony of routine, responsibility, and unceasing labor ironically serves only to stir his unrest:

> When you're done working for the day, you can sit on the lawn with Udi and Anat and talk politics. You'll go to the all-kibbutz chess tournament and maybe win another medal. When you come home, it will be time for winter plowing. Your brother Amos will get out of the army and maybe he'll marry Rachel. You'll start picking lemons and grapefruit, and then oranges, and you and Udi will be busy all day getting the shipments out on time. . . . And then winter will come back, and we'll light the heater and sit here together, and it can rain all it wants and we won't get wet. (67)

After Rimona's banal paen to duty, continuity, and sameness, Yonatan can only mutter "And then?"—to which she soothingly responds with maddening logic, "Then it will be autumn again." His resulting fury is exacerbated in part by guilt due to his earlier insistence that she agree to an abortion, a procedure which later causes a second child to be stillborn.

Oddly, the sterility of Yonatan's loveless marriage links him to the ailing condition of his own father, at once richly individualized and yet emblematic of his generation. Ironically, in spite of the kibbutz movement's manifestly egalitarian nature (which was certainly still the case in the mid-sixties), the community of Kibbutz Granot resembles a decadent monarchy presided over by Yonatan's father, the kibbutz secretary. Yolek Lifshitz is one of the Zionist "Founders" of Ben-Gurion's generation, a scarred and embattled warrior of many ideological as well as martial battles. His generation lived and died by the logic of an apocryphal Zionist motto, "[f]or a people without a land, a land without a people," that effectively rendered the indigenous Arab population invisible (effacing the memory of the abandoned village that borders the kibbutz), a fateful denial that now festers in his disaffected son's struggle with reality.[11]

Yolek is a man of unrelenting pragmatism and action; though an occasional stray thought like "starlight on a winter night was no doubt to be taken auspiciously . . . life was basically a rum business" (193) suggestively gestures toward a poetic nature, such reserves remain well-hidden in the face of constant duty. However, he now passively languishes. Alienated from his son (of whose true progeny both he and the kibbutz are uncertain) he is beset with doubts as to the long-term prospects of his socialist dreams and accomplishments. Though ravaged by the aches and pains of old age, the actual source of his discontent lies deep and mysterious: "Quite apart from his physical woes, some obscure worry was gnawing away inside him. He felt he had forgotten some terribly important, even urgent, matter, one that was imperative to remember lest some great harm be done. Yet what it was, and why it was so urgent, he could not for the life of him recall. . . . Outside, the rain began to come down harder" (52–53). Not content to rest on his laurels as part of an aging elite, with a proud record of nation building behind him, Yolek is strikingly reminiscent of Saul Bellow's depiction of Moses Herzog, an old Lear drafting stormy letters to old political adversaries (which, like Herzog, he rarely sends). These are invariably gloomy, filled with near-apocalyptic dread.

One winter day, riding a bus along Israel's Mediterranean coast to attend a meeting of the Labor Party Central Committee, the aging warrior-kibbutznik is apparently reassured by all the evidence of the young state's vigor, all the minute as well as monumental ways it has taken control of its environment:

> Yolek Lifshitz looked out the window at the washed pine trees whispering in the wind, redolent of peace and good will. All along the road running through the coastal plain new settlements had sprung up, gleaming white with roofs of red tile. All were constructed in straight lines, the houses equally spaced, as if designed by a bright, logical child. Between the houses the residents had already strung laundry lines, built shacks and storerooms, erected fences, put in trees and bushes, planted lawns, and hoed up beds of earth for flowers and vegetables. (105)

Unlike his son's estrangement, Yolek seems anchored by his sense of the country's surging vitality, corporeality, stability, and permanency. And yet, despite celebrating these signs of vigorous urban growth, Yolek is inwardly haunted by unease. For in such moments it seems as if the centuries of Jewish exile prove more tangible and enduring than the sunny, but somehow unreal, present suggests:

> Yet on these winter nights winds sometimes swept up the wadis and through the crevices of the mountains until you heard them break into a desperate howl right outside your window, as if they had been driven

> all the way from the snowy steppes of the Ukraine and still had found no peace. And right before dawn a formation of jets would sometimes shoot with savage furor across the low canopy of sky like a pack of hounds in heat. (108)

Still, for the most part, Yolek's inner and outer landscapes successfully commingle, each an extension of the other; perhaps he has labored too long for his vision of socialist Zionism to fully recognize a private realm sundered from the public. However, upon finding himself in an unfamiliar neighborhood, rather than being impressed by its manifest industriousness and quality of life, he recoils from the materialist values he feels are already undermining the hard-won Zionist dream of the new Jew:

> Its residents had taken all their savings, borrowed more money, obtained mortgages . . . to be able to live in these blindingly white high-rise buildings, in luxury apartments that would have made the local moneybags in the shtetl they had come from . . . turn green with envy in his unmarked grave. In vain, Yolek realized, had been the whole arduous attempt to rebuild Jewish life on a new foundation; in vain, the pioneers' tents and co-op restaurants; in vain, the creed of physical labor and life in the sun; in vain, the going barefoot, the peasant clothes, the shepherds' songs; in vain, the long nights of argument and debate. All these ex-pioneers who had skimped, saved, and borrowed to build homes, in each of them a living room; in each living room, a glass-paneled cabinet; in each glass-paneled cabinet, a fancy dinner service for twelve. (112–13)

This is what another member of Yolek's generation acerbically dismisses as "keeping up with the Cohens." As in the medieval parable of the fisher-king, a trope that Judd Ne'eman argues is surprisingly prevalent in Israeli culture, Yolek's angst and unease seems mirrored by a sense of weary malaise that has settled over his entire community.[12] Behind his back, members of the kibbutz mutter darkly to one another about his leadership, the growing scandal of his son's apparently failing marriage, and the general ruinous state of things: "Things are going to the dogs, my friend. . . . For all his big talk, Yolek never got off his butt to do a damn thing around here. Everything in sight is falling apart. The kibbutz. The country. The youth. I don't want to stoop to gossip . . . but just take a look at what's going on with a certain Very Important Person's son. *For the Lord hath created a new thing in the earth, one woman shall compass two men*" (177).

Through Yolek's response to kibbutz gossip and grumblings, the novel ruptures the idyll of kibbutz and nation, showing both to be riddled with social pretense, moral ambivalence, illness, and loathing. Most of all, Yolek is fearful of the lack of idealistic fire he senses in the young generation. But for the latter, the large political organizations to which Yolek has selflessly surrendered a long and embattled life, fail to provide the answers to the larger questions of life. The Jewish children of the kibbutz's new generation have only contempt for the lofty realm of politicians and politics. Yolek's son in particular detests the kibbutz's formalism along with what he regards as its hypocritical and dishonest call for perpetual "selfless" commitment. Even worse, the Miami hotel magnate Benya Trotsky, who was once intimately involved with Yolek's wife Hava, is now campaigning to persuade Yonatan, who he suspects is his biological son, to join him in America.

Self-righteously, Yolek warns the hilariously dubbed Trotsky, "Lay not thy hand upon the lad!"—Oz's wry intertextual nod to the angel's call to Abraham as he prepares to sacrifice Isaac (Gen. 22:12). As if the personal psychodrama of infidelity and paternity that divide Trotsky and Yolek weren't enough, there are also seething layers of bitter ideological conflict: the tension between Diaspora and Zion, of kibbutz idealism vs. city materialism. Even more than writing polemics against his old political foes, Yolek masochistically delights in drafting letters to this long-absent adversary that conventionally blur the men's personal history with Zionist repudiation of the *galut* Jew perpetually on the make:

> No power on earth can possibly forgive me for the moronic pity I showed in not digging your grave thirty years ago. . . . You are the lowest of the low. It's people like you who've been the poisonous cancer in the body of the Jewish people for generations. You're the age-old curse of the Exile. You're the reason the Gentiles hated and still hate us. . . . You with your money grubbing, you with your Golden Calf, you with your foaming lechery . . . stopping at no betrayal, sleeping on your filthy ducats that spread like germs from country to country, from exile to exile . . . homeless, conscienceless, rootless, making us a laughingstock and a pariah among the nations. (191)

Raging against decades of unease over his son's paternity, Yolek determines to exorcize the diasporic demons that might otherwise take root in his son. For in Yolek's eyes, Yonatan embodies the first Sabra generation to be born in freedom: "the first of a new line of Jews whose children and children would grow up in this land to put an end to the malignancy of the Exile. And now the Exile is back again, masquerading as a rich uncle. . . . Goddamn your soul, Trotsky, may it rot in hell!" (192). Of course it is Yolek, not Trotsky, who would bind Yonatan to the altar that has so often proved fatal—that of the first generation's ideology and wars. For his part, Trotsky merely proposes to offer the young man an alternative, open-ended destiny. Yet, as it happens, the disaffected young man's flight from ideology and home leads not to materialist America but a far more searching, spiritual quest in a transcendent landscape.

From the reader's perspective, as I hinted earlier, it soon becomes ironically apparent that Yolek's own (if often repressed) romanticism, the lure of something stirring both within and beyond, provides a strong hint of a paternal bond:

> Far away, across the border, lights twinkled in the mountains. Yolek raised his coat collar, pulled down his cap against the cold, and stood looking at them. For nearly ten minutes he did not budge, entirely drained of the old passions and high principles that had guided him all his life. . . . Frosty, hushed, and desolate the night, pinioned against the sky and earth, Yolek waited until he saw a falling star. And begged for mercy. (194)

But Yolek's jealousy and political rage both conspire to repress the social unease that would enable him to identify with his son. The angst that Yolek, and everyone else the reader encounters, apparently feels in the ailing socialist kingdom, is exacerbated by an almost supernaturally long rainy season, highly atypical for Israel, which reduces the kibbutz paths to mud, discouraging agricultural activity and all other forms of social engagement. For Yolek, hope arrives when Azariah, a strange young immigrant from the European Diaspora (later revealed as a Holocaust survivor), suddenly appears at the ebb of this winter of discontent, literally on his doorstep like a foundling, and the kibbutz patriarch embraces him as a new hope. Eventually, this exilic figure assumes redemptive proportions, at least for the kibbutz secretary.

In the beginning, much like a rabbi with a would-be convert, Yolek wards off the young man's fervent pleas for immediate acceptance in the community. Soon he is won over by the fact that Azariah, a Spinoza-quoting intellectual, is filled with precisely the kind of fiery socialist dreams ridiculed by Yonatan and his generation.[13] As Mazor aptly describes the abrasive outsider's interaction with his new surroundings, Azariah "injects himself into the brightly lit, summery kibbutz environment . . . redolent of that musty, moldy odor that native-born Israelis used to find repulsive and objectionable; his personality projects a certain furtive abjectness, a smarmy, conniving, insincere courtesy that . . . barely masks an innate crassness and vulgarity . . . from a Sabra's point of view, Azariah Gitlin embodies the stereotype of the exilic, Ghetto Jew" (147). However, in spite of his slightly ludicrous appearance and manners, the young feverish intellectual appears to Yolek much like a determined Hotspur to Yonatan's debauched Hal. Rapidly winning the kibbutz patriarch's favor, he eagerly ingratiates himself with the father figure (representative of homeland) he yearns will adopt him:

> The main thing was that he had developed an interest in the history of the kibbutz movement. He had talked to many people about it and read a number of essays and even a novel—and, of course, Comrade Lifshitz's pamphlet Facing the Future—so that he was by no means a stranger to the subject and had some idea who he had the honor to be speaking with. . . . He simply wished to be accepted by Kibbutz Granot. To strike roots in its soil, so to speak. . . . In all honesty and frankness, he should point out that he was accustomed to the harshest conditions and most backbreaking work. Not only had he just left the army but as a child in Europe he had grown up under Hitler's boot. No job, if you asked him, could be too difficult in a place where one could go to work every day with a sense of joy and community. If he wasn't mistaken, that was the whole idea of the kibbutz. (41, 42)

For his part, Yolek is utterly entranced by the stranger's striking contrast to "the hulking, tongue-tied, thick-skulled Huns, Scyths, and Tatars who had grown up in the kibbutz acting as though they were merely the most recent of immemorial generations of peasants" (43). Enthralled by the young eccentric's impassioned idealism, so in contrast to his unhappy son's cynicism about the obligations of socialistic life, Yolek imagines that Azariah uncannily evokes "those tormented soul-searchers from the small towns of Russia and Poland who had founded the first kibbutzim out of nothing, in the face of disease and desert heat" (44).

At first, Yonatan and his friends are merely amused by the stranger's hubristic rhetoric and quaint idealism. But they too are grudgingly impressed when, after Yonatan fails to fix a tractor, Azariah succeeds. Later, during a nature outing in damp weather, he manages to light a fire when the Sabras fail, earning their masculine approval. Though initially Yonatan condescendingly regards Azariah as a sort of pet project, suddenly it seems utterly logical to the alienated kibbutz son, who after all has been raised in a system dependent on the socialist logic of adaptive exchanges and who has already delayed his escape for months, that his new friend may be the right man to light Rimona's erotic fire as well.[14] Later, Oz brilliantly parodies the utilitarian mechanics of the collective system's beehive-like replacement of one individual by another. Dismissing the sexual scandal Yonatan's mysterious absence has provoked, Azariah offers this explanation of his fortuitous appearance to Srulik, the new kibbutz secretary who replaces Yolek: "'I want you to know,

Comrade Srulik, that it was Yonatan who invited me into his home. It's as simple as that. You can even announce it at the next general meeting. He wanted someone to be there. He even showed me where he kept all his tools so I could replace him. Just as you've replaced Yolek" (249). In this and the other reductive absurdities that operate within the microcosm of kibbutz life, the novel suggests that the claustrophobia of the modern Jewish state, as well as the epic geospatial scope of Jewish history, conspire to goad the lonely individual into a nomadic (and hence regressive) embrace of desert space.

Long before Yonatan's exodus to the desert, we receive an important hint of events to follow when a minor immigrant character contemplates the "forced gaiety" of the remarkable city of Tel Aviv. For the world-wise immigrant, the "clamor" it makes "to drown out the outer silence" is an illusion that allows for a temporary respite, at best, from the long history of Jewish pain and exile. The modern state of Israel seems like an all-too-fleeting haven, merely an oasis between past and future catastrophes: "Behind this western wall, the city cowered, cringing with fear of the open spaces that lay beyond. Even as a man turns his back to a strong wind, rounds his shoulders, tucks his head hard between them, and awaits a coming blow" (114). As we have seen, Yonatan himself seems to be suffering from a psychic trauma. Reluctantly he confronts the disparity between the threadbare Zionist myths he was raised on, the lies and deceptions of the present, and the intimations of a violent future that looms just ahead. Raised on the highest ideals of human community and justice, Yonatan has loyally served his country as an army officer during various skirmishes. But now he struggles to regain a lost sense of at-homeness and selfhood apparently missing since childhood. Fully aware that he has been going through the motions of agrarian socialism like a man trying to walk under water, he withdraws from the incestuous trivialities of kibbutz politics and the lives of its members. Their incessant debates on agendas and proposals only seem to promise him a prison of conformity. The son, like the father, is heartsick.

The more exquisitely detailed Oz's description of the natural beauty of the kibbutz and its surroundings, the more the reader is jarred by the depths to which the young man's cynicism (for whom "longing of any kind is a poison" [267]) apparently plummets. Even the most cherished icons of kibbutz life are malformed by Yonatan's morbid state of mind. For instance, one dazzling Sabbath morning of birdsong, breezes, and sunlight, his gloom overshadows even the innocence of the *Bet Yeladim,* the idealized collective and egalitarian child-rearing institution that is at the heart of all kibbutz life:

> The kindergarten children sent up a solitary kite. It climbed tenaciously to heavenly heights, at which it seemed to be a flying genie or sea monster. Don't believe any of it, it's a trap, thought Yonatan Lifshitz as he dressed. . . . They're just decorating your death with the crepe-paper of love. If you don't make tracks now like an animal, they'll trick you into staying until you relax and forget that your life is your own. (115–16)

Here Oz provocatively evokes the heated debates over child-rearing practices that increasingly troubled kibbutz members in the 1970s and 1980s. Many disillusioned members in this period concluded that the uniqueness of the individual, the quality of his or her self-esteem, was compromised in the intensely collective society. With the kibbutz movement's spartan dedication to service in communal life and the rigor of elite military units, many individuals raised by kibbutz education later reported that they found themselves in crisis, lacking the opportunity for personal development or the means of self-expression and anxious about ever-diminishing spiritual and cultural horizons.[15] As Balaban notes, the crux of Yonatan's unhappiness throughout the novel "is the feeling that he was never treated as a free human being, but as a 'human factor or manpower' . . . 'a means for implementing a fervent plan'" (*Between God and Beast* 120). The childhood of the hapless individual and the struggles of the young state are deeply interwoven in *A Perfect Peace.*

Precisely because the novel addresses these issues so effectively, by the time Yonatan departs, many of Oz's readers too may be breathing some relief when they are transported from the gloomy and embittered claustrophobia of this fading utopia to the spacious, unregulated desert landscape that beckons. In this sense, Yonatan's flight toward the ineffable proves richly illustrative of Attias and Benbassa's premise that in the Israeli cultural imagination, the biblical desert "does not cease being a temptation, perceived as an ever-open possibility of starting again" (19).

When at last he flees, Yonatan's mysterious disappearance throws his father and the entire kibbutz into a state of frenzied panic. Yet it is as if their collective uproar is less over Yonatan's safety and more in uneasy response to the abyss at the heart of their society: "maybe our whole way of thinking had a fatal flaw hidden in it right from the start" (282). As for Yonatan, he carries a great deal with him into the wilderness. For one thing, there is his father, with whom he struggles to converse, like Aeneas and his dead father Anchises in *The Aeneid,* out of the ruins of Troy: "He recalled how his father loathed the desert. The very word made Yolek grimace, as if it were a dirty word. It often catapulted him into one of his taming-the-wilderness spiels" (265). Landscapes, like the individual, had no innate significance of their own and must be culturally harnessed into the service of the master Zionist narrative:

> Deserts were a badge of shame, a mark of inequity, a disgrace to the map of Israel, an evil presence, an ancient enemy that must be subdued by armies bringing tractors, irrigation pipes, and fertilizer sacks until the last of its surly acres had been compelled to bear. *And the desert shall rejoice and blossom like a rose. For in the wilderness shall waters break out and streams in barren places.* Jewish water engineers would turn the parched ground into fountains and the thirsty land into springs. (265)

For his part, disturbingly drawn not only to the desert but enemy soil itself, where he peculiarly imagines that he will be redeemed in the place where human skeletons are "bleached by the sun and preserved by the dryness and heat in a state of polished perfection," Yonatan's repudiation seems a perverse echo of Bialik's "Dead of the Desert."

Imagining himself "pierced" by a greater reality as he has not been since his war wound (a mysterious injury which, like that endured by Hemingway's Jake Barnes, the narrator never specifies), Yonatan suddenly knows that his destination is Petra, the city "half as old as time," a discovery that enthralls him: "Just then, as swiftly as flame, a flash of piercing joy shot through him such as he had not felt since he was wounded in the raid . . . a wild, exquisite joy that percolated through every cell of his body to its very nerve endings, that made him feel a sweet tremor in his knees, a warm lump in his throat, a transfixing dilation in his chest, and an allergy of tears in his eyes" (217). He is more awake to his surroundings—and more importantly to the very meaning of his own subjectivity—than we have ever seen him.

Yonatan's orgasmic dream of entering foreign desert space in this moment might also be usefully compared to readings of an earlier cultural history of Zionist youth movement marches into remote areas that had a pseudo-martial nature during the prestate period. As Oz Almog recounts: "The youth movement marches to the Judean Desert, the ends of the Dead Sea, the Tzin Canyon, the Large Crater, Ein Gedi, and other distant points, while ignoring the British restrictions, granted the marches a national and heroic stature, a kind of proud national defiance—'we are here nevertheless' and also an element of danger, making the marches almost military" (175).

Though Yonatan's escapist idyll seems driven by alienation from the nation rather than Zionist fervor, it underscores Almog's sense that such youth hikes, a mainstay of Zionist pedagogy particularly in the kibbutz movement, "were a tool for creating drama and a sense of adventure, danger, suspense, and romanticism—adrenaline-producers for young people who were otherwise sitting around doing nothing" (177). Almog claims these activities engineered "an entire folklore of suspenseful and mysterious stories about clashes with Bedouins in the Judean wilderness and the stashing of weapons" (177). To better come to terms with the cultural significance of Yonatan's strange exultation, it bears consideration that, though meant to institutionalize Zionist culture, these intoxicating marches into forbidden territory inevitably instilled an ecstatic sense of the *individual,* unfettered by society, unleashed into the untamed exuberance of nature. In his engaging review of diaries and journals kept in the 1930s and 1940s by youth who undertook dangerous treks as individuals or in small groups, Almog finds that "[t]he experience of the march resembled . . . the intoxicating experience of the long-distance runner—self-denial ending in catharsis and elation. . . . The mechanism of the march shifted from a ritual and public obsession that served collective needs into an instrument of individual exaltation and euphoria. [Whereas] in a march undertaken by an army company or unit, the achievement is shared by many participants; in an individual march, the achievement is individual . . . a private, and therefore more satisfying, ecstasy" (184). In this light, Yonatan's private exodus from the collective vision takes on a sharper poignancy.

Desperate to come to terms with the mystery of a subjectivity that the carefully engineered, utilitarian society has denied him, Yonatan hitchhikes across the country, resting overnight in a remote desert outpost where his liberated libido leads to an amorous night spent with Michal, a charming and intelligent female soldier. Just as before, Oz presents the troubled masculinity of the Zionist hero in an uneasy mélange of sex and violence. Rimona's earlier characterization of her husband's confusion of Eros and Thanatos seems fully justified, for when Yonatan has an orgasm, he is "like a dog shot in the dark [he] let out a cry . . . burst into a flood of tears and sperm as if every wound in his life had opened at once and the very blood of that life was pouring out" (272). Impatient to elude any form of commitment and containment, he soon abandons her. Though their furious lovemaking enables him to momentarily overcome the sterility of his marriage, in the end Yonatan is left from the encounter with little but a compulsive and lonely drive to resume his deferred exodus. Stealing out of Michal's warm bed in the chill of dawn, his masculinist quest lures him away from the domestic feminine yet again.

Longing for his "perfect peace," Yonatan flees them all—banal utopia, wife, stern father, army, and mistress—eager to exchange the uncertainties of life for the final consummation of self-transcendence. Pausing only to filch an army guide to the desert, he hastily exits the army's maze of tents and shacks to plunge into an unknown, romanticized landscape:

> Beyond the camp stretched the desert vastness, serenely attending night's end. Yonatan squinted into the wind, pulled down his woolen cap, and lifted his jacket collar. His nostrils flared, like those of an animal feeling the call. His whole body was being swept away by an urge to set out at once, to the mountains, the wadis, the canyons, the steep, slippery rock ledges, the dwelling places of the gazelle and the mountain goat, the lair of the wildcat, the mighty pinnacles where nested the vulture, the griffin, and the lammergeir. (274)

Conceivably, Yonatan's willingness to yield to the desert's otherness may derive from his calm submission, a quietism that transcends the rule of ceaseless activity, motion, and force demanded by the army and kibbutz alike. But even if this is indeed the case, I think that Oz only ironically invokes Wordsworthian Romanticism, where Nature takes on the guise of an instructor, to teach the protagonist to harmonize his inner turmoil with the world beyond. Though Yonatan seems prepared to accept that instruction, this conceit soon collapses. In this sense, the novel seems to serve as a Hebraic rebuke to any literal belief in natural transcendence, any permanent consolation in the world beyond human organization. In the anonymity of these vast spaces, Yonatan's long-sought-for selfhood threatens to dissolve almost as soon as it is recovered.

For a time, this vision translates as a humbling spiritual awakening, especially after his first night alone in the desert: "What have I done with my life all these years? From the citrus groves to the dining hall, to a dead double bed to this committee, to that meeting. Here, praise be, I've come home at last. Here, I'm no longer theirs. Thank you for all this beauty" (274). Oddly, Oz chooses to express this in imagery that pointedly evokes a religious Jew wrapping himself in *tzitzit* to recite the liturgy from Psalms 121:1–2: "[His] lips parted like those of a dreamer in an untroubled sleep. The dawn chill was sharp but bracing. Yonatan put on his jacket, wrapped himself in the blanket with the solemnity of a Jew donning a prayer shawl, and stood with his face to the mountains in the east" (274).[16] Significantly, as Yonatan's flight ensues, Oz makes us aware that this vision of a transcendent reality is too easily gained and so it rapidly deteriorates. The provocative equation between the secular Zionist's existential struggle with religious certainty unravels as soon as it is set forth. In Yonatan's emergence from the cultivated contours of kibbutz life into the vast landscapes of the desert, a classic notion of the sublime arises. Increasingly, he experiences sensations of his own perishable existence and insignificance, especially as a mere individual set apart from the self-important enclosure of kibbutz society. Where the collective experience threatened to absorb him, now the sublime untamed landscape engenders a similar loss of resistance.

Though fully aware of the dangers—Arabs may capture and kill him once he has crossed into Transjordan—Yonatan is narcissistically mesmerized by a dream of his own fairy-tale city, the mysterious Nabatean ruins of Petra, set against rosy sandstone hills in a remote desert valley described evocatively in his guidebook as "unmarked by the tooth of time for two millennia . . . desolate and without a human presence," a phrase which he fetishistically links to his own condition: "like my life" (323).[17] Curiously, Yonatan imagines Petra as a fiery place ("Oleander bushes blazed . . . sculpted rocks flared upward in tongues of red, purple, and vermilion flame" [323]) where the souls of the dead congregate and another character calls "the bottom pit of hell" (329). As if to expiate for his own violence, Yonatan visualizes the ruinous landscape as the perfect scene of romantic violence for his heroic exit:

> He envisioned his death that night from a burst of bullets in the chest or a curved dagger between the shoulder blades. There was no fear in the thought of such a death, alone in the wilderness on enemy soil, face down in the dark sand, his blood soaking into the dust like a venom purged from his body. In such a death, he might at last find perfect peace, as sometimes he had found it when, during a childhood illness, he had lain between the cool sheets of his parents' bed, in the dim light of the shuttered blinds, beneath his mother's quilt. Yonatan yearned for a death as gentle and painless as this, one that would turn him into just another rock in the stony desert, one that would leave him without a single thought or longing, cold, inanimate, and forever still. (325)

Oz deftly underscores the plaintive nature of this interior voice by suggesting that the fatal innocence of the lost soul might be obvious to any casual observer: "Anyone looking at Yonatan . . . could have easily detected beneath the mask of dust, the scraggly growth of beard, and the tangled, grimy hair the face of the delicate eight-year-old boy he had once been, the sleepy-eyed child always enveloped in a quiet sorrow, as if the grown-ups had made him a promise that he had been sure would be kept but still had not been" (325).

In a surface reading, Yonatan's flight to desert space perversely inverts the Exodus story of homecoming to Canaan—the entire trajectory of the Jewish people. But in a Freudian reading, Oz might also be said to strategically replicate that Mosaic "family romance" where the child forsakes the royal father for Jethro, the desert chieftain. Here the unhappy kibbutz youth runs from the pharaonic Yolek, stern embodiment of kibbutz ideology, to the hostile desert. After Michal, he had thought to forsake all human company. But unexpectedly, he encounters the desert wild man, Tlallim. A sort of benevolent trickster figure, this self-described "desert rat, devil of a fellow, geologist, lover and lush" with a beard as long as "Tolstoy's" is Oz's gently carnivalesque portrayal of a "free-thinker" whose radical independence on the margins of the national story is most unlike the socialist conformity Yonatan has fled. While empathizing with a deep tenderness, condemning the "bastards" who have "smothered" Yonatan's passion for life, he nonetheless urges him to abandon his suicidal scheme to journey alone to Petra. Stationed at the edge of the Israeli polity as a kind of desert prophet, Tlallim vehemently beseeches Yonatan to return to life:

> My boy, what are you? A desperado? A babe in arms? A poet? Here, have a shot of gin. Drink up, *krasavitz,* and then get it all off your chest. Ay, *mama,* just look at the tears this child is choking back. . . . What bloody devils, I'd like to know, seduced you suddenly to go to Petra? . . . Live, you bastard! Live and go on living! . . . You spoiled brat! You little snot! Have a good cry and live! . . . My child! *Zolotoy* mine! What have the bastards done to you? (328–29)

In spite of the boisterous Russian's fiery insistence that he shoulder the burden of life, Yonatan is still nihilistically lured to the balm of utter solitude that lies ever "eastward." Ironically, however, just as he slips over the border, he cannot quash the ringing tones of a patriotic Zionist song that rings in his head: "What more, O what more do you want, our land, that we haven't given you yet?" (337).

Alone in the early desert evening, the young man recedes again into a solipsistic reverie of self-pitying tones that suggest the stubbornness of a delinquent adolescent rather than an adult prepared to endure the gritty ordeal of self-knowledge: "Up in that wadi in the mountains of Edom the nomads are on the move. And I'm a nomad now myself. I'm as good as dead to them all, but I've never been more alive to myself. No one will ever tell me what to do any more" (338). Yet in spite of his self-pity, in the stillness and solitude that gradually overtake him during his flight into liminality, Yonatan achieves a certain glimmer of secular revelation. Though perhaps no less a stranger to himself, by the end of the night he begins to accept a great burden of responsibility: for the alienation of his father; for the loss of his child; for Rimona's apparent madness; and for the sin of having another man tend to her conjugal needs:

> Why did I kill them all? Why am I killing them now? What did they do to me? What did I ever want that I didn't get? What am I looking for

> out here in the wild? . . . I killed Efrat, and that other baby before her, and turned Rimona into a corpse . . . here I am, as happy as a lark, going straight to hell. Let Zaro give her a baby? Let my father die? What was I thinking of all those rainy nights when I wanted to pick up and go? Warmth? Life? Love? Pain and anger mixed? Is that what I was missing? To kill? To be killed? To destroy? (340)

What proves most interesting is that it is not these individual failings but rather the collective sins of Zionism that prove so disquieting to Yonatan in the end. Though the reader may be inclined to view him from the perspective of Tlallim and his other elders—as irreverent, cynical, or otherwise insufficiently dedicated to collectivist goals—Oz hints that there may be more beneath the surface.

In Oz's rapid-fire presentation of anecdotal memories that overtake the young man in the eternity of the desert night, we begin to see Yonatan replace the innocent ideals of the Jewish socialist endeavor with a nascent political consciousness. In the haunting stillness, he is visited by all the literal and figurative ghosts that have subliminally haunted him throughout the novel, culminating in the crisis that facilitates his "escape" from the rigors of the Jewish state. And it is here that the subterranean issue of Palestine surfaces insistently as the young man suddenly recollects visiting the site of "Sheikh Dahr" as a child, ostensibly to search for the lost treasure of gold coins the kibbutz children believed hidden there (in ironic reversal of a popular anti-Jewish myth), only to encounter old agricultural tools, other rotting signs of past human lives—and a growing sense of uncanny dread that lingers into adulthood.

Though first introduced to the reader early in the novel, years later, Yonatan is suddenly transfixed by the inexplicable sense of persecution that nearly smothered him at the scene of ghostly absence: "Far-off jackals were howling. I was only a boy and those dead old villagers were thirsty for blood, for a bloodbath. . . . I was out of breath, and all I had to show from Sheikh Dahr in the end was a stitch in my chest and that terrible fear and sadness that keeps eating you, that keeps nibbling and gnawing at your soul to get up right away and go look for some sign of life in the wasteland" (24).

It is entirely characteristic of Oz's interest in the romantic imagination of children that this childhood episode is strikingly reminiscent of Wordsworth's uneasy "Nutting," an autobiographical lyric about the poet's disturbing intimation of the darkness and violence that resides within through his adolescent encounter with nature. More directly, Yonatan's experience recalls A. B. Yehoshua's early story "Facing the Forests" (1963), about a curiously childlike Israeli fire scout who stumbles onto the truth of a ruined Arab village beneath the Jewish National Forest he watches over. As Jonathan Boyarin observes, "the existence of Palestinian ruins within an Israeli landscape bears witness to a collective struggle for control of space" ("Ruins" 331). Here too, Yonatan's restless angst can be traced to the shock of encountering the "true" meaning of the landscape which his Zionist education has occluded: the destruction of the previous occupants of the land, stubbornly lingering in the form of the ruined village. Though it is difficult to fully assess Oz's intentions in this powerfully poetic section of the novel, it is interesting that the contemporary, domestic ruin of the Arab village contrasts with (and ultimately links to) the epic, romanticized site of Petra that lures his protagonist toward the desert.

Educated in the certitude of Zionist progress and achievement, Yonatan's awakening to the reality that his comfort hinges on the dispossessed Arab Other constitutes a violent existential shock. In these moments, there is a strong resemblance to Levinas's Abraham who, in discovering the alterity of the beyond, encounters the face of the other, a face that as Gary Mole describes it, "puts me into question, worries me, denudes me, opens me up to it" (62). In opposing the myths of the Greek Ulysses and the Hebrew Abraham, Levinas discerns a greater movement away from the dangers of excessive self-identification. The Greek deity of the philosophers is characteristically "a god who is adequate to reason, a god who is understood, incapable of troubling the autonomy of conscience, finding itself again through all its adventures, returning home like Ulysses who, through all his peregrinations, merely heads toward his native island" (*En découvrant l'existence* 188). In contrast, Levinas's Abraham embraces alterity, "leaving his country forever for a yet unknown land and forbidding his servant to bring even his son back to this point of departure" (*En découvrant l'existence* 191). Similarly, in my reading of Oz's deconstruction of the colonialist dimension of the Zionist enterprise, I find *solicitude;* he anticipates what has often been identified solely as the post-Zionist spirit of Israel's youngest ("post-Zionist") writers, attunement to the fate of Zionism's Others. Yet as the interior logic of the novel unfolds, it is not entirely clear whether Oz fully sanctions the political implications of his character's angry questioning.

As an adult, Yonatan would often return to the ruins with friends who collected for garden decorations the "old Arab junk" they found scattered. What they "read" in the landscape confirmed the triumphal Zionist narrative they've been raised with. For instance, as Udi, one of Yonatan's childhood friends, chauvinistically proclaims: "All the Arab terraces have been washed away, but that bottom course of stone still left down there must be from Second or First Temple times. Whatever Jews built, lasts" (125). Udi is comforted by the classical Zionist doctrine that nothing which transpired in the land between its eras of Jewish settlement has any enduring significance; a corollary for the "fact" that the long centuries of *galut* have no relevance to the reborn Sabra. But on one occasion, the joy of a picnic is disturbed by a melancholy that settles over the site, as if nature had conspired with history to preserve the grim, apocalyptic message of the former habitation:

> On the hilltop, against the sky, backed by blue clouds, stood the ruins of Sheikh Dahr, light slashing through the gaping windows like an eviscerating sword, the out-of-doors just as bright on one side of the smashed, charred, homeless walls as on the other. Rubble from fallen roofs lay in heaps. Here and there an unsubmitting grape vine had run wild, cling with bared claws to a remnant of a standing stone wall. Above the ravaged village rose its shattered minaret. (127)

Ironically, the modern Hebrew expression for ruin (*hirba*) is an Arabic borrowing. In another revealing variation on how landscapes are "read" by the novel's pivotal characters, it is noteworthy that, whereas for Yolek, the ruins are a fitting end to what he calls "this murderer's den," his son is guiltily stirred by its insistent silence: "from the ruins came not a sound of protest, not even the bark of a dog. Nothing but the silence of the earth and another, more subtle silence that seemed to blow down from the mountains, the silence of deeds that cannot be undone and of wrongs that no one can right" (127). In Oz's rendering of his protagonist's consciousness, the cultural constructs of "desert" and "desertification" mingle uneasily. Yonatan's awakening to the darker dimensions of the reversal of Jewish powerlessness dims the luster of the "glorious" achievements of his father's generation and precipitates his own crisis of homelessness. Sensitive to what he imagines are the ominous signs of nature's disapproval, Yonatan is incessantly compelled to return to the scene where he queasily observes the presence of expectant crows, buzzards, and other carrion eaters, noting that even "the dripping carob and olive trees kept up a steady pitterpatter, as if the last word, one for which they were still groping, had yet to be said" (128). In the young man's mind, a conflict rages over two conceptions of the same space, and Oz suggests that the clarity and stillness bestowed by the empty "useless" spaces irrelevant to the nation brings this contradiction to the fore.[18] As readers know, that "last word" has yet to be uttered but its apocalyptic force still looms.

In the desert, this disturbing lack of closure provokes yet another disquieting memory, of the very last day the local sheikh, once a family friend, visited Yolek. Though Yonatan was only seven years old at that time, the image of the old man dressed in a white robe, surrounded by notables, now surfaces as a nagging presence in his mind. He recalls that following a brief ceremonious exchange of greetings that soon exhausts his father's lexicon of Arabic phrases, he was sent out of the room prior to the mysterious final negotiation awkwardly conducted with the aid of translators:

> The sheikh touched my cheek with a hand that was furrowed like the earth. . . . Father told me to introduce myself, and Abu-Zuheir ran his weary old eyes from me to the bookshelf and back to father, who was the headman of the kibbutz. . . . It must have been Passover week, because someone brought matzos from the kitchen and a big jug of coffee. And now there's not a dog left in Sheikh Dahr and all of the fields, those we quarreled about and those we didn't, and all their sorghum and barley and alfalfa, are ours. Nothing is left now but those blackened walls on the hill and maybe their curse hanging over us. (129–30)

Zionist films and novels of an earlier period were replete with conventional images of corrupt Arab sheikhs and mukhtars who are overcome by idealistic and virile Zionist farmers. In such narratives, the impoverished landscapes and Arab peasants the Arab patriarchs ineptly administer are replaced by the abundant orchards and fields of the purposeful young pioneers. Clearly, in stressing the dignity and wisdom of the Arab Muslim village patriarch, as well as the fertile, well-tended "fields" of "sorghum and barley and alfalfa" handed over to the kibbutz, Oz sought to subvert this outworn and blinkered representation. Moreover, the novelist's ironic layering of the Passover holiday of redemption from slavery and exile with Yonatan's memories of the old sheikh's poignant mission brilliantly underscores how the triumph of homecoming for one people ensures a tragedy of dispossession for another. And it is an important factor in Yonatan's present turmoil. Following the disturbing reverie, he recalls moving impatiently away from the others, standing alone in an olive grove where "his eyes fell on the easternmost mountains, which seemed in this flowing, honeyed light to be within shouting distance. A dim, steely blue the color of an autumn sea, they loomed like steep breakers that seemed so imminently about to tumble westward that Yonatan felt an urge to run at them at once and plunge in head first" (130). Subsequently, though he vacillated before taking that precipitous plunge for many long months afterward, it is here that Yonatan's crisis was really born.

From this point, it is as though he is infected by the "Old Jew's" sickness of diasporic wandering. As with his view of the kibbutz children's house, Yonatan's inner turmoil distorts his perception of the natural world: "A sickly-looking gibbous moon hung caught in the boughs of an olive tree, like Absalom in his oak. Ringed by craggy branches, it could have been a pale Jewish fiddler trapped by a band of peasants in some distant land of exile" (131). Meanwhile, his friends idly debate the fate of the village of Sheikh Dahr and speculate "about what the Arabs would have done to us had they won, and about what Udi proposed doing to them in the next war" (132). But on this occasion, a benumbed Yonatan can think of little more than the insidious grasp of "the evil ruins of this village and its antediluvian goat dung" (132). He fantasizes about receiving a midnight phone call "from his other father" whose Florida hotels will open up a new life to him.

Udi, Yonatan's hawkish friend, forever preoccupied with dreams of conquest and combat ("He happened to be high up enough in the reserves to know of a fantastic plan to finish off the greaseballs with a single blow" [135]), seems a harmless "primitive," a woeful representative of the sad generation that provokes Yolek's impatience. But in his brutal indifference to the history of the Arab village (and its relation to his own story), he embodies the deconstruction of the Zionist present that festers in Yonatan's imagination, the ominous disparity between principled social justice and the effacement, even the desecration, of the past. For Udi, well-schooled in Zionist narratives of heroic struggle, even a picnic excursion serves to reaffirm the victor's position:

> Udi managed not to return empty-handed from his ramble on the hillside, bringing back a rusty wagon pole found among the rocks, some remnants of a leather harness, and the skull of a horse grimacing with hideous yellow teeth. All three finds were intended to give his front yard what he called "character." He was even considering digging up the skeleton of some greaseball from the village cemetery, wiring it together, and standing it in his garden to serve as a scarecrow and shock the entire kibbutz. (133)

The human remains have no more significance to the combative Sabra than the other ornamental relics of the Orientalized wastes, but a mortified Azariah cryptically warns, "if you don't watch it . . . one of the birds it scares may be the soul of a dead Arab and peck your eyes out" (134).[19] Significantly, while avoiding identification on his journey in the southern Negev, Yonatan informs someone that he is looking for his "lost" friend, whom he calls "Udi." Though Yonatan has seemed a passive figure through much of the novel, prolonged attentiveness to Udi's obtuse actions as well as Azariah's dark rejoinders stirs his dormant conscience. For in his memory, it is clear that the Palestinian village was as vital a community as the Jewish kibbutz—surrounded by its own agricultural abundance. In spite of the seductive powers of the pastoral landscape, the memory of the Palestinian peasantry unsettles him. Bewildered by conflicting images, fantasies, and fictions of disparate "homelands," Yonatan somehow intuits that wrestling with these, together with his own competing identities and yearnings, requires the uncluttered repose of the desert.

Significantly, during Yonatan's absence, those left behind expose even further the loss of values that have overtaken the kibbutz and the nation itself. After his son's disappearance, former premier Levi Eshkol (a historical figure) arrives on the scene, ostensibly to console his old political ally, only to be drawn into bitter debate when Azariah, engaging in one of his characteristic harangues, informs the politician that "bottomless pits of hatred" (288) within the heart of the nation are destroying Israel. As if to demonstrate the urgency of his case, Oz makes an unmistakable reference to Joseph Conrad when Azariah insists: "It's the heart of darkness . . . a snake pit, not a country. A jungle, not a commune. Death, not Zionism" (289). And ironically, at that very moment, Yonatan is struggling to rid himself of his own internal blackness in the desert, the place where insanity and revelation often edge close to one another.

In the desert, Belden C. Lane declares in his *Solace of Fierce Landscapes,* a masterful study of centuries of spiritual awakenings in wilderness spaces, the "personification of desire is an illusion, a mere projection of one's ego, offering the alluring and twisted seduction of self-love. The desert echoes back to us our own emptiness, our longing to be made complete, to move with confidence and self-poise through an unfriendly world" (197). And *A Perfect Peace* artfully exposes this presumption as an illusion. For where Yonatan expected to find solace and refuge, he finds himself terrified of the black shadows and furtive movements that surround him. Even more unsettling are the "shadowy specters that split off" from his own consciousness: "the ghosts [of] the Syrians we've killed. The Arabs my brother bayoneted" (341). These are the slain Syrian and Jordanian soldiers whose deaths contributed to his Zionist heroism. The ephemeral peace of the moonlit night is morbidly transfigured as "lifeless silver flow[ing] over the lifeless earth" (340). And here too, the memory of "Sheikh Dahr," the recently evacuated village whose memory is already fading, is juxtaposed with the epic spectacle of Petra's more pleasing "eternal" or "timeless" absences: all "soaked in the dead pale silver" of the desert moonlight. Frenzied with mounting regret over his own past violence, loss of innocence, and his abandonment of Rimona, Yonatan disconsolately releases the safety catch on his rifle and fires rounds into the desert emptiness.[20] It is as if he has been brought directly to the verge of the conflicted state often produced by the solipsistic immersion of the Western self in the desert realm Yi-Fu Tuan so aptly describes: "Confronted by the immensity and power of desert . . . one cannot simply stand to the side and evaluate as though one were standing before a landscape garden. . . . Conflicting emotions, including fear, are aroused or taken over by the overmastering presence of nature. Whereas absorption into the sensory realities of home means life, the loss of self in alien space—even if it provides moments of ecstasy—means death. Explorers of desert may be said to be half in love with piercing beauty and half in love with death" (155). Just so is the meaning of Yonatan's struggle between Eros and Thanatos, between solipsistic withdrawal and the binds of community.

After exhausting his ammunition, Yonatan nearly collapses, "pissing and puking." Suddenly panicked, fully aware that he presents a perfect target for unseen eyes in the light of the full moon, Yonatan dashes in a frenzy through the night (though there are no actual Arab pursuers), collapsing in physical and emotional exhaustion at the camp of Tlallim. Apparently he is not ready for death after all. In the days that follow, he remains in the desert, humbly aiding the patient old man on his rock and mineral expeditions, until one day when he is stunned "to see that smile reflected in a broken mirror in a corner of the trailer." He is "struck dumb. It was an exact replica of Rimona's, the woman who had been his wife" (342). At last, Yonatan, called back by the domestic feminine, rises from the nadir brought about by his own death impulse and returns home to reconcile himself to community and responsibility. In the end, Yonatan's circuit confirms Boyarin's argument that "to the extent that we confront the Other in relics, we are cast back even more on our own codes than in conversation with another living person" ("Ruins" 327). Earlier, the violence of the past seemingly caused the contemporary ruins of a Palestinian village to disrupt Yonatan's complacency; yet whatever that momentary coming into consciousness might have meant, the lasting significance of Sheikh Dahr itself is now silenced as the hero is summoned back to the imperious political "utopia" that birthed him.

As in many contemporary Jewish works of fiction from I. B. Singer to Allegra Goodman, Oz stresses *t'shuva* (which means "turning" in Hebrew) as central to the Jewish conception of human life. The idea of turning, whether to God or to the "right path," is connected with the Jewish conception of human redemption and underlies both the intrinsic hopefulness about humankind and the longing for messianic salvation which universal *t'shuva* will help bring about. In some ways, *t'shuva* in Jewish literature might be said to parallel the modern conception of epiphany in Western literature. But where literary epiphany is more a matter of consciousness and of recognition, *t'shuva* is a more explicitly spiritual and moral apprehension. The result of such decisive movement obviously has far-reaching consequences for the idea of the nation and the spiritual and social coherence of the kibbutz experiment. For Oz, this "turn" must almost necessarily be double: for in *A Perfect Peace* one character's spiritual and moral presence brings about the hero's catharsis and the restoration of the precarious community's equilibrium. Under Tlallim's firm guidance, as with Moses with Jethro among the Midianites, Yonatan finds himself, or rather, a version of a self that he is prepared to live with.

On one level, Yonatan's self-exile and boundary crossing fulfill the etymological destiny of "Hebrew," which literally means the "crossover" people (*ivri*). But in the more troubling reading that I propose, his aimless quest into the mysterious eastern desert in search of a gratification he cannot fully articulate may be viewed instead as a displaced version of the Zionist relation to territory. Ironically, the narrative's trajectory of escape positions the desert, particularly the taboo lure of Petra, as a feminized space invaded by the masculine interloper. This is not too distant from the gendered binaries that the late Edward Said claimed are always in the service of the East/West dichotomy of Orientalism. Indeed, the manner in which Yonatan's journey into the ineffable East is preceded by his lustful encounter with Michal, a sexual exploit of languid sensuality, is characteristic of the East configured as (un)veiled feminine.

In Mazor's approving rendering of what he considers the typical structure of Oz's narratives, he sees the repetition of "subtle, hesitant steps toward moderation and accommodation . . . for the warring sides to inch their way to the middle ground, to steer away from the path of perpetual strife. Reconciliation, however fragile and tenuous, is given a chance . . . the power struggle between the two rivals is far from terminated, and probably will never cease, but a soft, placating, almost caressing breeze is suddenly felt on the frantic, sweaty neck" (2). In particular, this Israeli critic embraces "the conciliatory note" that distinguishes the conclusion to *A Perfect Peace:* "One realizes that there is room for compromise, that there is no need to take sides, to triumph absolutely. Gradually, perhaps with time and maturity, one accepts the middle road, the golden mean, the existence of a reality that can accommodate opposing extremes" (43). That reconciling logic may be said to persevere, for in the end, Yonatan's struggle to leave his father's house to form an independent selfhood collapses and he returns to try to reassemble the shards of his own identity and that of the social world he has hurt, a willed synthesis of the private individual and the coercive collective. Mazor puts it plainly, "If not perfect peace, this is at least a truce" (43). Yet if so, the question surely is suggested, between what forces precisely? And what are the terms of that armistice?

I suggest that something more insidious than a return to wholeness and harmony actually transpires. In the final unfolding of the novel's ideological logic, it is clear that life must be found with people, with one's prescribed nation, whatever the psychic costs that entails. It is as if individualism itself, that great heresy of American Protestantism, has to be sternly pruned from the garden of the Jewish polity. Just as it comes into view, the alternative conscience of desert escape is overcome by a dutiful individual properly attuned to the political and social structures he belongs to. In this regard, it is worth considering the intrinsic relation between Yonatan's ephemeral isolation and the peculiar socio-political position of Amos Oz, and by extension any artist, in Israeli society. As Amos Kenan somberly observes, "Israel is, from a cultural standpoint, one of the most totalitarian states in the world." Kenan charges that, perpetually in thrall to the army (first as regular inductee, later as reservist), the artist perpetually vacillates between an identity as an autonomous, creative being and a soldier, in complete service to the will of the state. Of the latter, Kenan remarks "this teaches a person a lesson . . . that it is possible to take him wherever they wish, to make of him whatever they wish—and he has nothing to say about it." Ultimately, the national imperative is always there to diminish the significance of the self:

> This is a system of repression the like of which I am unacquainted with in any other country. It is very subtle, very democratic. There is no secret police or concentration camps. There is simply no need for them. In this state you can't become an other. Now how can a culture grow if a person doesn't become an other? What does it mean to be an other? It means first of all to be who you yourself are. Something that is not uniform. If there is no "you," then there can be no "we." (11)

For Kenan, no one in this arduous position of unceasing social responsibility (especially that society's artists), can utterly resist resentment toward the moral and psychic toll such a burden entails. Little wonder that Oz felt compelled to create a character as troubled and troubling as Yonatan; his flight from responsibility and national space toward the "otherness" of his own selfhood at once illuminates the psyche of the divided artist and that of all Israel's citizen-soldiers.[21]

Altogether, Oz seems most eager to settle his characters' anxious lives. Yonatan's homeward trajectory is balanced by the impressive integration of Azariah, the lonely orphan from the Diaspora (who in Yonatan's absence has impregnated Rimona and judiciously manages the tractor shed), into the kibbutz milieu, symbolized by his decorative choice of "a colorful picture of the sea" (358) to replace the snapshot of a public intellectual he had once clipped. Of the latter telling image, Mazor explains that "the conjunction of summer and sea certainly typifies the Israeli experience, suggesting . . . an approach to life. It is the essence of the 'blazing light' that is the antithesis of the dark, wintry . . . world that Azariah came from . . . a transition from a 'wintry' . . . lugubrious nature that is associated with exilic, European, musty existence, into the height of Israeli summer with its white scorching light [and] golden Mediterranean beaches" (151–52). Homecomings of all sorts abound in the mellow season of Zionist fecundity.

As it happens, Yonatan Lifshitz returns when the "agricultural season was at its height" (368), leaving the reader a comforting sense that the crisis of the fisher-king has passed—the land restored to fertility. Deux ex machina. Seamlessly resuming his old life, it is "as if he had never been away. . . . [Yonatan] had as little to say as ever" (369). In fleeing from national space toward indeterminate desert—and the growing apprehension that subjectivity, like the shifting sands of its landscape, is itself a space of flux—Oz's hapless citizen-soldier displays a longing for a more contiguous life that eludes the powerful grip of a reactive and coercive nationalism. But at the same time, though the hero lingers attentively to the politically revelatory space of the desert, Oz's novel ultimately affirms the imperative that the individual's salvation depends on a return to community. This traditional Jewish imperative is as ancient as Moses' return to the people from his sojourn among the Midianite flocks of Jethro and as modern as its transference to Zionism's unceasing emphasis on the solidarity of national identity. The desert is the testing grounds of that proposition.

Thus Yonatan's desertion of his wife, parents, and kibbutz is resolved by the reaffirmation of a version of the Jewish extended family, albeit wounded by Freudian sexual drama. On one level, Yonatan certainly occupies an unusual position among the kibbutzniks at the novel's end.

The clear sight lines of the desert have brought him to a point where he faces the world, more fully accountable to himself for his actions. As Oz himself once said of his novel, there is the attractive prospect for "a mystical merger between certain, different people . . . a *ménage à trois* . . . this mystical merger between decent human beings is a lot more exciting to me than the desertion theme" ("Amos Oz Talks about Amos Oz" 186). Considering the tension between the quotidian and the apocalyptic or transformative epiphany in his works, the novelist has remarked of his fascination with

> those moments when a Jerusalem housewife or a retired neighborhood doctor or a kibbutz member in search of self-discovery experiences a moment when the world opens up to them with great intensity and force. Then they return to their preoccupation with gardening, dishwashing, and earning a living. My work is full of such examples. There is a deep, organic connection between epiphany and laundry, cooking, and political discussion. This is the daily routine, the texture of the fabric and, through it, something else is perceived. ("Amos Oz Talks about Amos Oz" 178–79)

But the question remains whether Oz has somehow begged off the tension and discovery of a genuinely transformative journey (the kind where you can't go home again) and, in so assiduously healing Yonatan's raw, wounded self, leaves too much of interest behind. His hero's previous condition may not have been a fully integrated one but at least his quest evinced a courageous willingness to dig and struggle. Yonatan at peace is perhaps a less memorable character. And one wonders whether the outcome of Yonatan's exotic experiment wasn't somehow too predetermined—whether the Israeli artist really allows himself free rein in unleashing his imagination in exploring the weaknesses of the kibbutz system and of Israeli society itself.[22]

In Oz's liberal Zionist perspective, the protagonist's flight from home is significant only insofar that the individual's homecoming asserts the primacy of the collective.[23] In spite of the protagonist's pangs of conscience, the Zionist telos remains undisrupted, just as the narrative's imagery of the austere desert landscape is replaced at the novel's end by harmonious scenes of Azariah and Yonatan quietly laboring in the kibbutz vineyard and the birth of Rimona's daughter. In the novel's final nod to Oz's own ambivalence (and what amounts to a bittersweet perpetuation of Yonatan's own condition), the question of the infant's paternity is left unresolved. Indeed, Oz has always been quite at ease with his own ambivalence and vacillations. In what seems to still serve as an authorial manifesto, he has declared:

> Reading two or three paragraphs will suffice to convince the reader that the author is not a thinker possessing a systematic theory, but rather an easily excitable person, who tends to reach emotionally to various subjects; one of those ardent fellows who, when they don't contradict themselves—then they trip over their own line of thinking, and approach untheoretically topics that perhaps require a definite theoretical approach. (quoted in Mazor 1)

Still, though I share Aschkenasy's enthusiasm for Yonatan's conscientious "constant questioning of heroism, which he finds shallow and empty . . . an illusion" (131), I am less sanguine that he fully possesses a revitalized consciousness on his resigned return. For it must be recognized that Yonatan's beleaguered adventure, away from the familiar into the East's alterity and back toward reunification with homeland and collective, proves, like the logic of Zionism itself, ultimately circular.[24] The violent revelation of Sheikh Dahr recedes from our view.

Finally, the primal reality of the desert encounter vanishes as the soliloquizing of the sojourner himself takes over. Yonatan can survive the dangerous nomadic flirtation with the chaotic desert only by remaining detached, by negating all his longings, ostensibly subversive nomadic desires. The further he moves into the unknown, the more his inner self gains coherence and integrity. But in the end, counter to Levinas's expectations of the Hebraic, that "self" is seen as indistinguishable from the Zionist "home" that originally provided the impetus to flee it.[25] Restored to equilibrium and cleansed of his dangerous romantic infatuation with the desert, this pacified figure may also cause the reader to wonder about the fate of his moral angst, his awakened sensitivity to the scene of dispossession on the outskirts of his kibbutz.[26] For the collectivist instincts of kibbutz (and the nation at large) have formed this circuitous wanderer, shaped his reactions, and, at the critical moment in the desert, prevented the dissipation of his ego, though perhaps also the prospect of authentic transformation.[27]

4 *Immobilized Rebels on the Outskirts of the Promised Land*

"They looked as if in a state of exhilaration": Unholy Defiance in Bialik's "Dead of the Desert"

> Among these [tribes] there was not one of those enrolled by Moses and Aaron the priest when they recorded the Israelites in the wilderness of Sinai. For the Lord had said of them: "They shall die in the wilderness."
>
> —Numbers 26:64–65

One of the most subversive moments in the long series of protests by the people against Moses in the wilderness occurs in Numbers 16, where a confrontational Dathan and Abiram reverse the leader's privileged representation of the immediate past and the future that beckons: "Is it not enough that you brought us from a land flowing with milk and honey to have us die in the wilderness, that you would also lord it over us?" The pair's appropriation of the exalted terms assigned to Canaan, their backward elevation of Egypt as the redemptive land, dooms them to be consumed by holy fire, along with 248 others who are fatally unconvinced by Moses' national vision.

In a particularly mysterious meandering of the rabbinic imagination, the Talmud preserves an unexpectedly poignant version of the fate of that obdurate first generation.[1] Unusually, a nomadic Arab, who leads Rabbah b. Bar Hanna to his morbid discovery, is credited with the strange account that follows:

> "Come and I will show you the Dead of the Wilderness. I went [with him] and saw them; and they looked as if in a state of exhilaration. They slept on their backs; and the knee of one of them was raised, and the Arab merchant passed under the knee riding on a camel with a spear erect, and did not touch it. I cut off one corner of the purple blue shawl of one of them; and we could not move away. He said unto me: [if] you have, peradventure, taken something from them, return it; for we have a tradition that he who takes anything from them cannot move away. I went and returned it; and then we were able to move away."[2]

What seems most salient about the eerie narrative, more than such details as the fate of divine punishment that lingers over the scene, more than the glaring fact of the severance of the impious generation from the sanctimony of burial custom, are the monumental proportions of the desert dead themselves. In their strange attraction to the living sojourners in the wilderness, they present the same fatal lure of the past that paralyzes Lot's wife. The desert generation's hindrance to the fulfillment of the national narrative, the completion of the collective's destiny, is commemorated in this eternal sleep under the glare of the sun-drenched wilderness.

From the beginning of chapter 11 in Numbers, the liberated people begin to complain and die. The essentially harmonious flow between divine authority, Moses the earthly guide, and finally the people as complacent collective is interrupted by the rancorous voices of individuals infected by doubt, memories of Egyptian abundance, and free will. As noted in my earlier discussion of Shulamith Hareven, their protests culminate in the crisis of chapter 14 where God condemns the entire generation: "Say to them: 'As I live,' says the Lord, 'I will do to you just as you have urged Me. In this very wilderness shall your carcasses fall.'" "Falling in the wilderness" connotes an anonymous death without burial. And so it is that by the vast plague recounted by chapter 25 nobody of that generation (except for Caleb, Joshua, and Moses) survives. The appalling desert punishments meted out to the Israelites between chapters 11 and 25 include earthquakes, deadly snakes, God's consuming fire, and various plagues. Consumed by mounting attritions inflicted by divine anger in the wilderness, it is not unreasonable that the people fear what might await them in the land that waits to enclose them. As Adriane Leveen observes of the grim logic of the dissenters' terrible penalty: "Obsessed by their cravings for the remembered food of Egypt, the people trigger a series of episodes in which they are consumed by the fire of the Lord or fear being consumed by the devouring land" (250). It is the latter that the Bedouin of the talmudic legend stumbles across.

This fable about one of the bible's primal scenes of Hebraic disobedience bears interesting implications for thinking about the subversive inclinations of subsequent desert narratives. Bialik, the great national poet of the first generation of Zionist settlement, was drawn to the talmudic legend for what Ilana Pardes calls its "momentous, almost mythical, struggle . . . against the Creator" (123). Though his unabashedly nationalist lyrics were immensely and immediately influential among the readers of the day, his retelling of the desert generation's experience in the biblical Exodus, "The Dead of the Desert" (*Matei Midbar*) reads today as a troublingly ambivalent meditation on myth and politics. Its unexpected gesture toward an ancient story of skeptical refusal seems all the more strange for its composition precisely at the moment that the Jewish people seemed to be re-entering history for the first time in two thousand years by renewing their historical relation to the land. Bialik (who credits the talmudic source in his epigraph to the poem) imagines that giants, having transgressed the fixed boundaries of habitation set by divine fiat, are petrified as desert boulders. Centuries later, their defiance is resurrected in an obscure legend told by the Talmud's peripatetic Arab, who intuits the hidden secrets of the earth's rocky strata. For pious readers accustomed to the rabbinic interpretation of God's announcement ("In this wilderness your carcasses shall fall" [Num. 14:28]) as a fitting response to the people's anxiety that they will "fall" by the sword of human enemies, the subversive shift from sheepish acquiescence toward political agency and refusal may seem very strange. Perhaps for the Zionists of Bialik's day, this may have seemed even more troubling. For here, triumphantly embracing exilic existence, the immobilized but untamed dead still seem to be rising, against the very notion of national destiny and homecoming:

> We are the brave!
> Last of the Enslaved!
> First to be free!
> With our own strong hand,
> Our hand alone,
> We tore from our neck
> The heavy yoke.
> Raised our heads to the skies,
> Narrowed them with our eyes.
> Renegades of the waste,
> We called barrenness mother.[3]

In Bialik's poem, the warriors seem to be proud secularists, defying first pharaoh's, and later God's, enslavement of the people. Rebelling against God, their human autonomy is heroically set against pious obedience to a desert deity seemingly opposed to their individuality.

Like the modern Canaanite movement in early Zionism, they reject religiosity, and their desert-preserved corpses defend the struggle toward a radical freedom. A popular interpretation often offered in classrooms during the early days of the state aligned the poem with secular Zionism's rejection of the Talmud (and obligation to the Law as part of transcendent authority) as part of Judaism's exilic mentality that the poet sought to overcome; the rebirth of contemporary Jews would inhabit a more natural form of faith and relation to their homeland. However, this ideological thrust is surely complicated by the glaring fact that in their wilderness of resistance, neither do the giants embrace the salvation of Zionist space. Proclaiming "barrenness mother" transforms their sterile desert into an earthy alternative to God.[4] Moreover, Bialik further discomfits the reader by hedging in his representation, leaving open the question of whether they are truly "dead" or in a strange state of vigilant dormancy:

> The mighty phalanx awakes.
> They suddenly rouse themselves, the stalwart men of war,
> Lightning ablaze in their eyes, their faces aflame, hands on
> swords.

Yet this arousal would seem to be at odds with the last lines of the opening stanza:

> Only the scars on seared faces . . .
> The chipping of arrow and javelin, the carved hilts of the swords
> Remain, like inscriptions on tombstones.

Leveen suggests that this apparent rupture in the poet's rendering actually pays very close heed to Numbers' graphic attention to the variety of deaths resulting from God's condemnation of the wilderness generation:

> In imaginatively providing inscription and tombstone for the dead, Bialik makes apparent the gap in the biblical account. While Numbers narrates the variety of ways in which the people die, it only records the burial of members of the generation once, with extreme brevity. . . . The lack of specificity when it comes to the people's location at the end of their lives is especially startling when contrasted to the introduction of that very same generation at the opening of Numbers. Those who were so meticulously accounted for—each tribe named, numbered, and assigned a specific placement around the tabernacle in the camp—are now left, in their deaths, unburied and unmarked somewhere in the wilderness. (247)

Most striking of all is the way that both the rabbinic legend and the poet's lyric underscore how the unburied are nakedly exposed not only to the elements but to human witnesses of a much later era, who must struggle to construct a narrative to explain the incomprehensible. In other words, Bialik's unconventional meditation on disobedience, so strangely resistant to both Zionist optimism and religious piety, is actually an ingenious midrash, for as Pardes observes, "It is a generation that was born via a struggle with God and dies in a forceful struggle against Him" (125). The talmudic legend of an Arab wanderer encountering these stony archetypes (that paradoxically embody both nomadic journey and stasis), wonderfully encrypts the fraught relation between Jew and obedience. For Pardes, this strange episode contains the essence of the unresolved nature of the bond between the Jewish subject and the land for the duration of all the Diasporas and exiles of the future:

> The spirit of the desert generation unsettles future generations as well. Even when the Israelites finally invade Canaan, the wandering does not fully stop. Exile piles up on exile. The Promised Land . . . is never seen as truly a stable home, or as the center of holiness. "I remember thee, the kindness of thy youth, the love of thine espousals, when thou wentest after me in the wilderness, in a land that was not sown," says Jeremiah in the name of God to Israel (2:2). In this passage Jeremiah ventures to claim that the desert offers a youthful passion the Promised Land lacks. He realizes with his wandering precursors that a land that is not "sown" leaves more room for dreaming than a tilled land. (Pardes 125)

In Leveen's generally congruent reading (she alludes to a significant body of biblical scholars who all note the suspicious lack of a single mention of a birth in the wilderness story), she reasonably contends that, coupled with the absence of "particular, discrete sites of burial, the biblical wilderness signifies only "a vast and terrible burying ground" (262). For being more persuaded by their material surroundings than the divine voice, for crying out, "If only we had died in the land of Egypt . . . or if only we might die in this wilderness" (Num. 14:2), the people will be annihilated, their God transforming them into enduring subjects of the menacing wasteland (in place of the Law they reject).

Where Leveen bleakly concludes that Numbers assigns the desert wilderness "as the premier site of death," merely "juxtaposed in the starkest of terms with its counterpart, the land promised Israel by God" (247), Pardes reveals that something more dynamic than repugnance toward a fatal obscurity may be afoot. There are strange undercurrents in the Bible that seem to credit the desert as the adversarial site of a supreme skepticism that unsettles all nationalist complacency, resisting the idealized narrative of ancestral rootedness that Moses would impose. This uncanny paradigm would still resonate at the other end of the century, where the desertification of the individual poses a substantial challenge to the integrity of both the individual and the collective, which I will now consider in the work of the youngest Israeli writer addressed in this study.

Postwar Malaise in David Grossman's Yani on the Mountain

> Aaron shall lay both his hands upon the head of the live goat and confess over it all the iniquities and transgressions of the Israelites, whatever their sins, putting them on the head of the goat; and it shall be sent off to the wilderness through a designated man. Thus the goat shall carry on it all their iniquities to an inaccessible region; and the goat shall be set free in the wilderness.
>
> —Leviticus 16:21–22

> Between the news bulletins, amid the ambulance sirens and the helicopters that relentlessly circle above, I try to isolate myself. I battle to write my story. Not as a way of turning my back on reality . . . but rather out of a sense that, in the current situation, the very act of writing becomes an act of protest. An act of self-definition within a situation that literally threatens to obliterate me. . . . For a moment, I am not a *victim.*
>
> —David Grossman[5]

Our examination of the modern Hebrew narrative's fusion of spatial/geographic and cultural/spiritual forms of displacement in the desert experience reaches a curious turn in David Grossman's first-person novella *Yani on the Mountain* (1983), in which a hard-bitten commander of an intelligence outpost in Sinai strangely lingers in the desert for seven years following the shock of the Yom Kippur War, long past any rational explanation.[6] Grossman is one of Israel's most highly acclaimed and widely translated novelists, internationally respected as a writer of extraordinary gifts, whose structurally intricate style is accompanied by a bold social and political vision. He is highly regarded as a pioneer of such innovative techniques hitherto unknown in Israeli literature, such as magic realism and other experimental narrative strategies. Political injustice, as well as its lingering psychological repercussions, forms the central themes of many of his works. An acute interest in the ironic presence of diasporic vulnerability and exilic identity within modern Israel has been evident as a constant theme ever since the appearance of his powerful Holocaust novel *See Under: Love* in 1989 (Ayen Erekh: Ahavah [1986]), where the sensitive Sabra survivor of a traumatic event is made alien in his own homeland by a wounding encounter with traumatic truth.

Grossman's entire oeuvre exhibits a strong dedication to recognizing the consequences that Jewish history and memory has had for the Jewish national homeland as well as for those directly affected by its triumphs. For Grossman, that national redemption has always been a messy business and he mourns the suffering of Israelis as well as their victims: "So much creative power, so much imagination and thought, are directed today at destruction and death (or at guarding against destruction and death). Sometimes there is a sense that most of our energy is invested in defending the boundaries of our existence. And too little energy is left for living life itself" (*Death as a Way of Life* 146). Though primarily a novelist, Grossman actually first came to international attention with *The Yellow Wind,* a searing account of what he observed in early 1987 on the West Bank.[7] Mediating between the complex collective myths and political animosities on both sides of the Palestinian-Israeli conflict, Grossman placed his readers in direct contact with impassioned, representative human beings from both wounded communities. More recently, his collection of editorials and articles, *Death as a Way of Life: Israel Ten Years after Oslo* (2003), revisits the wrenching conflict between Israelis and Palestinians. In an earlier period, *Smile of the Lamb* (Hiuch Ha-Gedi), a memorably prescient 1983 novel set largely in a small Palestinian village, also considered the moral cost incurred by the occupier and occupied through the relationship of an idealistic reservist and an old Arab storyteller.

On the surface, *Yani on the Mountain,* rarely discussed by critics, seems altogether a different sort of narrative. In Grossman's portrait of a deeply embittered, lonely Sabra clinging to the cocoon of a private mythos that has robbed him of friends and a fully realized life in the most desolate reaches of the Sinai Peninsula, the novelist created a powerfully imaginative critique of a society that has crowned itself with its own sufferings—and is hence paralyzed from acting constructively. The success of Grossman's achievement can be measured by his indelible portrait of a tormented individual that also serves readers as a persuasive allegory of the plight of a traumatized society retreating into itself, struggling to gain a fresh perspective—in the wilderness as it were—of the high penalties incurred for its own existence. Grossman's penchant for creating allegories of the national scene can be traced back to the heartbreaking figure of Kazik in his early masterpiece *See Under: Love,* where Kazik, a mysterious child discovered by an elderly, childless couple, grows in accelerated time, eventually withering into old age and infirmity in his twenty-second hour of life. Just as earlier critics have seen Kazik's precarious existence as an allegory of the birth, growth, and current moribund condition of Israel, Yani in the later novella presents us with a symbol of the nation that indulges in stubborn and self-defeating actions. Accordingly, where Hareven retells the wanderings of the pre-Canaan Hebrews, the psychology of Grossman's protagonist evokes the desert places (beyond the sovereignty of the ancient Israelite kingdoms) that the Hebrew Bible portrays as "refuge," as in the prophet's lament "Oh, to be in the desert, at an encampment for wayfarers! Oh, to leave my people, to go away from them—for they are all adulterers, a band of rogues" and his advice to those seeking a haven: "Be like a wild ass in the desert" (Jer. 9:1; 48:6) or the psalmist who, in flight from the enemy, yearns for "the wings of a dove" that he "would wander afar . . . would lodge in the wilderness" (Ps. 55:7–8).

For our purposes, in considering the traditional desert-versus-society dialectic, what is most important to note about such passages may be profitably gleaned from Shemaryahu Talmon's judicious reading: "The prophet is not drawn into the desert, as it were, to meditate there and come face to face with his God. He does not seek communion with the Deity, but rather he longs to dissociate himself from his contemporaries" (46). In Grossman's ironic recasting of these terms, Yani, the officer who stays on at the outpost for an unseasonable seven years (well beyond his regular military service), is anchored in a liminal space somewhere between his romantic yearning and his realistic despair that he has been in thrall to an "illusion": "that I continue to cherish as if to convince myself" (56). Emotionally distant from his men and severed from his past, Yani remains in the desert as an even more radically disaffected and embittered version of Oz's Yonatan. Grossman seems to imagine his protagonist as a surrogate for an entire generation tainted by cynicism and despair. Sinking into madness, Yani is a figure of deferment, refusing to reunite with the society that sent him to war. Indeed, he embodies "wasteland," impotent to fulfill the fecundity of Zionist ideals.

Set in a landscape of death, war, and sterility, *Yani on the Mountain* explores the psychological rationalizations of the title character's retreat from friends and the Israeli civil polity, and particularly the profound impact of the desert on his emotional and intellectual condition. Even in a literary generation often singled out for its indelible portraits of lonely and alienated Israelis, Grossman's aloof officer stands apart.[8] The plot accelerates through rising peaks of naked emotional pain and suffering as well as strangely melancholy beauty when the protagonist confronts the internal and exterior landscapes that have led to his sad condition. We first meet the narrator at an apocalyptic moment he dreads: his beloved fortification is due shortly to be blown up and abandoned. This is to be a day of reckoning that seems to presage the protagonist's own psychic implosion. Psychically injured to the core, Yani's war-infected perception distorts even the most benign aspects of his environment. For example, a sunset looms "in the sky like the bloody eye of a dead fish" (83). The crisis that marks Grossman's officer is an abyss dividing him from the harmony and cohesion of youth movements and national service, the consolation of belonging to a collective, with its total identification with a land and people, and the present, outcast and adrift in a hostile world of violence, war, and the certainty of horrifying death.

As Susan Niditch observes of the salient details of Leviticus 16 (quoted above), the biblical text alludes to two goats: the first sacrificed to Yahweh and a second to be delivered alive into the wilderness to "Azazel." This god is conceived as "a wilderness deity, a threatening power that had to be appeased in an ancient pre-Israelite ritual . . . in a sympathetic magical process, the sins are invested in the goat [which] then takes [them] with him beyond the group's borders and body politic" (107, 108). The Talmud claims that during observations of Yom Kippur during Temple times, a red thread was twisted around its horns while a duplicate was attached to the entrance of the Temple and would turn white to signify purity when the goat wandered into the desert.[9] There is more than an allegorical allusion to this ancient rite in Grossman's portrayal of his hero's self-sacrifice in Yani's ordeal; an analogous passage of "cleansing" seems called for before he can return to the mundane world of state and society. Yet Grossman complicates this ancient model by representing the desert as a tempting site of self-serving illusion and deception, a topography of dangerous self-indulgence.

For a substantial portion of the narrative, Yani (who, like Oz's Yonatan, embodies the kind of inarticulate Israeli personality that gravitates toward the mute desert) appears as desiccated as the bleak surroundings that engulf him. When the story begins, the imminent demolition of the outpost forms the backdrop for both Yani's journal-style narration of his own story and his memories of the emotional triangle that ensnared two other young people: Elisha, his close friend, a poet; and a woman named Nimra, who enters and exits their lives in a manner as abrupt and inexplicable as the war itself. Cut off from family and friends, the officer leads a nearly monastic existence, unwilling to consciously confront the grounds for his loneliness and solitude, a grief he persists in keeping to himself, as if unaware or indifferent to the fact that the war has also been catastrophic for an entire society.

Yani is a mournful prince presiding over a fiefdom of thorns, blackened cartridges, oil-soaked rags, and barbed wire, which he perversely clings to as "this peaceful place, free of all human schemes and spitefulness" (89). Living an obsessively ritualized existence of blinkered memories, the nostalgic soldier would apparently gather all his days into an uninterrupted span of Eastern nowness, always beyond the reach of time and contingency: "happy to be here . . . as I was yesterday and the day before and all the other days" (61). Having failed to rejoin the national scene, the collective experience so vital to Israeli selfhood, he persuades himself that he is consoled and completed by desert solitude, thinking of the desolate mountain peak he inhabits as a "nest" (57), deluding himself that he is somehow dedicated to the cause of the state that others hedonistically abandoned. Aside from occasional anecdotes about the lives of lost loves and comrades in far-flung locales like Paris, the novella's landscape encompasses a bleak scene of generator sheds, vehicle bunkers, and a forlorn subterranean maze "where once upon a time the intelligence work was done" (67).

Like many individuals beset by neurosis, Yani begins each brilliant day with an obsessive ritual, surveying the desert beyond the windswept camp, content to know that in the afternoon the clear blue sky will fade, and unvaryingly "gloom will descend on this fenced-in square of land" (60). On these mornings Yani hastens purposefully to his cherished desert sanctuary, a lonely enclave of rusty, fissured limestone to ritualistically confirm the splendid feat of his own persistence and isolation:

> Half within the area of the camp and half without, facing the desert . . . I pause for a moment and perform the morning ritual. First the powerful, quivering stretch, touching the sky above and the earth below, the roar of a yawn flung in the direction of the desert, ah, what a mighty lion cub is waking to his day . . . the avid gulp of fresh air that hurts the lungs, the brisk, ruthless rubbing of the scalp, the genial pee, the steaming arc spraying from the heights of the rock to the gaping depths of the wadi. I'm still here. (61)

Here a putatively exuberant private ritual is overshadowed by Yani's pathetic masculine mimicry of fecundity; the lingering imagery of sterile urine coursing into the nadir of the wasteland underscores Yani's manifest decline and hollowness. Though an astute reader of this rugged setting, knowing "all the secrets of the mountain, the steep crevices, the crows' nests in the bushes, the viper's paths, and the marks etched by the wind in the rocks" (72), there is little evidence that Yani's years of isolation have brought him any closer to confronting the essence of his own humanity. He is quite the antithesis of Michael Ondaatje's romantic reading of his own desert sojourner's sensibility: "A man in a desert can hold absence in his cupped hands knowing it is something that feeds him more than water" (*The English Patient* 155).

Over the years, solicitous letters from busy comrades sternly admonish Yani to resume his life, but he resists:

> Elisha, Giddy, Hanoch, Papush. . . . How long was I going to go on sitting here, on top of the mountain, when was I going to come down, stop playing childish games, and do something with my life. Mild rebukes, hints of envy, perhaps even longing, faint stings winging toward me from all over the world, Cambridge, Jerusalem, Paris. I was their silent line of communication on the heights of the mountain. They wrote to themselves, to each other, and to who they were once upon a time, and I gathered all their words inside me and never wrote back. (92)

Ironically, what seems to be only his solipsistic grief and abiding paralysis can be traced to Grossman's awareness of what of course was in reality a collective response to an unprecedented trauma. With the exception of the 1948 War of Independence, all previous wars were initiated by Israel and fought on enemy territory. Throughout the decades, Israelis had placed enormous trust in their military and intelligence services, in spite of being virtually surrounded by Arab states, a confidence that has Yani still marveling at its breezy insouciance years later: "What plans we had, what faith in our unlimited strength, our unshakeable integrity. How we despised our parents, the distorted truths they taught us. How sure we were that we would never be like them" (98). But that societal sense of domestic security was destroyed forever. Years later, hiding in his desert fort, Yani bears the crucible of the collective grief and paralysis of that war. As an intensely private, morbidly repressed individual, Yani seems characteristic of a number of memorably repressed Israeli men in recent Hebrew fiction. However, he exceeds most literary critiques of Zionist masculinity in the striking degree to which he has armored himself against his own emotions.[10]

In recent years, three feminist critics have deftly illuminated the critical way traditional codes of masculinity and Zionism coalesce. In Grossman's grim testimony to the upheaval of his time, Yani seems to be the last of the mythic Sabras or "New Hebrews," the figure that cultural historian Yael Zerubavel describes as "an ideal . . . fictive hegemonic identity . . . young and robust, daring and resourceful, direct and down-to-earth, honest and loyal, ideologically committed and ready to defend his people to the bitter end" ("The 'Mythological Sabra' and Jewish Past" 116). Correspondingly, in her penetrating study of the uses of space in Israeli film and literature, Nurith Gertz observes that classical Zionist narratives portrayed the native-born masculine figure "as a natural, original, and universal figure. It was through him that 'Hebrewness' in general was defined. The geography that unfolded beneath his feet and gaze denoted his connection with the homeland and his power to control it" ("Space and Gender" 157). Finally, Yosefa Loshitzky describes a literary revolution of the 1960s "that established a tradition of 'meta-Zionist narrative' characterized by a sense of disillusionment with the State . . . an attempt to challenge Zionist ideology. One of the major consequences . . . has been a demythification of the figure of the Hebrew hero . . . the heroes of Hebrew literature have ceased to be mythic Sabras" (197). In many respects, *Yani on the Mountain* should be appreciated as a rueful literary farewell to this once commanding figure. As such, the novel provides an especially elegiac portrait of the decline of a once vital myth.

Whereas Hebrew masculinity typically dominated "an empty submissive space," Grossman's lonely figure, knowing he is feared by many while he himself is paralyzed "with dread," shrugs off the smothering embrace of national space, constructing an alternative identity in an alternative space. Dutifully reporting on his obsessively violent routine of militarism, Yani's language is almost a self-parody of masculine sufficiency: "I went out every day for private target practice with my revolver. I shot dozens of lead bullets into cardboard men, riddled them with neat round holes from their heads to their hips; I squeezed the trigger with my right hand and my left, I shot from the hip, from eye level, from behind my head" (72).

As if the shooting range was not enough, Yani re-enacts the "proof" of his "potency": on the basketball court (playing ferociously even against himself); beating all others on the running track; and provoking fights with the toughest men on the base. Yet in spite of his dry reportage of these activities, he confesses that "I felt no relief" (72). Never a team player, he dislikes the soldiers of his own age. To distance himself from their "laxity," his behavior is compulsively ascetic: "abstention from meat for months on end, sleeping without blankets, weeks-long silences." Imposing absurd wagers against himself that he cannot possibly win, he eagerly accepts the penance of endless nights on guard duty, going so far as to sleep in a cave outside of the base, which of course has no practical purpose except to appease his masochistic narcissism.

An intimidatingly unbounded figure, Yani is one of the most challenging and critically neglected characters in recent Israeli fiction, insofar as he destabilizes and dissolves the reader's expectations about the nature of his bond with the Israeli nation. Though his character is radically isolated from society, Grossman subtly links his condition to the psychological trauma inflicted on the communal psyche of Israel. An indelible portrait gradually emerges of a numbed society "in the wilderness," that has repressed its own need for unofficial forms of mourning and grief. For Israel, the events of 1973 proved a spiritual earthquake that had a lasting impact on the society's emotional climate. The public sphere saw a distinct deterioration from the post-1967 euphoria and a general position of strength and optimism to a condition of dejection and a diminished sense of both national and personal security. Yoram Bilu and Eliezer Witztum argue that

> Some of Israel's most cherished myths crumbled in this war and the subsequent ambiance of disorientation, demoralization, and mistrust made it difficult for the bereaved to cling to the older collectivist discourse of bereavement . . . the 1973 War, despite the confusion and defeat that marked the first days of fighting (and partly because of them), was replete with episodes of heroic fighting, in the course of which the Israeli army eventually overturned the wheel, took over territories in Egypt and Syria, and removed the initial threat of annihilation. But in the Israeli collective memory, the military achievements and gallantry of the combatants were overshadowed by the dark aspects of the war: the political and military arrogance that left the army ill-prepared for the war and in utter surprise when it erupted, the high number of casualties, and the resultant weakening of Israel's political stance, both regionally and internationally. (14–15)

Emblematic of an entire shell-shocked generation that felt itself betrayed by its leaders, the lingering effects of the war have benumbed the officer to such a degree that he can no longer conceive of re-establishing relations with either his best friend or the woman he once loved. As for the engineers who currently serve under him in the remote base, Yani expresses a certain degree of sympathy for their plight—"for the desert lying at the door of the mountain isn't easy on an individual" (40). He cannot, however, bring himself to enter into the kind of camaraderie that one normally achieves in such close quarters. As more details of Yani's story emerge, the technicians busily prepare the grounds for the underground outpost's physical destruction (virtually the entire mountain); the reader's knowledge of this inevitability intensifies the narrative's darkening mood.

For Yani, these functionaries of the distant state are mere interlopers, mechanistically burrowing into the mountain to which he has come to assume an oddly proprietary relation. He coldly perceives them as so many insects: "Competently, with dull precision, they glide over my mountain, planting stakes, skipping between the defense positions and the underground halls, making strange signs in yellow chalk on the walls, giving me looks of feigned apology when I pass, and getting right back to the job the minute my back is turned" (40). Infiltrated and besieged, the unprotected target of stealthy attack, Yani's resentment toward the engineers' efficiency may also stem from the fact that—aside from his false sense of sovereignty over the surrounding desert—he can lay claim to little else of his own, whether material possessions or human relations.

Having first arrived at the mountain base of Ras Ajeh as a boy of nineteen, Yani seems surprised to discover in these late days that eleven years have rapidly passed. Though his friends have long moved on to create families and other careers, he remains a keenly poetic observer of the desert's moods—but not of the humanity of those he commands. The cognitive rift between Yani's static consciousness and that of his estranged comrades, who have since tested themselves in cosmopolitan worlds, is striking. Though he recalls the moment he failed to come to terms with a decision that would have returned him to his family, and perhaps to himself, Yani is childishly helpless to locate its cause:

> Soldiers came and went; they begged to leave the rocky cliff, loathed the mountains and everything on it, counted the passing days on tables and charts. And I—I gave all I had here. When my turn came I didn't apply for transfer . . . I remember long months when I didn't take the leave due me. (I broke off relations with my father shortly after I arrived here: suddenly I realized that the gulf was unbridgeable. I wonder how much the desert had to do with it.) (72)

Yani's self-exile has made him more at home in the wasteland than in the society that has begun to regenerate itself. Not unlike Oz's Yonatan in *A Perfect Peace,* the troubled protagonist here seems to associate an absent father with the indifferent power of the implacable state itself. Here too, the morbid psychology of the tormented protagonist merges with his sense of place. In language strikingly similar to Yonatan's yearning for a death "that would turn him into just another rock in the stony desert" (*Perfect Peace* 325), Yani is stubbornly comforted to find his own identity shrinking under the sheer immensity of the sublime landscape: "Here's the edge of the mountain. The craggy cliff looms up with a yawning power. It stretches toward the desert gaping at its feet, crashes down with the sudden fall of a rock, holds itself back with a strength it does not stop exerting for a minute, like a horse rearing backward" (43–44). Though unable to identify with the vulnerable human beings who surround him, Yani approves of the rock's resistance to the powers of erosion, a corollary for his own delusion of heroic self-mastery and sufficiency in the face of emotional loss. Were either he, or the boulder, to relinquish even a minute degree of control, a fatal collapse would surely follow.

Yani apparently possesses just enough self-awareness to prevent him from fully succumbing to the dangerous fallacy of his own anthropomorphism. Still, when it becomes apparent that the geological power of the craggy rock arouses him more than any prospect of a sensual encounter with a living human being, Grossman signals the depth of the protagonist's crisis to the reader (knowledge that always eludes the protagonist himself): "Such a posture fills me with actual physical excitement, for . . . unfinished movements, processes interrupted midway, have always made me feel uneasy, psychologically and physically, as if waiting, for the continuation of the movements to be dragged out of me" (44). Not surprisingly, Yani resents the ways that the engineers are sabotaging the desert's own geological pace, for their frenetic activity reveals the vulnerable chinks in his own armor, his awareness of the inexorable momentum of erosive time.

Undisturbed by human complications, serenely accustomed to the monotony and silence of the desert, Yani lives without love but also without pain; reluctant to confront any lingering trace of fellow feeling, let alone love. If any deep emotion remains it would seem to be interred in the deepest strata of his rocky being. In the critical final days before the mountain's destruction, he ruthlessly casts the yellowing pages of once-treasured love letters to the desert winds, masochistically severing the only real bond between him and the past or another human being. Nevertheless, as if only to confirm the reality of the tender memories that have bound him to Sinai, Yani lures Elisha, an old friend now working as a journalist in a provincial town in France, back to the place of their long dormant friendship:

> I can trust him. He felt the place like me . . . from the days when we were young soldiers here, when we combed all the low sand hills, when we escaped from the camp and hiked to Refidim, to visit Nimra who was incarcerated there . . . before we grew heavy and cynical . . . when together we studied the birds and the herbs of the surrounding mountainsides. The roads we forged through the tangled growth of the wadi, the talks through the night, the chess games, Nimra, Nimra . . . (59)

Grossman's reiterated ellipses (that most withholding of grammatical figures) suggest the enormity of untold losses, signifying that those tender emotions for the girl were petrified by the war—symbolically signifying a life that has become a void. Still, there is a hope that Elisha might restore his connection to this great lost love—and to his better self.

In these days, horror often overtakes Yani, particularly in the form of a visceral memory of suddenly stumbling onto the corpse of an Egyptian pilot at a time he had thought to have long been liberated from the war's nightmare of death. In an eerily verdant wadi (because it is fed by the base's sewage pipe), "an old trap lies waiting":

> The day after the Yom Kippur War ended I went out again to roam the wadis around the base, which had not yet been aired by the joy of those who have survived one more war. Without permission, ignoring the threats and warnings, the real and imaginary dangers they warned us of day and night, I stole out of the camp . . . burst into the wadi, laughing out loud to myself, reckless, opening the buttons of my stinking army shirt, pleasurably scratched by thorny branches, thudding into soft, fragrant tree trunks, clearing a path, beating down the tangled growth with my hands. (46)

That subversive and rejuvenative laughter may have been the last truly spontaneous, youthful moment in the soldier's life. Grossman's imagery here suggests that Yani is fully alive to the miniature oasis of life around him, at least for a transient moment. Like Oz's kibbutznik, who uncovers the destruction of the Arab village as the true meaning of a popular picnic spot, Yani discovers the morbid secret just below the leafy idyll of his magnificent isolation. Within the blackened cockpit of an Egyptian Mig 21 is "a young man, his two charred hands clinging to the joystick" (47). In spite of the grotesque encounter with the Egyptian pilot's "sooty, fear-distorted face," Yani is incongruously struck by the humanizing details of his enemy's moustache, still "arrogant" and "hopeful," "jaunty" and "flirtatious": "You could imagine the man, in the air force club in Cairo or Luxor, narrowing his eyes as he passed the gleaming samovar" (47). A mere twenty-three years old at the time, Yani has been paralyzed ever since. Mortality and the dull landscape have encased him, the meaning of one informing the other, effectively sealing him off from process and continuity.

In later days he experiences awe at the discovery of how powerfully he has struggled to suppress the memory of this encounter. Here he confronts the "shameful reactions" of the days that immediately followed the wadi's startling revelation: "I struggled to toughen myself more and more. I sentenced myself to undergo daily trials of torture. I almost believed in my strength. And then, in the thicket of bushes, exposed to that sight, came the primal fear, calling: Run" (47). A childhood episode that haunts his imagination throughout the long span of his mummified desert years eerily anticipates this moment. Aptly for Yani, his earliest memory is also his first apprehension of death: once, having crawled under the legs of inebriated adults at a party held by his parents, he had listened "to the roar of unintelligible words . . . shaken by the sound of the volleys of hoarse, nasty laughter" when overcome by the dizzying array of perfumes and bodily odors he is suddenly struck "by the bitter, surprisingly adult knowledge: one day I would die" (77).[11] Still helpless before that terrifying certainty, Yani now recognizes that brutal cognition as the moment he was "eternally maimed" (77). It is as if his arrival at the forlorn mountain was already set in motion by that precipitate intimation of mortality. Here the reader first begins to grasp the meaning of the protagonist's flight from uncertainty to the clean lines of military life: "I was nineteen when I arrived here. I tasted military life that leaves no room for doubts. They put their faith in me, they entrusted men's lives to me. I came to know the mountain and I immersed myself in it. I knew with absolute clarity—this was the way" (78). But when Elisha and Nimra depart, to reunite with the world, this fragile edifice crumbles:

> They went away. Both of them. They left the mountain. They left me all by myself. They mocked my dreams. I wanted them both to volunteer for the regular army, like me, and go on serving on the mountain. . . . I think a lot about growing up. I'm a man of thirty, who weighs two hundred pounds, and who everyone's afraid of, while he himself is afraid of doing things that everyone else does without a second thought. (79)

Even now, there remains something poignantly childlike in this large man's morbid fixation on mortality and avoidance of the vulnerability that might otherwise humanize him: "I'm afraid of the life waiting for me after I come down from here; I'm afraid of going back to my empty flat in Ramat Gan. The explosion about to take place paralyzes me with dread" (79). Burying himself in a mordant, stultifying sorrow—and with that biblically resonant allusion to a sacrifice "in the thicket" (47) recalling the ram that replaces Isaac in the sacrifice required by God—Yani poignantly situates himself as a son still bewildered, immobilized on one of the state's martial altars of nationalist conflict.

In that fateful year, Yani returns to the morbid scene with such alarming frequency that he wears a deep path in the thicket of reeds. Meditatively, for hours on end, he observes how:

> Slowly the facial features and that narrow mustache disappeared; the blue uniform frayed, tore and blew away in the wind; all the personal features were effaced, and only the suggested movement of the body remained,

> the forward crouch over the jammed joystick, the tense slope of the back, the strength in the shoulders. . . . I sit there, hidden from sight, hearing only the gurgle of the sewage streaming nearby . . . and gaze hypnotically at the dead pilot, who was gradually shedding his human covering, his mustache and his uniform, keeping only the flow of the skeletal body, only the unknown, stubborn hunch over the controls. (48)

It is as if the "meaning" of that incomprehensible war can only be gleaned from this place of human waste and dry bones. As noted in Hareven's work, Grossman employs the concept of the ancient *akedah* as the deeply entrenched myth that marks contemporary Israeli reality. When the acutely sensitive Elisha first encounters Yani after seven years, he is immediately disturbed by his cognition of that festering wound. Stammering, Elisha awkwardly struggles to mask his discomfiture with levity—"how should I put it—you've grown into . . . a mountain of a man." As if aware that he has come to ironically resemble the fate of the rotting corpse that he has kept secret, an undeceived Yani ruefully muses that "he doesn't say what he wants to say, what I know for myself, that I've lost something of my human image on the top of this mountain" (51).

For the reader confronting the daunting depths of the embittered officer's disengagement from society, old friends, and lovers, Bilu and Witztum's analysis of Israel's postwar trauma proves useful here, illuminating the condition of surviving soldiers and parents alike,

> whose "work of mourning" was poisoned by the excruciating awareness that the war could have been avoided or could have taken an entirely different course. This awareness detracted from the meaningfulness of the loss, since it became extremely difficult to articulate it within the Zionist ethos at large and the myth of heroism in particular. For the first time, the delicate balance between personal sense of loss and societal mechanisms for its symbolization and commemoration was undermined. As a result, a new discourse of bereavement has emerged in which rage, bitterness and accusations—kept hidden and mute in the past—come to the fore. (15)

Yani cannot possibly fulfill the Zionist imperative that the Sabra be a force of fertility and continuity because he bears the paralyzing legacy of a previously unknown form of bereavement; a repressed state in which rage and bitterness swell within to inhibit the humanizing and cathartic transformation of grief. It is as if the secret of his own arrested life, his own "stubborn hunch over the controls" of an exclusively martial existence, somehow resides in the moldering corpse of his doppelganger. In the present, Yani catches himself uncannily mimicking the pilot's final moment of life: "I bend forward, remembering the despair in the black, clutching fingers . . . the information, which is too much to contain, explodes inside me and streams mercilessly into all the cells of understanding and feeling, leaving me exposed and helpless" (48). Though the army has devoted enormous resources to locate the crash site of the Mig, Yani has inexplicably guarded its secret: "During the entire war I wasn't as tense as I was in those days of baffled, confused searching. There was no point in telling them. They would have come and taken him out of there with a crane, and ground the metal down into scrap iron" (55). Having persuaded himself that the desiccated Egyptian is "more comfortable the way he was"—which Grossman surely intends as an ironic reflection on his protagonist's own paralysis—Yani remains as a mummified relic of an age of pristine Zionism and militarism. Meanwhile Elisha and other comrades move on to more cosmopolitan spaces.

Unaware that his old friend fully intends to keep him prisoner until "the saving blast comes" (124), Elisha breathlessly struggles to resurrect Yani, distracting him with the far-flung achievements of their old comrades ("Me and Nimra in France, Hanoch in Cambridge . . . Yair a lawyer . . . all those who have been dispersed like dandelion seeds"). These are the living names that connect Yani to his golden years of promise; the once zealous but now uncertain soldier can "no longer remember for sure what the glue was that kept us together in those months we spent here. Perhaps it was only the hostile desert lying all around us, and the fear of the unseen enemy; that kept us together with a false patina of friendship" (56). In contrast, remaining geographically and socially isolated, Yani has stoically functioned unimpeded by outside influences. Still, he is alive enough to fantasize that his lost love Nimra will materialize to call him forth from his romantic fog and resurrect him: "I can see her, brisk and solid . . . stepping toward me with her firm gait . . . now she's seen me, now she's heading in my direction, standing opposite me, and slapping me hard, her hand flat on my forehead, hey, you're dreaming again" (57).

Tormented by her memory, pathetically seeking signs of her "in columns of ants" and in the clouds that occasionally drift over the desert sky, the soldier imagines her furious indictment: "'You've turned your weaknesses, your fears and anxieties, into an ideology . . . you're banal. A god full of self-pity'" (58). At such moments it is clear that the intractable Yani serves as an imaginative version of Grossman's usually direct political critique of Israel's national malaise which he often represents in his editorials as a failure to be fully conscious of the moral implications of its own actions: "If Israel is interested not just in punishing the Palestinians but also in extricating itself from the trap it's in, it must wake up and reinsert into the tragic story of the conflict those parts that have been expunged from its consciousness during the last two years" ("Fictions Embraced" 23).

In spite of Yani's latent fantasies of an erotic reunion, it is Elisha, not the lost love of his life, which fate has brought to explode the thin veneer of self-deception that holds Yani's world together. Naturally, this intensifies the latter's rage. For instead of Nimra, he has trapped Elisha (who four days earlier was living the cosmopolitan life of a poet in Paris) in his "monkish cell." Still in the throes of nostalgia for a past love, not yet fully assuming responsibility for his condition, what he now bitterly recognizes as "seven years of rocky exile"—he feels that "the taste of the desert surrounding me" with its "slow, hypnotic" time deserves some of the blame. Yet Eli's presence gradually stirs him into confronting the scars left by his old loves (53). Memories of old tensions surface now as Yani recalls the contrast between his gung-ho patriotism and Eli's feeble militarism: "he never grasped the insignia of all the ranks . . . the army always seemed to him an amusement for childish men. He would split his sides laughing when we drilled" (55). In those days Yani was appalled by Eli's irreverence toward the nation's most sacred institution and for his part recalls his own unqualified dedication to "the drill, the military language, the strict, ritual nature of military life" (55). Though Nimra too was repulsed by military life, her heartfelt objections never rankled Yani as did Eli's crass mockery. Now, however, he finds himself less preoccupied by his loss of Nimra to the poet. Instead he is disturbed by his embryonic suspicion that the zealous nationalistic ardor, the ethos that formed the compact horizons of his youth, was woefully misplaced.

Yani was deeply wounded by Nimra's caustic candor—"I'm not prepared to understand that you love only me and loathe the rest of the world. That story would have flattered me when I was sixteen. Today it makes me sick" (58). Yet the effects of confronting the years of solitude drives him back to re-examine the truth of her trenchant criticisms: "On the platform, in the cold wind, in the darkly rolling night mists, I am suddenly seized with longing for that pain" (58). He cannot avoid revisiting this painful moment because the stark reality of his existential sterility is made explicit again when he ineptly fails to seduce Rinat, a young female soldier eager to finish her service and return to civilian life. When he suddenly lunges at the vulnerable woman she recoils in terror: "The sobs distort the words. They told her about what I was like, like a wild animal, that I've forgotten how to behave like a human being, and the meaning of civilization, and consideration, and altogether—I should have shut myself up in one of the caves around here and stayed there after the explosion too, alone with the crows and the jackals, which were obviously the most suitable companions for me" (70). Torn somewhere between denial and confronting the sterile artifice of his misplaced desire, Yani makes no comment in defense of his sorrowful performance. Interestingly, this episode is followed by a penitent retreat to the desert.

Job-like, Yani huddles miserably on the precipice of a cliff, gazing out at "the desert—purple in the pale sunlight, full of shadows, humping, gaping, streaming continuously toward the horizon, toward the two blue gleams, the bitter lakes" (70). Grossman's ironic allusion to the Bitter Lakes region north of the Gulf of Suez—a site many scholars associate with the actual crossing of the "sea of reeds," the liberation of the Israelites from their Egyptian pursuers—forms a poignant contrast to Yani's paralysis. Overtaken by memories of Elisha and Nimra as they were, Yani knows that their humanizing influences kept him from the abyss long ago. But in the wake of their absence, life—though he has willed it not to—has moved on without him. Letters arrive from Nimra teasing him with news of her feverish political activism in support of Hector, a Marxist guerrilla leader caught in dangerous struggle against the violent Argentinean regime. Struck by the contrast between Nimra's activism in the world and his own "passive solitude" and unexpectedly moved by news of the young idealist's imprisonment and the humanitarian activities of Amnesty International on his behalf, Yani finds himself disgusted by the enormity of his own wasted potential. He is jolted awake by the apprehension of an alternative way of being: "Hector, hundreds of kilometers away from me, as foreign to me as two people can be foreign to each other, hypnotizing the tense attention of so many people, touching life and death, swept me away too, shot spurts of hope and strength into my life, returned me to the yearning I had found in the eternally soaring figure of the dead man at the bottom of the wadi" (75).

Until this moment, Grossman has portrayed his protagonist as essentially analogous to an insular Israeli society that is so embattled and withdrawn it does not know how to place its own suffering in relation to that of others. But something about Nimra's ardent efforts on behalf of persecuted intellectuals seems to awaken Yani's interest in a wider world. True, three days before the explosion of his mountainous desert solitude, a voice like an evil desert *djinn* still warns him "they're hurting you, blowing your home sky-high. Protest, chain yourself to the rocks, don't let them" (79). But he imagines her there to coax him with a smile, relishing the thought of how she would gently chide him: "Oh, you romantic child . . . you're still spellbound by your childish dreams." In a wry reference to Saint-Exupéry's *The Little Prince,* he imagines her tender yet insistent rebuke: "There are so many baobab trees to uproot, stop making a fool of yourself, kicking your legs like an insulted, cheated child. You've lost nine years of your life, wasted them here, can't you see, this is the moment to do the right thing, Yani, come down from the mountain" (79). Apparently unable to form a complete sense of selfhood distinct from his monasticism, Yani shudders, still imagining the "violent rending" to come (83). As noted earlier, he construes the first real transformation in his life in many years as an impending apocalypse, visualizing it in religiously obsessive imagery.

Traditionally, apocalyptic narratives can accommodate spiritual yearnings but not genuinely material or historical evolution, certainly not that of an individual. Like an ancient desert hermit, Yani's own imagined apocalypse affords him an expedient insulation, in which the past and the turbulent present may both be safely forgotten. Effectively, this mythos prevents a this-worldly orientation. Surrounded by desert eternity, indulging in the past, Yani has learned to forsake the immediate future. Perhaps because of that refusal, he comes dangerously close to placing Elisha, the narrative's embodiment of life lived elsewhere, in harm's way as the two revisit their old haunts in the base and its surroundings.

Unaccustomed to the precarious terrain, stumbling badly in the dark without his glasses, Elisha is soon "bruised, scratched, and bleeding." But Yani, at his most hyper-masculine, heedlessly imagines that his friend is "excited as a child." Ironically, like the willful child of his own imaginings, Yani presumes that the clean slate of the pristine desert might still wipe the traces of his friend's absence, indeed all the ensuing years away: "how glad I am that his eyes are blind to the white patches left by the uprooted huts on the bare ground. I see the camp with his eyes. Everything's fine. Everything's as usual, and everyone's only sleeping" (85). Of course such optics entails a dangerous presumption, but Yani doesn't care. He cannot help fantasizing the obliteration of the friend whose very presence is nagging testimony to change and exigency: "one rash step would be enough to send him crashing into the rocks below, into the lap of the mountain where the wind whirls . . . if he falls he'll be swallowed up in the dense thickets below. Nobody will see him, and the sound of his cry will go unheard. He'll fall softly toward the dead man, waiting in tense anticipation in the darkness of the thicket. My double secret at the foot of the mountain" (86). Grossman's solipsistic protagonist is more complex than a conventional sadist; entertaining the prospect of Elisha's demise for a fleeting, fantastical moment is really a way of clinging onto his own isolation a little bit longer. In the end, however, Yani hastens to remove his friend from the menace of the abyss, if only so that his Scheherazade might resume the terrible narrative of Nimra's undoing.

Only at this point does Yani learn that after their army years Nimra and Elisha spent an unquiet year in Jerusalem, a period in which Nimra met with "extreme left-wing circles" (90), visited hot spots of Palestinian-Israeli conflict like Nablus, and eventually prevailed on Elisha to hide mysterious Arabs for weeks at a time. Elisha tearfully recalls that when he grew uneasy about the nature of the covert arrangements, Nimra pleaded with him to understand that he is "her home and her bed . . . and to remember the charity of her youth, when she walked with him in the wilderness" (91). For the Israeli reader, this recollection poignantly echoes Jeremiah: "Thus says, the Lord, I remember the devotion of your youth, your love as a bride, how you followed me in the wilderness, in a land not sown." All too soon, Nimra's liberal compassion leads to unmitigated disaster when one of their group is arrested with explosives, revealing the details of a terrorist plot. As Elisha sheepishly confesses to Yani: "I was sad. In an instant my life was empty—you might even say strange. An Israeli, a sabra, like me, a soldier in the Intelligence corps, an innocent, a stay-at-home, even a self-declared coward, aiding and abetting secret, shady gatherings, giving shelter to an anonymous Arab. But you understand of course: Nimra" (93). For her part, Nimra is devastated. Lavishing her money and risking her life for their cause, Nimra had demanded only one condition—that no violence be plotted. In the end, however, she is cynically exploited as an unwitting courier.

In spite of the painful blow to her leftist convictions, Nimra flees Jerusalem for Europe only to plunge further into altruistic activity, this time working for Amnesty International. Oddly, as Elisha exposes the painful details of Nimra's final activities, Yani becomes sharply attuned to the impending violence that will soon launch him, willingly or not, back into the world:

> Outside the wind is gathering force. As if it's collecting its tides and currents from the four corners of the desert and assembling them here, in preparation for tomorrow. . . . The sky is darkening now. An obscure anxiety stirs in the clouds gathering silently from all corners of the horizon, in the uprooted thorn bushes rolling over the grounds of the camp, escaping over the barbed wire fences, floating aimlessly over the desert and the abyss. (105, 106)

Where once Yani could reliably depend on the sameness of all his desert days, this morning will bring a much different cognition of the passage of time. An hour that would once have been "indistinguishable from all the hundreds of thousands of other hours" will be irreparably impregnated by the violence of human caprice, will "suddenly feel a heavy lump condensing inside it, tearing its guts apart, spraying it in all directions" (106). "Tomorrow" is no longer an abstract temporal sequence of the unchanging, but an immediate prospect of mutability and transformation: "now all that remains is the slow counting of the hours. Only remorse toward the mountain beneath our feet, which trusts us so blindly, oblivious to our treachery, the treachery of the grasshoppers who have been stepping on its surface for all these years" (106).

Significantly, throughout the Hebrew Bible, grasshoppers appear (frequently in the company of locusts) as harbingers of literal disasters like famine and desertification (2 Chronicles 6:28, Psalm 78:46, Psalm 105:34). They are also allegorical tropes for pettiness and the hubris of human ambition: "We seemed like grasshoppers in our own eyes, and we looked the same to them" (Num. 13:33); "He sits enthroned above the circle of the earth, and its people are like grasshoppers" (Isa. 40:22). As so often occurs in desert narratives, inner and outer landscapes converge when Yani imagines that the usually hidden species of the diurnal desert are sent on a peripatetic flurry by unseen forces:

> Geckos and spiders, beetles and jerboas, a countless multitude of tiny creatures is swarming everywhere today. The sand beneath my feet is full of activity. The birds of prey—the buzzards and the hawks—circle the sky expectantly, gather in their wings and claws, swoop again and again, bringing a swift death to these little denizens of the dark, which some mysterious force has banished from their usual haunts and sent scurrying into the sunlight. (107)

Like the insects, reptiles, birds, and other non-human denizens that have shared his wasteland these many years, the reluctant soldier feels a deep foreboding that he too has been "banished" from his aerie and "sent scurrying into the sunlight" by a power indifferent to his fate. The grace of the old desert vision of "streaming light" that once "infuse[d] me with strength and decisive confidence" has been cruelly withdrawn: "something's gone wrong and the vistas opening up only yesterday are now closing before my eyes" (107). But what Grossman wants us to notice is that the more alien and hostile his surroundings appear, the more Yani wakens to other fates, other lives. The prospect of something larger than himself is suddenly irresistibly enticing. Once again many readers may be provoked by the likely necessity of reading Yani as a literary surrogate for the insular and embattled Jewish state.

It seems that the final station on Nimra's spectacular road of altruism—the evidence of which is contained in a letter written in "panic-stricken haste" (112) to Yani in the desert—included the same degree of cynical manipulation to which she had been subject earlier. Yani finds himself irretrievably moved by the poignancy of the disaster that encompassed her. Once again, she was doomed by "the ardor of her eager, generous faith" (112). But the universe does not reward altruism, and nobody knows this more than Yani, who has stayed in the wilderness to prevent the toll of any future exigencies (or emotions) overtaking him. Among the *desaparecidos*, or "disappeared," of Argentina, Nimra spent her final days, staggered by the enormity of the fate that engulfed them: "Fifteen thousand of them have been counted in the past two years. The prey of the military junta, which decides human fates. Men and women, of all ages and classes, housewives, students, workers, intellectuals. All of them snatched away" (109). While serving as a member of the Amnesty delegation, Nimra befriended, and then fell deeply in love with, an elderly professor of Russian literature, father of the Argentinean political prisoner the international group once sought to remove from danger. Now it is clear that when Nimra first met him, the professor himself was also already in grave danger. What ensues, in Grossman's gripping narration, is a tragedy that grotesquely echoes the outcome of Nimra's earlier expression of moral agency in Jerusalem. In the aftermath of her second fatal act of misjudgment, matters unravel more precipitously than before.

After smuggling the professor away to France, Amnesty appoints Nimra to care for him in a rented house in Lyons. One evening a young stranger with a South American accent approaches her, promising to deliver urgent information about the activist son's fate to his elderly father. Though initially wary, the stranger's disarming expressions of admiration and respect for the "dear doctor," together with his genial and smiling façade, persuade the ever-trusting Nimra to set up a meeting. At the assigned place, "a tall, strong man with a grotesque mask on his face . . . whispered something, a kind of slogan, and fired one bullet into Mark's chest" (113). After the police interrogate her, Nimra discovers the professor's final letter in which he confesses that he fully understood that only violence awaited him that evening: "How painful. He wanted it. An end to the hopeless struggle. He grieved for her. The world was not worthy of her" (114). At this juncture, the reader can easily forget that it is no longer Elisha, but rather Nimra herself, who narrates the disaster in her final effort to explain her actions to the world. This is all the more tragically futile, because she addresses her letter to the hermetic

Yani. It is here that the reader's understanding of Yani's retreat from the world becomes more complicated.

That very night, "trembling with fear and rage," Nimra writes to him, she says, because only he will understand. That cryptic remark is perhaps the worst blow of all because in the end, it can only signify that Nimra died in despair, repudiating her short life of selflessness and her naïve faith in the essential goodness of those she trusted: "And I, here, on the mountaintop, like a balloon pricked with a pin, in a pain I didn't know I was capable of, sank again into my apathy and my resignation. Although I wrote to her, and asked her to send for Elisha . . . I already knew, from the tone of her words, from her beaten spirit, I knew—he would not be able to save her. And I too had nothing left to look forward to now" (114). In the end it is quietly revealed that Nimra took her life. Such suffering would seem to lend justification for any sensitive individual's withdrawal. In this heartbreaking world, Grossman's reader might reasonably begin to sympathize with the aging warrior's retreat from society, but Yani, long armored against life's obscene contingencies, awakens to his responsibility for the man he has inveigled into the wilderness.

In spite of the horror, this awareness shines as a moment of redemption, an act of *t'shuva,* that strikingly echoes the conscious turn to life taken by Oz's Yonatan after his desert trek proves unsatisfactory: "There's still a lot of strength in my arms and legs, and this is just as well, since it will make it easier for me to lead Elisha down all the paths of the camp, to reach all the places and the scents for the last time. My farewell present" (115). Seizing the limp Elisha (who is exhausted from illness and his three days of fast), he rushes helter-skelter through their old haunts down into the darkened labyrinth of empty corridors of the intelligence station—the desert that lies beneath the desert. There the meaning of those lost years rises to the surface in a frenzied rush of transfixing, megalomaniac nostalgia: "Only someone who spent thousands of crowded hours here, in the hum of the instruments, the commotion and the excitement, the tapping of the typewriters, the transmitters and telephones; only someone who experienced the anxiety of responsibility and difficult decisions here, the flushed young faces, the tremendous ferment of energy that assumed so many forms, of effort, and love, of quick, nervous repartee, of youthful hopes, anxieties, and suffering, only someone who was here during days of peace and war . . . would understand my devastation" (116–17). No longer a self-sufficient monologist, Yani discovers that he *needs* Elisha—feverish and barely sentient as he is—to testify, to witness, to somehow validate the past as a repository of meaning. At least Yani might gain an assurance that the past existed.

Grossman's memorable conclusion plunges readers into a stormy exchange between the two men, a verbal duel that thrusts Yani even closer to painful truths. Emerging from his fast with a sense of lucidity and vision, the usually amiable Elisha rises to confront "the prophet of wrath" who has long overly awed him (123). Fully aware that "thousands of soldiers have passed through this place," Elisha demands to know "why you out of all of them stayed behind," to which Yani retorts, still in denial: "I had nowhere to go from here" (though both men recall how he received generous offers of employment [117]). With a blend of pity and a creeping degree of contempt, Elisha is amazed that the heroic soldier he revered has lived his life abjectly cowering from the world: "Yani—so big and enormous, a mountain of a man, brave, an outstanding officer—and afraid as a child. Hiding up here on the mountain, wrapping himself in layers of flesh and uniforms, armoring himself with hostility. . . . Afraid, afraid" (121). Elisha is utterly disgusted by his friend's desiccated nostalgia, his fetishization of the past: "that phony yearning, the sentimental inflation of every banal memory . . . how your eyes caressed every stone . . . the love that poured out of you. Wasted love . . . love for dead things, narcissistic love" (121). Back in those days, Elisha clearly idolized Yani as a giant among men. Now his recollection of past events reveals a deeply tormented figure who, in his obduracy, resembled nothing so much as Bialik's perversely unrepentant "Dead of the Desert": "you had such amazing strength. Destructive strength. You were even destroying yourself, and it fascinated me. It had something to do with our age, I guess. Nimra used to say that people were afraid of you, not because you trod on corpses, but because you trod on your own corpse" (119). Like the legions of Hebrew rebels who crossed over the boundaries established by their God only to be transformed into rocky monoliths in the desert, Yani's tragic struggle presents the reader with a disturbingly pessimistic picture of stagnation. Elisha's struggle to roll away the stones that block his friend from living authentically seems heroic.

Does this suggest that Yani's condition resembles the fate of Bialik's cadavers who, "renegades of the waste . . . called barrenness mother," remain unfit for political independence? At such moments Grossman artfully juxtaposes both personal and collective paralysis. The ancient/new Sinai sojourns are imbricated, layered onto one another. Yani clings to his inchoate yearnings as the last bulwark against circumstances and a society that would otherwise rob him of the fading vestiges of his own emotional depths. Raging against Elisha's insinuations and accusations, Yani explodes in a self-pitying diatribe:

> Neither she nor you are capable of understanding what it means to live here on top of a random mountain, knowing all the time just how random it is, and to live alone, in the greatest possible loneliness, even if you're surrounded by hundreds of your kind, to live in despair, when the closest thing to you is a memory of ancient hopes growing fainter all the time, and the constant nagging feeling of having missed out, and a desire that drives you crazy for something that you can't define, that only the dead man in the bushes has any clue what it is. (119)

This is the first time that Yani has let slip the secret of the dead Egyptian, and he is momentarily stunned by his own admission, as much for his sudden loss of steely self-control as for its naked confirmation of Elisha's charge—his penchant for wasting his love on dead things. This revelation of his misdirected compassion in turn takes Yani to a much deeper appraisal of his past. What he suddenly reveals to himself and Elisha constitutes one of the most penetrating observations (indeed offers an elegant deconstruction) of the relation between the individual and Israeli military life in recent fiction: "I'm afraid, *afraid,* of that casual army camaraderie, of the 'wisecracking in the canteen,' because 'being a soldier' means being alienated. Alienated from the weapons they push into your hands, a friend-within-limits to the men sharing your tent, or your tank, until you part, until you go your separate ways, and when you meet again you won't have anything to say to each other" (120). It is nearly commonplace for Israeli writers of Grossman's generation to allude in some way to the essential loneliness of Israeli society. Few though, have so pertinently delineated the paradoxical way that the intensely collective experience of the army underscores the essential solitude and trauma of the individual's experience.

It is worth pausing here to consider how, in his role as a public intellectual commenting on the "brutishness" of the interminable armed conflict, Grossman has expressed his dismay with how the individual's "life is being dissipated, squandered in a pointless struggle," the ominous ways that "identity and self-respect and the one life" the individual possesses "are being endlessly expropriated . . . in a conflict that could have been resolved long ago" (*Death as a Way of Life* vii). Tellingly, his desert sojourner complains that the objectifying logic of the national narrative is bound to leave the Israeli subject "alienated from yourself, because you're nothing but an object, for them to do what they like with" (120). Often hinting that he has long seen himself at "war" with his society's harsh norms, Yani applied the lesson to himself long ago: "if you want to preserve your sanity, be alienated, contemptuous, detached from the pain of transience, protect yourself" (120). The real significance of Grossman's novella emerges when an authentic dialectic is created; as the two men, representing two polarities of the same generation, verbally spar for the right to interpret reality—both past and present.

Determined to divest Yani of the powerful hold that nostalgia has on him, Elisha dismisses his friend's portrait of their desert idyll: "People our age all over the world were living full, complete lives during those wonderful years, while we were here in the sand storms, and the thunderstorms, always half-starved, afraid of unseen enemies . . . look, I'm getting angry again just thinking about it" (124). Struggling desperately to counter this painful disavowal, Yani can conjure up only this wistful rationale: "But there was something about it, Elisha . . . something beautiful. If only because it was innocent, it's worth missing." Elisha will not have it, responding tersely: "Missing yes. Not wallowing, not addiction" (124). Though Elisha's steely logic is inescapable as he reminds Yani that alienation and loneliness are to be found "everywhere," readers may find it difficult to dismiss the justification for the latter's bitter defiance. Still, in the end, there is a hint that Yani has emerged from his forlorn depression, prepared to create a life in the community from which he had previously estranged himself.

Unlike Oz's sublime landscape, here the desert is employed as a suspiciously impervious and decidedly static environment, a wasteland of stagnation hostile to incorporating new elements into itself, in ways that reflect back on Yani himself. In contrast, Elisha and others demonstrate the fluid and natural capacity of the human psyche to interact in a process of continuous and cumulative fusion with the rich, conflict-ridden cultures that surround them (whether in Israel or Diaspora), in short to renew themselves. Still, it may be granted that though Yani is nearly ruptured by the surfacing of old memories, the desert has offered him a haven in which to confront and assimilate the epiphany of self-knowledge. In this regard, the denouements of Oz's and Grossman's narratives are strikingly similar.

The question of regaining one's humanity after reneging it is always at the heart of Grossman's fiction, as in the tormented child Momik's traumatic encounter with Holocaust bestiality and his own shadows in *See Under: Love,* and more recently in the young adult novel *Someone to Run With* (2004), where the young protagonist ponders, "If a person—any person—decided to enclose himself in armor, seal up and protect his soul, for a certain amount of time, in order to be able to execute a difficult mission—whatever it might be—after the mission has ended, will he be able to be himself, to go back to exactly the same person he was beforehand?" (152). After nine long and lonely years, Yani comes to be astounded by what his conformist self once took for the meaning of "my life, and especially my death, crude and blunt and very romantic" (72). More importantly, he has opened himself to the compassion of his fellow, allowing a place for the grief and sorrow the war inflicted on the traumatized collective to surface through the cracks in his wall of stoic heroism and individuality. Like Oz's Yonatan, it is the catalyst of another human being's solicitous presence, not merely a mystical encounter with a transcendent landscape, that ultimately returns the alienated citizen-subject to himself.[12] Yet perhaps in the end, being an officer in command of a remote base in the desert carries with it a form of knowledge not granted to most of us—a lucid awareness that there is no one in charge.

5 *Sinai of the Diasporic Imagination*

"We'll leave these sheep and wolves to Canaan": Masters and Slaves in Moses in Sinai

> "Canaan means the end of everything. Once we have land we have owners, we have gold . . . if we have Canaan we'll have Lords again. We'll be like everyone else. We'll have masters and slaves. You don't want that."
>
> —Dathan to Moses, in Simone Zelitch's *Moses in Sinai*

> Someone told me he's going down to Sinai because he wants to be alone with his God: I warned him.
>
> —Yehudah Amichai

> Religion is not, at the outset, a refuge of grace and mercy for the despondent and desperate, an enchanted stream for crushed spirits, but a raging, clamorous torrent of man's consciousness with all its crises, pangs and torments.
>
> —Rabbi Joseph Soloveitchik

Whereas modern Hebrew writers often make strident political uses of the desert in ways that resonate in the Israeli national scene, a significant number of Jewish writers in the Diaspora have discovered the luxury of moving in the universal tropes and renderings of "exile." Where Israeli writers are dutifully compelled by urgent social necessities and the imperatives of political specificity and concrete Zionist realities, much different renderings of the mythic past emerge from Jewish writers situated in other cultures. In diasporic explorations of the primal landscape where God and the Jew called to one another, terms such as exile, exodus, and estrangement are often valorized in these writers' imaginations, acquiring a different form of questioning. Without having to shoulder the anguished burden of answering to immediate political realities, self-consciously diasporic Jewish writers continue to explore the universal identity of all writers as somehow exilic. Though the two writers examined here come from markedly different backgrounds, cultural histories, and even aesthetics (one devoted to the strange configurations of a new aphoristic poetics, the other to the traditional novel), both reveal striking commonalities in their questioning of the essence of Jewish textuality, alterity, and the meaning of the burdensome liberty of Exodus. In Simone Zelitch's and Edmund Jabès's disparate representations of desert ethics and transcendence, the desert is not a literal landscape from which the Jew makes a clean break, but rather poses the metaphoric identity of a terrifying and obsessive questioning, an origin that also provides the essential parameters of the Jewish reality for eternity. Each shares a symbolic frame of reference in which to forsake the desert would mean to abandon the deepest engagement with the questions of truth and justice that constitute Judaism's ancient relationship to responsibility, hospitality, and justice. Zelitch's and Jabès's haunting approaches to post-Holocaust identity, even if radically different in form and genre, ultimately share a deeper engagement with Jewish rootedness in exile, the liturgical Jew of memory and wandering, than is present in the Israeli narratives we have explored thus far.

If the feminist politics of Hareven's return to the Bible enables a fresh reading of the social frailty of modern Zionism, the Jewish American novelist Simone Zelitch's own midrashic rewriting of Exodus and Numbers in her harsh and earthy *Moses in Sinai* (2002) makes the old stories stranger still by creating a more eclectic collage that juxtaposes mystical knowledge, ancient history, Oriental folk traditions, and even Marxism.[1] With her eye on the primitive and the savage dimensions of being and God, Zelitch's novel can be justly compared to the poet Jerome Rothenberg's earlier foray into what he has dubbed "ethnopoetics," the ancient currents of Jewish mysticism and esoteric ritual repressed (at the time of the novel's composition) in assimilated Jewish American life. Though some readers have found the novel's intentions, especially vis-à-vis its Jewish sources (especially in her audacious recreation of Korah), a rather tough riddle, the novel also has received critical acclaim as a "lush, lavish, atmospheric literary symphony" and a "mature and absorbing story of sacrifice, illusion, and resignation."[2] Zelitch playfully calls her *Moses in Sinai* "a Last Temptation of Christ for Jews," perhaps alluding to the ways her midrashic expansion aspires to fill in gaps about the spiritual yearnings and confusions of the leading characters. Rather than the abstract liberation of the collective, it is the challenge of delineating individual psychology in response to the upheavals of wrenching political transformations in the desert that concerns Zelitch. Prior to writing *Moses in Sinai,* Zelitch had often affirmed that her previous novels (*Louisa* [2001] and *Confession of Jack Straw* [1991]) were explorations of the contradictions that exist in political movements amidst the struggle toward a compassionate society. *Moses in Sinai* is her most direct exploration of the existential possibility of living without becoming masters or slaves, or without the "slaves" (oppressed) becoming the masters or oppressors. Like Hareven, she invents additional figures to elucidate the complexity of the wilderness experience from different perspectives, but here the primary focus is on the sacred and political consequences of Moses' and his brother Aaron's complex relations to the divine, particularly in relation to the meaning of freedom understood by other liberated subjects. Especially striking in this regard is Zelitch's recasting of Korah's infamous rebellion in the wilderness as a revolutionary struggle to keep faith with nomadic ethics.

Brimming with a number of deftly perverse deviations on the familiar story, Zelitch's novel leaves readers with strategic disjunctions that enable them to see critical psychological dimensions of the story, specifically in her exploration of scripture's representation of authority and acquiescence. For example, long before they set foot in the wilderness, her Israelites seem to hate it with a deep, existential dread that carries both mythic and modern psychological resonance, more than they do their present condition of enslavement. Dumbly accepting the pharaoh's will that they should dispose of their newborn sons, the fathers ritualistically obey: "Before a mother rose from her childbed, the father would take the newborn, swaddle him, stuff his mouth with stone and straw, and bear him to a basket to the wadi where a current would carry him away to the Red Sea" (11). As for the mothers, they answer their daughters' curiosity ("What was that?") with the bleak reply: "It never was. . . . Blessed be our Lord Pharaoh who keeps us from death in Sinai" (11).

Juxtaposed to these passive responses to power is the disturbing figure of Korah, whose insurrection in the wilderness receives much more sympathetic treatment than it does in scripture.[3] Korah's instinctive dream of a civilization without either masters or slaves, the vicious cycle in which the "slaves" (oppressed) invariably become the "masters" (oppressors), bears more affinity to the visions of human liberation first articulated in the age of Romanticism such as William Blake's Orc-Urizen cycle of rebellious liberation and authoritarian repression or Shelley's Prometheus than it does to the Book of Numbers. In Zelitch's novel, Korah's subversive response to authority inaugurates a questioning of the master narrative of the original crisis which ensues in the coming out of Egypt in the Book of Exodus. *Moses in Sinai* displays a fresh perspective on the sins and backslidings that followed—and the inscrutability of the Lord's violent judgments. This Korah embodies the egalitarian forces of outspoken dissent, who speaks out of concern for the well-being of the whole community, not unlike Hareven's subaltern voices of opposition in *Thirst.*

Through a compelling blend of lyrical magical realism and terse narrative, Zelitch adopts the spectacular desert showground as a lens for recognizing the Levinasian stranger who is intimately known, the antagonistic other who is also the double, and the double who is always intrinsic to the divided self. As briefly hinted at in Hareven's portrayal of the Hebrews' enigmatic leader, Zelitch's Moses ("running away from certainty") seems to recognize his own nature in the "cleft rock" he strikes to produce the life-giving waters that sustain his flight:

> The border of Sinai is lined with goat bones, thorn bushes, or the Red Sea. Deeper in, cliffs of brown stone shelter snakes so poisonous that they could pass over the shadow of a bird and make it fall. It was there Moses walked. . . . Sometimes he would take his staff and strike a rock again and again to force up a little water. . . . Yet, once he raised his staff to strike . . . Moses felt pity for the rock. "So I am divided," Moses said to the rock.[4]

This identification, however, proves an ephemeral conceit; nature and the lonely man remain violently at odds with each other (as they do throughout the desert experience). For the latter, with a "blazing unity of purpose," strikes the rock "even after water flowed" (83). In Zelitch's exploration of the repressed sensual and pagan currents from which Judaism struggled to emerge, Moses' experience of the desert seems to be a cosmic space where dreams and nightmares exist side by side. Yet, from this oppositional realm, clarity emerges: "No longer did the world call to him and make impossible demands; rather he called to the world itself, called everything by name. There were few names in the Sinai; they weren't hard to learn: bird, snake, rock, thorn, acacia" (84). At other times, such transparency dissipates, if only because of the sheer vastness of the spaces Moses traverses: "The Sinai was enormous, beyond human scale. The farther he walked, the more he felt himself as a slight aspect of the landscape . . . a trail scratched like a fine thread through the dust. When Moses praised what he passed through, that praise was so expansive that sometimes he would have to stop walking and sit on a rock, too overcome to move" (85). Zelitch's reluctant prophet is in perpetual danger of losing himself. Initially, as with Oz's Yonatan, the encounter with the sublime landscape threatens the integrity and potency of the self; even the "holy" denizens of the desert that cross his path seem dangerous portents of an utterly hostile landscape that will strip away his subjective integrity: "The snakes of Sinai are so black they look like gold; their eyes are the color of olives. As the snake slid past the bare feet of Moses, it shed its skin. . . . Moses took up the snake skin and held it to the sun. It felt hot, fragile and holy. . . . As night fell, Moses thought: it is not the skin of an ox, taken by slaughter, but a skin shed cleanly, left behind" (84).

As with the cleft rock, though at first an ominous sign, the snake's cast-off skin ultimately signals something vital about the essence of Moses' own condition. Emulating Moses' own layered identity, the snakeskin "shed cleanly" also seems to conjure up the startling prospect that "it is possible to live without doing harm" (84). It comes to him as a revelation that the benign process of "a skin shed cleanly" is "not the skin of an ox, taken by slaughter" and so Moses accepts the "hot, fragile and holy" gift as a token of his own identity (84).

Zelitch's perpetually tormented outsider is a bewildered man struggling against his own psychic loneliness and the burden of forming the great epic of Hebrew solidarity while perpetually wondering about an alternative to violent forms of authority. Bewildered and numb after slaying an Egyptian overseer, Moses suddenly finds himself drawn toward the desert, a mysterious calling that the reader experiences at a slight distance, from the perspective of Moses' brother Amram: "It was in the direction of Sinai that Moses stared as they walked on, his mouth in that set, scar-lined gape of wonder, his eyes unfocused. The afternoon sun rounded his shoulders with clean light, and Amram felt what he had felt the night before, a terrible presence. And it came to Amram then that this youth was bound for Sinai, would lead him back to Sinai, even against his will" (72). Throughout *Moses in Sinai,* a distinct reluctance to accept the violent rupture of desert initiation (as uprooting from place and culture) marks both the individual and the collective. For example, in the novel's early pages, Zelitch represents the warm relationship between the pharaoh and his Hebrew tribes as the product of cultural roots and continuity; four centuries after Joseph they still loyally interpret the disturbing dreams of their sovereign for the blessing of a permanent dwelling:

> The Pharaoh was not often troubled by dreams, so he was surprised to find himself sitting bolt-upright one morning with his hand on a wildly beating heart. Without rising from bed, he called for the twelve elders . . . they kissed the earth between his feet and piled his lap with their rods of judgment. He said "A black fish came to me and whispered in my ear that a son would be born who would shorten my life and drive you out of Goshen into the wilderness of Sinai." (10)

For their part, the tribal elders are as dismayed as their sovereign by the prospect of a nomadic fate, passionately denying that they harbor any thought of departure. At such moments, immersing readers in the illicitly dark human energies of its troubled human characters, not to mention the unlit shadow of its inexplicable God, Zelitch creates a palpable mood of raw fear. Hur, the elder of the Levi, starkly proclaims, "If such a son is born, we will all die."

The tribes of Goshen are unified in their certainty that the Sinai is a singularly threatening waste where "even the shadows of the rocks were poisonous, and snakes ate men" (10). Henceforth, to protect the pharaoh's precarious peace of mind, the twelve tribes meekly acquiesce to drowning their newborn males and mothers would recite "Blessed is our Lord Pharaoh who keeps us from death in Sinai" (11). Zelitch's provocative representation of the Hebrew's complicity with their own annihilation reads as an audacious echo of Hannah Arendt's description of the failure of the moral will of both the Nazis and their victims in her controversial study *Eichmann in Jerusalem: A Report on the Banality of Evil* (1994). If readers are jarred by this anachronistic intertextuality, it may be part of Zelitch's intentions to disturb them with the "timeless" implications of Arendt's troubling conclusions about the intertwined conditions of power and powerlessness.

Far from beckoning as a respite from such tyranny, the very thought of this virulent realm induces shivers yet again when, fleeing his childhood friend Mernepthah (the pharaoh's son), Moses himself pauses on the border of Sinai, very much a divided man, uncertain of his path:

> He felt a shiver like a spasm. He could go back to Goshen, kill every master, free the slaves. Another shiver. He was shivering with joy. But then his heart misspoke itself and divided with such force that he lost his footing and lay breathless on the rubble with his fist clenched tight. . . . Behind him lay Goshen and before him lay the Sinai. In Sinai

> there were snakes, thorns, acacia and birds of prey. No one could walk there and live. He got to his feet with the aid of the staff and climbed down the rock to the gravel below. He entered Sinai because he was afraid. (79)

Zelitch's remote/near deity, dwelling somewhere in the jagged cliffs of high latitudes, seems every bit as dangerous and violent as the Sinai landscape, and perhaps every bit as divided as the lonely prophet.

Certainly one of the most spiritually inclined of all the works addressed in this study, *Moses in Sinai* presents its desert as a stern rebuke to the dreamy sojourner. Zelitch suggests that the world reflects the divine even when its nature is harsh and jagged, even when we are left with little choice but to conclude that the divine sovereign of such a realm must be similarly inconsiderate. Indeed, the deity encountered in the wilderness by Zelitch's Hebrews bears a striking resemblance to Annie Dillard's unsparing meditations on God as deadly, implacable energy.[5] For Dillard's negative theology offers a similarly severe imperative:

> We do need reminding, not of what God can do, but of what he cannot do, or will not, which is to catch time in its free fall and stick a nickel's worth of sense into our days. And we need reminding of what time can do, must only do; churn out enormity at random and beat it, with God's blessing, into our heads: that we are created, *created,* sojourners in a land we did not make. . . . Who are we to demand explanations from God? (*Holy the Firm* 45)

In this representative passage, Dillard's sensibility greatly resembles that expressed throughout Zelitch's reconstruction of the Sinai experience. Impatient with the infantilizing assumptions of modern faith, Dillard admonishes that "we people in churches seem like cheerful, brainless tourists on a packaged tour of the Absolute" (quoted in Carroll 49). Though ostensibly addressing Christianity, she implicitly offers a sobering critique of the three monotheistic faiths' collective tendencies to instruct their adherents that God is "close" at hand. Of course this critique is often voiced by rabbis as well. Indeed, one cannot but hear a surprisingly distinct reverberation of the stern terms of Rabbi Soloveitchik's sober approach to religious experience ("a raging, clamorous torrent of man's consciousness with all its crises, pangs and torments") that introduce this chapter. For Dillard (as if, like Soloveitchik, more at home in the Book of Job than the Gospels), laying bare the conditions of time, danger, and death to which we are all subject, it is no accident that God in the Hebraic and other traditions is often located at the summit of mountains.

In the powerful conclusion to *Pilgrim at Tinker Creek,* Dillard momentarily acknowledges that "mystics of all creeds experience the presence of God on mountaintops." But then, she seems to intuit the harsher reality that illuminates the deep core of Moses' inexplicable reluctance that distinguishes Zelitch's own portrayal:

> Aren't they afraid of being blown away? God said to Moses on Sinai that even the priests, who have access to the Lord, must hallow themselves, for fear that the Lord may break out against them. This is *the* fear. It often feels best to lay low, inconspicuous, instead of waving your spirit around from high places like a lightning rod. For if God is in one sense the igniter, a fireball that spins over the ground of continents, God is also in another sense the destroyer, lightning, blind power, impartial as the atmosphere. . . . In the open anything might happen. (89)

Similarly, in Zelitch's disturbing foray into biblical fiction, her savage, unyielding desert weans readers from looking with much hope in the universe for a God of compassion, instead coaxing onward toward a more human-centered ethics.[6] Her meditation on the Israelites' nascent desert theology represents a spatial conundrum. Utterly withholding its "meaning," the desert drives the individual on a path toward the true site of revelation, which is inward (rather than rewarding the pantheistic error of using the natural world that yields to human will or reveals an intimate, sympathetic God). At the same time, in such passages as her provocative portrayal of the people gathered at Mount Sinai, Zelitch judiciously preserves a degree of ambiguity in the crucial question of divine versus human agency, a strategy that allows readers space for their own faith perspectives: "Here was the mountain, an ordinary mountain such as might rise out of an ordinary plateau. It was red-brown, dung-colored, like any Sinai mountain. No fire, no sheer sides, even a clear trail to the summit. Yet every Hebrew stood, deadened with fear. In the silence, the earth hummed, a hum that came from the mingled reverberation of the Hebrews" (185).

It is hardly clear whether the enduring implacability of the mountain is divine "presence" or a natural "absence" filled only by the Israelites' anxious bleating. Against a domesticated, "personal" God of consolation who rules a benevolent natural world, Zelitch's Moses confronts a remote and inexplicable deity whose significance resides solely in His capacity to lead human beings toward their truest potential through the rigor of the Law. Emerging blinking from centuries of slavery to dwell forty more years in exile from the land, the people learn in the desert that there is no need of sovereignty for God's will to be done in the present.

In her reanimation of Moses' flight into the wilderness, Zelitch's young "Egyptian" finds unquestioning welcome in the tents of a desert chieftain who lays out the lean and pristine nomadic ethics of what will grow into the complexities of Mosaic (and later talmudic) law and justice: "'Seek righteousness. Do not slander. Use sound weights and measures. Do not oppress strangers'" (87). In his insistence that Law must prevail over the untrustworthy realm of the heart, the plainspoken nomad anticipates the stark clarity of what will eventually distinguish the Sinai revelation—indeed all of Hebraic prophecy—from Christianity's focus on the plaudits of "love" and "salvation" (a chasm that has only widened for contemporary writers since the Holocaust): "'Hearts falter; laws are firm. Hearts cannot know what will come to pass. . . . Follow laws and you will know evil is met with evil, good met with good. Well am I rid of a wayward heart, having gained law'" (88). Still more urban Egyptian than desert dweller, apparently stunned by the sheer alterity of the revelation, Moses staggers back as if unable to bear the weight of what awaits him. Shy and tentative, his crude actions form a mimetic parody of the retributive anger of the desert prophet of scripture: "Moses took a step back, for as the old man sang, he felt his blood turn to clay, and his feet crunched on two tablets, and cracked them to bits" (88).

After wedding the Midianite maiden named Zipporah, Moses tends his father-in-law's sheep, living in the slow time of the desert. While elsewhere in Sinai Hebrew slaves as well as strangers from distant Nubia toil in the turquoise mines, Moses serenely cares for the flocks, acquiring "quiet, wholesome pity for the world. He would not let Jethro's daughters slaughter sheep, though it meant they ate no meat and that the flocks multiplied to no purpose. He silenced complaints by watering and grazing those sheep himself" (99). Here, Zelitch invokes Exodus 3:1: "Now Moses, tending the flock of his father-in-law Jethro, the priest of Midian, drove the flock into the wilderness, and came to Horeb, the mountain of God." Leading his flock in the wilderness as a shepherd clearly anticipates things to come. Zelitch imagines a man content to tolerate the "sand fleas, snakes, and sheep," all the creatures that permeate his environment. Paradoxically, Moses is so enamored of creation even in this austere environment that he protests even those mundane actions necessary to sustain human life: "To Zipporah, he said 'Do you not even pity the wheat you thresh to make those cakes? It was a seed. It troubled itself to grow. It struggled and suffered'" (100). Zipporah responds with affectionate (if mildly mocking) laughter. But the reader recognizes that her husband's helplessly ever-widening empathy with the animal and vegetable worlds are the first halting steps toward an expanded consciousness that will prove essential for the prophetic imagination, for shepherding a people in the wilderness.

Three years after the birth of his son Gershom (named "stranger" by Zipporah after the strange deity that both draws and repulses her husband), Moses visits the tent of Jethro, now on his deathbed. The evidence of the old nomad's inspired instruction is gathered in piles around the two: "as years passed, Moses had learned to carve the laws. Jethro would rest a cold hand on Moses' hand to be sure it was moving in the right direction. Moses felt the piles of fresh clay press in from all sides, clammy and malleable, as he dug into the tablet with the little brass knife. . . . By now, the clay tablets lay piled so thick against the walls that [Jethro] sat inside a narrow chimney" (108). This wry description of the scribe's symbolic space poetically underscores the fateful enclosure of the law that will hem the people in the desert (like Moses' "bleating sheep" which are "safe, penned in"), henceforth dividing them from all other peoples in a refuge that, in the ages to come, at times will feel claustrophobic and at others a radical freedom.

In her portrait of Moses' transformation, Zelitch underscores the profound loneliness of a leader alienated from his own people and who, seeking God, experiences only brief ecstasy—and then lasting violence in submitting to that God. In her ironic retelling of one of the Bible's most mysterious passages, it would seem to be Moses, and not the bush, that is physically afflicted by divine fire, burnt but not "consumed." One day, he suddenly bursts into flame and burns until at last Zipporah circumcises their son, which quenches the flame, eliciting Zipporah's observation that "you have been a bridegroom of blood to me." It is as if he personifies all the predatory force that the universe bears down on Creation. The strange episode invoked here (Exod. 4:24–26), also referred to as that of "the bloody bridegroom" by perplexed biblical scholars, has been midrashically read by a few as a sort of psychological allegory of the severe emotional stress experienced by Moses, who at this point most acutely feels his soul torn between Egyptian and Jewish identities.[7] Zelitch's retelling works admirably with this empathic hermeneutics. From this point, "trailing ash and blood," her Moses sets out to redeem his people: "He walked into his task as he might walk into a wind, and then slowly and without a moment when he marked a change, the wind was to his back, and he was borne forward over rocks and over mountains . . . bound for Pti-Ramesses where he would find his brother, Aaron" (116).

When at last Moses prevails to ensure his people's peripatetic destiny, Zelitch evokes Pharaoh's pursuit of the Israelites into the desert in an unusual light. Rather than the Pharaoh's acting out of resentment toward their new-found freedom or because he has second thoughts about losing his slaves, Zelitch's sly rendering seems to fulfill the logic of the people's reluctance to make a clean break with Egypt's fleshpots, as expressed in Exodus and Numbers. For this Pharaoh, finding his land and all Egyptian first-born males stricken by the strange invisible God of the Israelites, determines to drive the pariahs away. Nothing short of violent expulsion will otherwise persuade the Israelites to enter the poisonous desert expanses:

> At once, the Pharaoh knew what must be done. He turned from the Angel of Death and spoke not to Moses, but to God. "So now they cannot turn back. . . . So they must go to Sinai, for they will never be allowed to stay in Goshen now that you are killing in their name. And now I will tell them to take their flocks and gold and never to return." Through the last rag ends of dark, the Pharaoh mounted a bright chariot, and all of Egypt wondered at his holy anger as he drove the twelve tribes. . . . Through the rushes, arrows flew, until at last those tribes were trapped against a deep Red Sea. (146)

At such moments, Zelitch's novel reveals a strong kinship with Hareven's vision of a people alienated from their own origins, whose oral myths inspire indifference for most while provoking urgent questions for the few. For the latter individuals, even before Moses is prepared to lead, the desert instills a special sense of wandering as a cognitive process of recovery of lost identity. In response to his people's complacent fulfillment of Pharaoh's edict, a nomadic Hebrew, reminiscent of Hareven's portrayal of visionary outsiders as well as her interrogatory engagement with the *akedah* myth, muses that in the old legends, "Abraham was told to spare his son, and now we slay our own sons willfully. . . . In those tales, we had one master, and now we have another. Who was our master then? Who is our master now?" (38). Though the others assure him that "Lord Pharaoh" is part of the natural order that follows the patriarchal succession, this anonymous Hebrew tirelessly interrogates "elders, wives and children" for ten years, "sworn to wander until he knew the name of the master who made Abraham spare his son" (38).

This Hebrew, who remains nameless throughout the narrative, never lingers at night in the camps of those who have slain their first-born;

increasingly persuaded that his answer resides in the ineffable stillness beyond the compromised human community: "He liked the feel of a rock below his head, the wadi to his right . . . and a wind passing across his face. At times he believed the wind itself would give the riddle's answer, a truer answer than a slave could find" (39). Moses too experiences the desert as a quietness that "weans away his anger," rewarding him with unparalleled lucidity: "If he kept walking, he could live an honest life. The stones gave off a hot, sharp scent that cleared his head, emptied it like a porcelain basin to let light shine through" (84). Zelitch's spirited representation of the enigmatic prophet of Exodus draws from classical as well as modern rabbinic speculation. Her Moses is a singularly alienated and alienating figure. Accordingly, in naming their son "Gershom," meaning "stranger," Zipporah startles her husband, but calmly explains that "you are a stranger to me. Our souls are strangers" (101). Zipporah accuses Moses of a God fever so ardent that she fears he will one day inadvertently break her neck. In an ironic displacement of Moses' call to God's summons: "I'm here. Here I am," Zelitch's impassioned Zipporah protests "You're not here!" as if Moses' severe God orientation is too lacking in human immediacy and warmth. Her retort serves as a brilliant crystallization of the novel's theme of resisting the violence of transcendence—Moses' "here-ness" translates spiritually and emotionally as a diminished elsewhere, too remote for his earthy wife. His God is constantly beckoning "something else . . . immediate, urgent, advancing on him and forcing everything else into insignificance" (110). Increasingly, Moses locates this amorphous being in the dry austerity and white light of Sinai, where "[t]he vastness of the wilderness opened before him, but now he could not take the time to wonder, to fear, to feel at home, to feel displaced, to feel anything but himself, called by name. If once he had surrendered to the Sinai, now he saw it only as something he must pass over as a hand passes over a table to reach for something no one else can see. He walked at such a pace that by mid-day, he was close to Midian" (113).

As is often the case in *Moses in Sinai,* this odd invocation of a key phrase allows for playful new meanings. Instead of the Angel of Death "passing over" the House of Israel as Egypt's own first-born infants are struck down, Moses' own grasp amidst the naked stone of Sinai assumes almost divine proportions, an ambition that exceeds the comprehension of anyone else. Much like Judaism's sacred text, it suggests an implacable force bent on its own inexplicable purposes.

Remarking on the danger of any notion of transcendence not firmly anchored in humanism, Michael Rosenak, a professor of Jewish education, observes that "clearly each historical faith community has its own language that points to the beyond . . . while differing approaches to transcendence can guide their communities to the heights of profound insight and understanding, they can also lead them into perverse idolatries. What criteria have we to distinguish between holy and abominable approaches to transcendence?" Rosenak proposes that "when humanism is understood as having its source in transcendence, 'humanistic' life constitutes a universal religious imperative, standing guard against idolatry while bringing transcendence down to earth" (25). Perhaps for that very reason, the young Korah's initial attraction to and subsequent grave disappointment in the Israelite priestly hierarchy must be understood as an anxiety over repetition, a fear that the priest clan whose power grows day by day in the desert will reproduce the masters and slaves dialectic of Egypt. Yet ironically, this Moses is a leader most reluctant to lead, who insists to his obdurate brother Aaron that "I am not leading. . . . I am running away . . . from all of you" (161–62).

Throughout Zelitch's extended midrash, Korah—a figure that the rabbinic imagination up until the present day casts as one of scripture's most villainous figures for orchestrating a nearly disastrous insurrection—comes across as far more sympathetic than the increasingly remote figure of Moses. Acutely aware of dwelling in a liminal space between slavery and freedom, Korah spends most of the novel struggling with the true nature of human liberation, longing to know, "When will we be home?" or what would constitute "home?" and, most of all, "What is the god's name?" (163). Ever since the dislocations of childhood, when a mysterious old man (apparently the same figure who earlier challenged Egypt's settled Hebrews) instructed him that "you are home and you are homeless. You are a Hebrew in Sinai" (163), Korah's soul has been tormented by the enigma of that identity.

Like the marginalized skeptics of Hareven's novellas, Korah grows into a bold doubter, alienated by Moses' distant leadership and the mundane authoritarian culture that has begun to form. When a stranger arrives in the camp with his young son, seeking a new form of human community—"I have been told that here there are no masters and no slaves"—Korah bitterly insists on disillusioning him: "Take your son and go, for we have a master now" (216). When pressed by the stranger, who hopes that the new "master" might at least signify some hope for a more benevolent deity, Korah, who sees the return of hierarchical relationships as the woeful death of the old exhilarating days of cooperative desert anarchy, bitterly strips him of that final hope too: "'A god?' the man asked. 'The High Priest,' Korah answered. 'And he has an overseer named Moses who holds a whip called Law'" (216).

Later, Zelitch's Dathan, yet another rebellious figure the Bible claims was swallowed up by the earth (Num. 16:32), offers Moses a more explicit plea to justify his own heretical rhetoric and subversive actions: "'Canaan means the end of everything. Once we have land we have owners, we have gold. We both know.' 'What do we know?' Moses asked. He sounded tired. Dathan struck the tent post with his fist. 'You know that if we have Canaan we'll have Lords again. We'll be like everyone else. We'll have masters and slaves. You don't want that'" (239).

For Dathan, the prophetic doom of "everything" that he vehemently protests against here means the destruction of nomadic ethics—the lived reality as practiced by the tribes in the desert, rather than legalistic abstraction. His argument may be profitably compared with the French philosopher Maurice Blanchot's reading of the subversive force of Jewish scripture (the Talmud and Torah) as "nomadic" in its ethical spirit: "in this respect . . . it stands out against paganism . . . [if] to be pagan is to settle, to plant oneself in the earth, so to speak, to set oneself up through a pact with permanency that authorizes the sojourn and that certifies the certainty of the soil. Nomadism answers to a relationship that possession does not satisfy . . . this nomadic movement (where the ideas of dividing and separation can be found) reveals itself not as the eternal privation of sojourn, but as a genuine way of residing, of a residence that does not bind us to the determination of a place. . . . As if the truth itself were necessarily sedentary!" (*L'Entretien infini,* 183, 185).

Readers sympathetic to this ancient/postmodern resistance to stasis and moribund rootedness will appreciate what happens next in Zelitch's version. When an unmoved Moses offers only one choice—"do you stand with Aaron or with Korah"—Dathan angrily opposes him in measured terms curiously reminiscent of Bialik's retelling of the obdurate stand of the "Dead of the Desert": "We walked away from Pharaoh's law. We'll walk away again. . . . We'll write the Law of Feet" (240). Intuiting that Moses must be as disgusted by the regime as he and Korah, Dathan pleads, "Get up. We'll go together. We'll leave these sheep and wolves to Canaan where they'll kill each other" (240). An unusual but respected current in biblical scholarship supports Zelitch's challenging reading of the tensions embedded in the desert experience. In Harry Berger's innovative rendering of this countertradition, he argues that

> The failure of the Mosaic revolution was built into the very premises it started from, and into the very conditions of its origin and triumph. A

> phantom double of the pharaoh, what the Egyptians would have called an *akh,* a vital force emanating from the tomb, traveled with the fugitive Israelites, stored its potency within their early image of Yahweh, and waited for the time when they would inevitably return to spiritual Egypt, not as slaves who had been betrayed or forced into captivity but as the captors and victors themselves. (134)

Berger sees "the seeds of Egypt" fatally germinating and "carried within . . . the Mosaic revolution . . . the royalist and antiroyalist trajectories are certainly present in the text, twining and untwining throughout" (134). To Zelitch's credit, *Moses in Sinai* brings alive the vibrant impulse of this vital paradox for contemporary readers who may be unfamiliar with the competing strands embedded in their own spiritual traditions. What Dathan and Korah plead for is the preservation of nomadic ethics, the intensified understanding of human interdependence that the desert experience bestows.[8]

For theologian B. Jill Carroll, a religion for adults would affirm that "God has . . . loosed us to sojourn on a speckled earth that holds within it the possibility for death as much as life, horror as much as beauty, and pain as much as comfort" (43). Carroll finds a perverse solace in Dillard's "daredevil spirituality," the latter's steely insistence that a lonely humankind blinks in the darkness toward a mysterious "'God less lovable than a grasshead, who treats us less well than we treat our lawns. . . . God is a brute and traitor, abandoning us to time, to necessity and the engines of matter unhinged.'" For Carroll, the naturalist's God seems altogether aligned "in both design and behavior" with "predatory animals" (43). However, the ostensibly inviting alternative—abandoning God "as the poster-deity" (117) for political platforms, who sympathizes with some and not other programs—is to distort the oppressive, arbitrary nature of existence itself. Acutely aware of the need for an honest theology that would assert the true terms of reality, Carroll's advocacy that we "retain a sense of otherness in reference to God and to nature so that both are at times experienced as hostile or alien to humanity" (65) illuminates my own sense that accepting the novel's layers of violence and destruction is necessary to fully come to terms with Zelitch's horrifying and beautiful vision:

> When the world in which we live and the deity that is immanent in it seems hostile and alien, there is no room for fancying that the world or God is aligned in the least with human political or social concern. The

> otherness of God and the natural world appears most alarmingly in these instances, and serves as a critique of those models of God that are reductionistic and self-serving, focusing as they do only upon the aspects of deity that are comforting and helpful. (Carroll 65–66)

Zelitch's rendering of desert, redolent with Carroll's assertion that freedom and beauty come only when the random, indifferent, and terrifying aspects of the world are recognized, affirms an "adult" spiritual sensibility that need not depend on a docile and benevolent God of "childhood." This ethos suggests the possibility of a genuinely shared Judeo-Christian-Islamic continuum, a utopian category that many have often felt was untenable. Such a vision is also highly compatible with the lively spiritual imagination of Belden Lane, whose years of desert experience taught him the plain spiritual sense that "God is a desert, ultimately beyond human comprehension" (12). Interestingly, Lane, drawing from his meditations in desert spaces, declares that "I really don't want a God who is solicitous of my every need, fawning for my attention, eager for nothing in the world so much as the fulfillment of my self-potential. One of the scourges of our age is that all our deities are house-broken and eminently companionable. Far from demanding anything, they ask only how they can more meaningfully enhance the lives of those they serve" (53).

Reading Zelitch and Soloveitchik alongside these other spiritual writers—Christians very close to the stark monotheistic spirit of the Hebrew Bible—suggests the possibility that the "God" of rough terrain who also haunts Zelitch's narrative makes the best case for becoming attuned to human concerns. Ultimately, Zelitch's Moses, Dathan, and Korah are all recognizable as variations on the archetypal Jewish subject drawn toward the irrevocable movement into exile and estrangement. Each meets a similar fate of tormented consciousness and loneliness. Their incessant questioning represents the burden of the nomadic imagination, as both Zelitch and, as we will shortly see, Jabès construe as the alternative to complacent habitation.

In the end, the anonymous destiny that greets Zelitch's leader, who has persistently protested "I am not a leader" throughout the novel, bears a compelling logic that seems both richly poetic and scripturally steadfast. Abandoned by the Israelites on Mount Nebo, Moses is addressed by voices in the wilderness. Uncertain whether it is God's or Korah's utterances that beckon to him at the end, Moses departs the novel by taking hold of the carcass of a newly sacrificed ox. Turning back slowly to the desert: "he would carry the ox so far into the Sinai that nobody could follow, or separate their mingled bones or know their names" (267). Through the enigma with which these final rueful words leave us, Zelitch's novel zealously preserves the strange mystery of Moses' unknown burial place, making the reader ache for the palpable human loss of the uncertain prophet and perhaps shudder not a little in the wake of the unknowable, infinitely estranged deity of the wilderness.

"The desert wrote the Jew": Jabès's Enigmas of Liberty and Responsibility

> The exiled pilgrim, carrying with him a curse, an affliction, a mortal sin, does not turn to God in his distress. In the strictest sense of the word, he has no God; He, too, has fallen by the wayside. A dim, ancient memory of something broken, of vague yearnings, is stored inside him. He does not call it by name, he does not know its name, but he needs it and he is looking for it.
>
> —Yitzhak Orpaz

> Judaism, our texts, and our practices are all designed to create a kind of emptiness. It is not the emptiness of despair or the loss of meaning. It is the emptiness that mythic Abraham felt on being denied the right to sacrifice his son. It is the emptiness of the holy "tent of meeting" that held place for a new kind of God that had no idol. It is the emptiness, this nothingness itself, that holds open the possibility for the divine to emerge.
>
> —Douglas Rushkoff

No other modern Jewish writer has responded more creatively to *Lekh-lekha* (get thee out), God's command to Abram that he uproot himself and be cast out from homeland, than has Edmond Jabès (1912–1991), whose work is so singularly devoted to the ruptures and tribulations of exile. His postmodern poetry offers an invigorating but often daunting exploration of the meaning and consequences of both textuality and the ineffable in the wake of the Holocaust and personal dislocation.[9] In his audacious aphoristic works which bear the imprint of both Mallarmé and Auschwitz, Jabès reveals the intrinsic paradox of language as both the origin, and consolation, of exile. Determined to translate the post-Holocaust identity of the Jew as a permanently wounded form of writing, Jabès nevertheless upholds the necessity of the Jewish writer's indelible relation to an eternal book: "Faced with the impossibility of writing which paralyzes every writer and the impossibility of being Jewish which for two thousand years has rent the people of this name, the writer chooses to write and the Jew to survive" (*Livre de Yukel* 59–60). Fittingly, Sidra DeKoven Ezrahi dubs Jabès one of the pre-eminent "modern architects and exemplars of text-centeredness as an exilic priority" (*Booking Passage* 11). In Jabès's extraordinary art, Sinai and the Shoah converge; redemption and nullification must always oscillate in irresolvable and infinite tension.

Born in Cairo to Jewish-Italian parents, Jabès received a French education and lived among Egypt's French-speaking community. He published small collections of poetry in the 1940s and 1950s while forming important literary friendships with Paul Eluard, René Char, and Max Jacob. During World War II, Jabès worked for the British in Palestine but returned to Egypt shortly afterwards, a simple biographical detail that seems to speak volumes of his relationship to Jewish nationalism and "homeland" that I will describe. In the immediate postwar years he frequently visited Paris, where he cultivated important literary relations and friendships with the Jewish German poet Paul Celan, Albert Camus, Jean Grenier, and others. The Suez crisis and the 1956 war between Israel and Egypt led to Jabès's forced departure by Nasser's regime (along with most of Egypt's Jews) at the age of forty-five.

Living in Cairo, the desert that would form the crucial grounds of his fragmentary art was literally at Jabès's feet (much as it would figure in both the life and career of Amos Oz). Subsequently, this landscape evolved as a forceful presence in his art during his life as an artist in exile in Paris, as if only at a great remove could its true significance emerge. Once a deracinated Jew, Jabès's exile led him not only to come to terms with the burden of his Jewishness as a perpetual condition of being society's Other, but to see himself in relation to Judaism's quintessential exilic history and the sacred texts it engendered. As the novelist Paul Auster observes of the critical influence of Judaism's sacred works in this period, "Jabès began studying Jewish texts—the Talmud, the Kabbala—and though this reading did not initiate a return to the religious precepts of Judaism, it did provide a way for Jabès to affirm his ties with Jewish history and thought. More than the primary source of the Torah, it was the writings and rabbinical commentaries of the Diaspora that moved Jabès" ("Introduction" x). Even without that biographical evidence, it soon becomes clear that the briefest of encounters with the poet immediately presents readers with disturbing paradoxes of silence and speech, absence and presence—"postmodern" paradigms that have their origin in Judaism's central texts. Such oppositions are always contained within Jabès's peculiarly talmudic mode of presenting disparate, disembodied "rabbis" to the reader:

> "The desert" replied Reb Goetz, "is the soul's awakening, and sky, its envy. . . . The garden means speaking, the desert, writing. In every grain of sand, a sign surprises us." (*Book of Questions* 148–49)

> Reb Jacob, who was my first teacher, believed in the virtue of the lie because, so he said, there is no writing without lies. And writing is the way of God. . . . The divine utterance is silenced as soon as it is pronounced. . . . Eloquence is created by the absence of a divine word. (*Book of Questions* 148–49)

In his Parisian exile, Jabès created the most notoriously enigmatic aphoristic works of the late twentieth century, as these representative passages suggest. With disarmingly seductive titles such as *The Book of Questions, The Book of Resemblances,* and *If There Were Anywhere but Desert,* Jabès's imaginative sojourns into the myriad mysteries produced by silence, absence, dialogue, and the meaning of the Jewish book, captivate readers in the form of mystical, often playful aphorisms. For Jabès, the "Jewish book" signifies the totality of Jewish textuality in any moment in time.

Heavily influenced by the French surrealistic tradition, his writings have captivated writers beginning with continental philosophers such as Maurice Blanchot, Georges Bataille, and Jacques Derrida, and transmitted to a later generation of American postmodernist novelists like Auster as well as poets such as Robert Duncan and Jerome Rothenberg. However, it should also be emphasized that this ostensibly "French" writer long held a high regard for his *indigenous* influences, which has often been neglected by his Eurocentric readers: "I had a certain rapport with Arab literature and philosophy, and then I realized in the Moslem tradition, with the Sufis for example, there were completely amazing things, as in the questioning of language. And at the same time I was also beginning to read the Jewish mystics, who wrote in Hebrew and Arabic at the same time" ("Interview with Jason Wiess" 140–41). The "East" presented Jabès with a rich semiotics of geographic and linguistic terrain. As a striking (at times it seems inevitable) metaphor for writing, the Oriental desert is the most central trope of Jabès's thought, the continuum that links one work to the next: "The unsayable settles us in those desert regions which are the home of dead languages" (*Book of Questions: Yael Elya Aely El, or the Last Book* 77). However, this paradigm does not seem to have entered his consciousness before his exile from Egypt (following the Suez Canal crisis in 1956), which he subsequently acknowledged as a profound personal rupture even if a mere blip on the screen of Judaism's historical displacements.

Jabès's foundational work is the seven-volume *The Book of Questions,* composed between 1963 and 1972 and perhaps most aptly described by Josh Cohen as "an endless, discontinuous succession of commentaries on narratives alluded to rather than told" (97). A fragmentary chronicle of the fate of Sarah and Yukel, lovers engulfed by the Nazi concentration camps, this massive work ingeniously references both the Talmud and the Kabbalistic tradition, especially in the latter's meditation on God's withdrawal from the world, His absence from His own creation. As Cohen points out, there is both "affirmation and denial" here; indeed these "must be understood as one and the same: to approach the absolute is always to be turned away from it" (98).

In Jabès's exilic career there is always struggle to transcend the loss of place and to avoid reducing it to death: "I have the impression of moving in the shadow of syllables, in regions before secrets, where language cannot yet answer the call of thought, in swamps where you risk sinking with every breath" (*Book of Yukel* 23). Paradoxically, to truly grasp the inaugural moment of writing means to be already assailed by loss: "The experience of the desert is both the place of the Word—where it is supremely word—and the non-place where it loses itself in the infinite" (*Sin of the Book* 27). The American poet Robert Duncan offers a vivid sense of Jabès's literary response to his existential condition: "Emptied of the Jewish universe (his exile from 'home,' the Jewish community of Cairo, in his actual life, presents an immediacy of this void), Jabès lives now in the creation of his Jewish universe in the universe of the French language. This 'Jewishness' is the need for a new universal consciousness/conscience" (117). Such an awareness of Jewish "homeland" as portable textuality has often been associated with the writer's condition, but in Jabès's poetics it as more sustained than among any other writer I am acquainted with.

Exile, always understood as intrinsic to the vast spatial and temporal continuum of the Jewish Diaspora in its totality, was intimately felt by Jabès as a scattered, discontinuous terrain of lost family members. Even lamentation itself offered no proper center or coherence: "In the cemetery of Bagneux . . . rests my mother. In Old Cairo, in the cemetery of sand, my father. In Milano, in the dead marble city, my sister is buried. In Rome where the dark dug out the ground to receive him, my brother lies. Four graves. Three countries. Does death know borders? One family. Two continents. Four cities. Three flags. One language: of nothingness" (*Book of Questions* 145).[10]

Death and the shattering of selfhood are frequent tropes in Jabès's oeuvre, but because of these global entombments they are never reduced to poetic artifice. The painful sense of abandonment and loss, graves marking the closing off of possibility in one world, always to be succeeded by additional sites of bereavement, is almost unbearably palpable. Perhaps this is why the "cosmopolitan" writer, at home in Cairo and Paris, purposely turns from circumscribed urban space and national boundaries to the desert, where humanity can no longer organize itself into the violent categories of "natives" and "strangers." In this regard, Susan Handelman has proved useful in my struggle to comprehend just how Jabès's imagined topography overcomes exclusions: "[The] 'emptiness' of the desert signifies the potential for universality . . . an open space where all can enter . . . this emptiness of the desert and its shifting sands are the tropes for the shifting meanings of the text where one wanders" (*Fragments of Redemption* 295). As Jabès himself cautions in an aphorism that may reflect on familial history but also seems applicable to the very act of interpretation—and perhaps human life as a whole: "Never say that you have arrived; for everywhere, you will be a traveler in transit" (quoted in Ouaknin 209). This paradigm of transience seems to be the identical meaning shared by Jewish books and their authors. Josh Cohen offers this penetrating account of Jabès's sense of Judaism's textual dynamic after Auschwitz: "any text which claimed to heal rather than inhabit the rift between language and the divine would be an object of idolatry rather than interpretation" (95). Before an interpretation paralyzes the text, the latter instantly demands a counterreading. This is at the heart of what Jabès says of Judaism's resistance to idolatry. The unsayable (whether of the ineffable divine or the unvocalized splinter of Holocaust trauma), haunts the lines of every Jabès text. Drawing readers into a realization of becoming, Jabès sees language as a dynamic process always unfolding meaning beyond the surface vocable. After Auschwitz, the God of the sacred text is even more radically extraterritorial: "Being nowhere or everywhere nearly comes to the same thing" (*Sin of the Book* 228).

I am particularly stirred by James Diamond's penetrating reading of such pivotal moments of traumatic dislocation, his somber sense of Jabès "pointing to one of the key affects of the post-secular consciousness: a pervading sense of God's absence. And yet, paradoxical or even oxymoronic as it may sound, to postmodern man God is most present in God's absence" (598). There is a passage of cryptic interdependence where Jabès tells us that the book remains tauntingly mysterious even to its author: "Poring over the book, haven't I lived only in anticipation of the enigma's word which, although it is conveyed by every vocable, still to this day has never been deciphered?" (Motte 9). Most important of all is the powerfully antihierarchical autonomy that was realized somewhere in the transition from Egypt to Canaan. In a moment of perhaps deceptive clarity, Jabès notes that "[t]he desert wrote the Jew, and the Jew reads himself in the desert" (*Book of Questions* 302). Receiving this as a form of unprecedented agency, Jabès glosses the meaning of the radical liberty and responsibility realized by the individual in the desert of Exodus first and foremost as a "rising up against God to take voice and pen out of His power. We have to get rid of the divine within us in order to give God back to Himself and fully enjoy our freedom as men" (*Book of Questions: Yael Elya Aely El, or the Last Book* 146). In a similar moment of rhetorical play he teases us, "Who is closest to God? He who invents Him as He created man, or he who prays for permission to approach him?" (*Livre de Yukel* 140–41) Jabès's passion for this inaugural moment of humanity's moral sovereignty as individuals corresponds impressively with Zelitch's portrayal of the spirit of the tormented Dathan's passionate utterance about masters and slaves in *Moses in Sinai.*

Lest the reader presume that Jabès's "desert" is merely postmodern whimsy, it is imperative to recall the concrete and experiential dimensions of his poetics. Raw encounters with the actual desert sired the peculiar nature of his intervention with the text: "I would often stay for forty-eight hours all alone in the desert. I wouldn't take any books, only a blanket. A silence of that order makes you feel the nearness of death so deeply that it becomes difficult to bear any more of it" (*From the Desert to the Book* 3). Even in the poet's insistent linkage of the tenses of past and present ("the desert wrote / the Jew reads") it is unmapped desert space, the place of prolonged wandering and enigma, which receives primacy for its unprecedented freedom. In the denuded environment of Jabès's desert, language becomes the portable sanctuary as it was for the desert forefathers, the most natural of homelands. Warren Motte suggests that "the association of writing with the desert, or rather the inscription of the former within the latter, is *crucial,* literally, in that writing and the desert are two transcendent metaphors in this body of work, which afford structure and coherence from one [Jabès] volume to the next. Jabès offers the desert as the radical other, a place of wandering and indeterminacy, a place defined, first by its distanciation from places that are, or can be, known" (7–8; italics in original). Motte's sense of this paradigm provides a fitting corollary for the wandering of the Jewish text itself which, according to the talmudic explicator Marc-Alain Ouaknin, "must not stop, grind to a halt in a 'said.' The movement of the spoken word cannot be enclosed within the synchrony of the written word" (152).

To be sure, it can be a daunting task to locate Jabès conventionally in the tradition of Jewish thought. Where is one to turn for precedents to such an idiosyncratic formulation of the Jewish subject? Handelman rises to this challenge by drawing on the perspectives of postmodern thought as well as rabbinics. On the indelible relation of silence, text, and wilderness in Jabès's writings, she comments:

> This silent barren place is the theme of the desert in Jabès . . . a desert which is void, yet an open place to which one returns in order to breathe and find space, a space which the writer needs to preserve. The Torah as well is connected to the desert, given in the wilderness of Sinai to a people who, like Jabès, had to make their exodus from Egypt, and whose soul is formed in their desert wanderings and tribulations. . . . Though a vast openness, the desert is obdurate and inhospitable—save to those who accommodate themselves to it. And though obdurate, it is no source of stability: its sands shift; its routes are circuitous, like the circuitous routes of writing, like the indirections of God. ("Torments" 69)

Handelman explains how the fragmentary, aphoristic imagination reflecting a notion of the sacred text that precariously encompasses revelation but also the abyss: "The Sacred Book is not only fatherland; it is also desert. God is not just word, presence, law; He is also silence, absence, void" ("Torments" 71). To further pursue this question of diasporic textuality, it is worth recalling the early-twentieth-century Jewish philosopher Franz Rosenzweig's visionary lines (written on army postal cards while serving in an antiaircraft unit in the First World War): "Even in its land Israel was not a nation like other nations. The third exile could not be the end of the people of Israel, since from its inception the history of the Jews passes from one exile to another, and since the spirit of exile, the essential foreignness to the land, a struggle for higher forms of life against the confinement of the land and the time is rooted in this history from its beginning" (335). Sharing the modernist theologian's sense of exile as a desired state (a source of both relentlessly this-worldly ethics and interior consciousness), Jabès presents the desert to us as the place that permanently unmakes the kind of rootedness and complacency that Rosenzweig saw as the murderous illusion of the West: "Even in Israel the Jew is a nomad, that is to say, his wanderings are part of his thought. The Jews—even when they were dispersed throughout the world, and wherever they are now—have always been in exile in relation to the place they were in before. What are the dreams of the Israelis? One of them dreams about Morocco, another about Poland, another about Germany. Even the youngsters don't actually lose that. There is a kind of melancholia, a nostalgia which finally is the world. The Jew is the world" (Lichtenberg 253). This is not the chauvinistically universal claim that might rankle some readers, rightfully weary of excessively diffuse renderings of "Jewishness." Nor is it an alienating iteration of "chosenness." What Jabès does clearly invoke are all the multiple worlds the Jews have inhabited in their movement through space and time up until the present. Then too, there is a palpable sense of nostalgia for all those lost worlds. From Jabès's perspective, Zionism does not cure the Jewish imagination's complex dependence on cultural loss and dislocation.

Jabès always regards the Jewish people's singular relation to space and absence as intrinsic to the text's own ceaseless inquiry and restless circling. Rather than finished object, the self-consciously Jewish text is a mysteriously unstable or nomadic presence that disturbs the reader's innermost illusions of stability and coherence. Before Zionist certainties, the Jewish text affirmed adaptiveness, the philosophically rich meaning behind Abraham's nomadic displacement over other peoples' blood and soil. Judaism, ancient as it is, is not a culture that rests in certainty but one that perpetually confronts the mystery of being, a creation of untold stories still unfolding. True to its nomadic origins, Jabès's Judaism, indelibly personified by his wandering subjects, always evolves, never fulfilled: "At noon he found himself facing the infinite, the blank page. All tracks, footprints, paths were gone. Buried. . . . He was probably only a few dozen miles from his point of departure. But he did not know. And how could one, here speak of arrival or departure? Everywhere: oblivion, the unmade bed of absence, the wandering kingdom of dust. . . . When there is nothing left, there will still be sand. There will still be the desert to conjugate the nothing" (*Book of Questions* 55). Or as Jabès's contemporary Blanchot has it: "Any answer should bear in it the essence of the question, which is not extinguished by the one who answers" (quoted in Ouaknin 281). Such an interrogatory mode passionately resists the seductions of national identity, for in the modern Jewish state Jabès glimpses the violent foreclosure of the vital process of questioning, with all its dire consequences: "All of Jewish tradition is a [process] of posing questions, and this point has been totally ignored. Israel is a Jewish state, but it is not Jewish in its character."[11] Perhaps because "Egypt" still looms so large in Jabès's exilic imagination, his European writings are necessarily haunted by Moses, the archetypal and reluctant scribe of in-betweenness and becoming who never achieves his destination. As we have seen, this crucial gap also forms the uneasily open-ended question that haunts Zelitch's conclusion in *Moses in Sinai.* Here, too, readers encounter the ethical disruption of the sufficient, self-contained identity. Indeed, Jabès's "rabbis" speak for a Judaism perpetually renewed by skeptical questioning: "'Knowledge means questioning,' answered Reb Mendel. 'What will we get out of these questions? What will we get out of all the answers which only lead to more questions, since questions are born of unsatisfactory answers?' asked the second disciple. 'The promise of a new question,' replied Reb Mendel" (*Book of Questions* 116).

Jabès affirms this condition as the true source of Judaism's relationship to eternity; its long resistance to idols of certainty. Such perpetuation of unappeasable language further suggests why the desert emerges as the essentially tormented landscape of this "renewal." Describing this intertextual space of losses and interruptions, Ammiel Alcalay remarks that "the search for the truth once taken into the desert by the saintly mystic leads into the labyrinths of a book challenged by despair, suicide, and mass murder. The exile from Egypt is met by graffiti on the walls of Europe" (71). Moreover, Josh Cohen asserts that for Jabès "to premise writing on measurelessness is to recognize . . . the moral and political exigencies the Holocaust never ceases to impose . . . to refuse both the melancholic renunciation and the triumphal affirmation of writing, or better, to recognize the ineluctable binding of the one to the other" (106). As Alcalay and Cohen suggest, the ovens of Auschwitz seem to demand that the poet bear witness to the paradigmatic disruption of all previous certainties. But I believe that for Jabès, its true origins always lie somewhere more remote, in the primal scenes of Exodus.

Of Moses' shattering of the tablets of the Law, Jabès declares that "[i]t was necessary for Moses to break the book in order for the book to become human. . . . We destroy the book when we read it to make it into another book. The book is always born from a broken book" (Auster, "Interview," 23).[12] Elsewhere, he delineates the book's essential homeland as "Desert. All writing is first of all a wound of sand. Thus the Hebrews had to spend forty years in Sinai in order to identify with the Book" (*From the Desert to the Book* 301). In much the same manner that Zelitch's *Moses in Sinai* poses difficult questions about whether Judaism's true nature resides in radical freedom or obedience, the exiled Egyptian Jew's midrash conceives of Exodus 34 as a dialectic of ruin and renewal, independence and submission: "The second Tablets could not be the same as the first, for they were born from the breaking of the latter. Between them bleeds the abyss of the wound./ The first Tablets emerged from the divine abyss; the second, from the red abyss of man. Shall we have the impudence to assert that the second resemble the first, knowing that all resemblance marks the difference we would have abolished?" (*Book of Resemblances*

87). Whereas Judaism traditionally commemorates Moses as the laudable receiver/giver of the Law, Jabès is far more interested in the "destructive" persona that shatters the tablets given him on Mount Sinai: "Moses suddenly scared God./He incarnated subversion" (*Le Parcours* 63).[13]

To fully account for the peculiar agency of the Jewish reader/scribe requires a distinctly peripatetic discourse, an intimacy with creative doubt, that resists the complacency of stasis, without succumbing to a nostalgia for divine origins: "I believe that we create our identity through . . . interrogation. To be Jewish would therefore mean to become it, step by step. At each step we would only be on the point of becoming Jewish. This would also mean that we couldn't be Jewish constantly. The affirmation 'I am Jewish' is already a regression, a stop, a way of falling asleep in that condition" (*From the Desert to the Book* 67).

Always accompanying this paradigm of process is the idea of the wilderness. To follow Jabès into the desert means to visualize the text always surrounded by the blankness of white space, like an oasis in the desert. The physical appearance of the aphorism on the page steers us toward this realization. Jabès's work recalls the primal moment of Sinai, where the voice of God conjoined with human writing in the still emptiness, for as Jabès addresses Levinas: "There is no trace but in the desert, no voice but in the desert" (*Book of Margins* 160). Sojourning in the metaphysical desert conjured up by Jabès, the reader learns to be invigorated by coming to terms with his or her very distance from tradition. However, this requires one's never fully arriving at any final resting place of faith or assurance: "*Certainty may be a need for a man, but in itself, it is only a vacant reply to a penultimate question, with the ultimate left in suspense . . . vacant like a lot on which no building will ever rise because it would immediately tumble to ruins*" (*Book of Shares* 17; ellipsis and italics in original).

Death and absence are the daunting mysteries that the nomadic human imagination projects onto the white page and the desert alike. But readers are always encouraged to listen carefully in the ostensible sterility of Jabès's desert, a space actually filled with a cacophony of voices, mostly rabbinic, always rushing in as if to fill the existential void:

> "My name is a question. It is also my freedom within my tendency to question."—Reb Eglal
> (*From the Book to the Book* 47)
>
> Reb Ava: "We live in the sea. Its bottom links us to the land.
> "We are children of the sea who do not remember the water."
> (*From the Book to the Book* 67)

In Jabès's aphorisms, the rabbis (surrogates and guides for the readers' active deciphering) are the privileged interpreters of the book, but they dwell in a restless heterogeneity, one strong voice always supplanted by another, just as they are in traditional rabbinics. His invented rabbis disclose to us that "to find God means to find him *in* the book, through the word that is hiding *behind* the word—as if there was always a book in the book and it was really a question . . . a kind of writing inside of writing" (*From the Desert to the Book* 47). Here too the desert is the unifying principle. William Kluback asserts that Jabès's imagined universal book, like the sparse appearance of the poet's own aphorisms against the looming white space of the page, has "the shifting forms of the desert sands: the book abhors fixity and definition. It is the book because it never finds form but is always the book of questions. . . . [Man] wants to explore the absence of form" (13). The reader's physical experience of the aphorism, the welcoming tent or oasis of text set against the indifferent blankness of the page, is conducive to a sensation of the transience, movement, endless horizons that are essential for apprehending Jabès's sense of the Jewish text's endless horizons.

If "desert" is the essential human condition, then "homeland" always remains a decidedly ambivalent notion in Jabès's writings. Of the expatriate poet's fraught relation to his homeland of Egypt, Alcalay contends that "an insufficiently examined irony coursing throughout . . . is that of the exiled writer/narrator producing and inhabiting a *native* space contained by the text but clearly arising from and alluding to the very personal circumstance and situation of Jabès himself" (67). In this matter it is crucial to note how, through the voice of one of his invented rabbis, the poet soberly addresses the precarious nature of place and identity: "No matter how solidly you build your house," said Reb Alken, "it will always rest on sand" (*Book of Yukel* 101). Jabès is surprisingly lucid in explaining why the desert possesses such a transformative potential for human consciousness: "In the desert one becomes other; one becomes the one who knows the weight of the sky and the thirst of the earth, the one who has learned to take account of his own solitude. Far from excluding us, the desert envelops us. We become the immensity of sand, just as we are the book when we write" (*From the Desert to the Book* 3). This is both burden and privilege. Like the Jews, the book was birthed in the explosive force of the wilderness experience from where it migrated to cities and peoples everywhere. Jabès is always mindful that in the place where God has most absented Himself, humanity can dream its boldest dreams. Justifying the endurance of this open speculation, Kluback declares that "[t]he presence of God would destroy the question. Absence is the realization of what was or what can be. When we speak of the absence of God, we speak of creating a world in which the presence would reveal holiness and majesty. But in such a world there could be no human life" (21). For, as Lurianic Kabbalists have taught throughout the centuries, it is God's very absence that creates a role for human language's divine potentiality. Indeed, it is the generosity of that divine withdrawal which enables humanity to participate in Creation, and the endless horizon of desert expanse is the fitting spatial corollary of such absence—the generous indeterminacy that invites commentary in its infinitude but lies beyond grasp and control.

For Jabès, the desert is the primal geography from which all human wanderings and realizations have emerged. Yet, it is critical to understand that a dialectic between the city dweller and the nomad allows each to emerge from the encounter with an invigorated sense of in-betweenness. Kluback reminds us that Jabès's "visions and reveries remain with the desert, but he cultivates his words in the ambiance of urban life. Exiled from both the city and desert, the poet dwells in both. He is the poet of the exile. In the desert, his words are those of the city. In the city, he meditates on the sands of the desert. How do we walk between the two, become the juggler who must balance this life between contrasts, knowing that the book he searches for has already been revealed by the God of the desert and has been brought by his people to cities, to be studied and revealed in commentary?" (6). To be born in the vocables of human language means to be born in the absence of divine speech, to be brought immediately into an exile in which only traces of the ineffable remain.

Jabès always insisted that his desert experience did not have its birth in amorphous metaphor but rather in lived experience. In the "place of the desert" he proudly declares that he was able

> to depersonalize myself, to no longer be who I was in appearance to others in Cairo. . . . In Cairo, I felt a prisoner of the social game. . . . In those days, the mainly European quarter where I lived and worked—the commercial and business quarter—was barely the size of the Opera quarter in Paris. In such a confined atmosphere, the texts I published were considered at best a kind of intellectual entertainment. . . . Hence, the desert, which started at the very city limits, was a life-saving break for me. It fulfilled an urgent need of both body and mind, and I would venture into it with completely contradictory desires: to lose myself, so that, some day, I may find myself. So the place of the desert in my books is not a simple metaphor. (quoted in Alcalay 68–69)

Finding, losing, confinement, expansiveness, exteriority, interiority: in his encounter with these varieties of experience, the discovery of a buried self, Jabès's narrative of his desert sojourn captures many of the elements of the literary characters we have encountered in Hareven, Oz, Grossman, and Zelitch. As in the ethically oriented explorations of these other writers, the West's most liminal space provided the privileged foundation for the poet's potent revelation: "This *other* is not myself nor my invention. It is my discovery of the *other* in me" (*Book of Dialogue* 13). In this quintessential moment of ethical revelation we see how Jabès aligns himself with the ancient etymological significance of Hebrew as *ivri:* one who experiences passage, or exile, which is the permanent and necessary route to discover ethics, or the recognition of the Other that disrupts the quietude of the self. Gary Mole aptly identifies Jabès's perception of the desert as the site "in which alterity itself is produced" (58). Though exiled from the Egyptian desert, Jabès acutely felt its presence as a wellspring for his unique vision of the relation between the self and the alien.

What Yi-Fu Tuan observes of the ambivalent existential allure of the desert in Western culture has profound relevance to what we may glean of Jabèsian ethics: "It is the longing to be taken out of oneself and one's habitual world into something vast, overpowering, and indifferent. If home in the narrow sense absorbs the self in its diffuse multiple sensory impressions, and if home space provides the kind of psychological distancing that makes aesthetic appreciation possible, then alien space once again offers unity but this time by overwhelming the individual" (155).

Similarly, as with Levinas's sense of Abraham's desert psychology, Jabès's encounter with the face of the other places self-sufficiency into question. But if the self must be understood as somehow in thrall to this new equation, it is also true that the nomadic routes of the desert endow the "Hebrew" Jabès with the freedom to question: "How free is the nomad! The desert asks nothing of him" (*Le Parcours* 93). In such moments I sense a striking resemblance to Zelitch's representations of the perpetually disturbed nomadic imagination. For both writers, questioning always entails a rupture, a break between certainty and being troubled: "It is indeed my impossibility of being an 'untroubled Jew,' assuaged and anchored in his certainties, that has made me the Jew I think I am. This may seem paradoxical, but it is precisely in this break—in that non-belonging in search of its belonging—that I am no doubt most Jewish" (*From the Desert to the Book* 95–96). Jabès freely acknowledges an essence of non-belonging that strongly resembles the angst of Zelitch's Moses. From such declarations it is clear that the Sinai mystery encoded in the Jewish text is the essential question that informs Jabès's understanding of both his own and Judaism's journey into paradox. For in God's speech to Moses out of the burning bush, the enactment of an eternal destruction that does not consume (and is that not the long story of Jewish life?), this must be the provocation that impels Jabès's project. In God's words "I am that I am" nothing is expressly said and yet we are to understand that at the same time *everything* is revealed.

Then too, the centrality of the desert of Exodus in Jabès's vision ultimately reflects the fact that all of us, Jews and others, live our lives not in straight lines, but in peripatetic arcs, gyres, and epicycles. Only the expansiveness of the wilderness can allow for an imagined space where we can listen to the purpose of our existence: "all the secrets of the universe are buds of fire soon to open, do I know in my exile, what has driven me back through tears and time, back to the wells of the desert where my ancestors had ventured? There is nothing at the threshold of the open page, it seems, but this wound of a race both of the book, whose order and disorder are roads of suffering. Nothing but this pain, whose past and whose permanence is also that of writing" (*Book of Questions* 25–26). The desert promises that not only a sublime questioning but revelation itself is still unfolding, always a process in flux. Just as with Dathan and Korah, Zelitch's ethical "heretics," Jabès narrates the desert as the center of humankind's greatest epiphanies and imaginative leaps, the place where "the Jew is at the center of a vertiginous paradox . . . [where] by inventing God he invented himself" (*From the Desert to the Book* 57–58). Perhaps the radical questioning that has subsequently characterized Jewish existence *required* the wilderness for its divine conduit. As Jabès muses, "maybe exodus and exile were indeed needed so that the word cut off from all words—and thus confronted with silence—can acquire its true dimension . . . just as we are truly ourselves only at the most arid core of our solitude" (*From the Desert to the Book* 68).

The desert's widening of textual and geographical perspectives is a catalyst for consciousness, stimulating access to recesses once occluded. Jabès draws this paradigm deeply into his understanding of his own subjectivity, explaining in an interview that "[m]aybe there is something deeper still, something I constantly broach in my books, and that is my visceral repugnance to being rooted anywhere. I felt that I exist only outside of any belonging. That non-belonging is my very substance" (*From the Desert to the Book* 29). However, this "non-belonging" cannot be reduced to an ego-centered alienation but rather encompasses a shared ethics of estrangement, an "uprooting," in Levinas's sense of recoiling from the violence of nationalism: "Every word is an uprooting. Every rational institution is uprooting. The constitution of a true society is uprooting."[14] This would mean an outward movement, whether from the egoistic self or from the insular society. Or in Handelman's cogent reading, from "the rootedness of narcissistic self-enclosure" (*Fragments of Redemption* 295). Hence, Jabès employs the notion of God much as Zelitch's Moses sees him: as void or non-appearance whose conspicuous absence is a provocation that ignites zealous questions about justice and the universe's laws that lead us out of self-sufficiency. The desert accommodates this notion of deserted word/world precisely. Mole demarcates the true parameters of this paradigm, remarking that Jabès's "law of hospitality and silence . . . moves across the sand of the desert, ever shifting with the wind, no sooner effaced than retraced . . . not a law of perfection, but one of perfectibility, not a law of the finite, but of the infinite, of constant potential" (80). Challenged by such an inimitable voice, many of Jabès's most observant readers often struggle to explicate him in relation to other Jewish modernists.

Blanchot must have been the first to expose the sensibility shared by the postmodern Jabès with his modernist predecessor Franz Kafka when he declares that Kafka belongs to the Judaic continuum of the "the truth of the desert" that is simultaneously also "erring in the desert" or the "infinite migration" of Abraham (*L'Espace littéraire* 78–79). Similarly, Diamond observes that just as Kafka was a deracinated Jew in and of central Europe before the Holocaust, "Jabès was a deracinated Jew of Cairo and Paris. . . . The desiccation of spirit was Kafka's inner landscape. . . . Jabès stands where Kafka stood, except that now the door to the Law has opened, opened onto a sunlit, barren desert" (598). Persuaded by Blanchot's and Diamond's cogent demonstrations of Jabès's proximity to Kafka, I would add yet another luminary for consideration by those seeking a greater understanding of the peculiarly modernist dimensions of the Jewish poet's disquieting relation to language and the unsayable.

In the great Hebrew national poet Hayim Nahman Bialik's "Revealment and Concealment in Language" (1915), surely the most idiosyncratic and perhaps mystical of his essays, he posits that human language consists of "husks," or words without their "core": "On the other side of the barrier of language, behind its curtain . . . the spirit of man wanders ceaselessly. 'For man shall not look on men and live,' says the void, and every speech, every pulsation of speech, partakes of the nature of a concealment of nothingness, a husk enclosing within itself a dark seed of the eternal enigma" (132). In a startlingly "Jabèsian" revelation,

Bialik speculates that "*[n]o word contains the complete dissolution of any question.* What does it contain? *The question's concealment*" (133, Bialik's emphasis). There is a striking parallel between the Jabèsian text and Bialik's epiphany that the word is "nothing but a manifestation of the void." Bialik's language precedes Jabès's immersion in the desert of negative Kabbalah in the sense that, rather than see language as the mutual conduit between humankind and the divine mind, "the word's existence takes place by virtue of the process by which it closes up the small aperture of the void—constructing a barrier to prevent the void's darkness from welling up and overflowing its bounds" (133). Language diverts us from, conceals, or otherwise compensates us for, the abyss. Bialik ruefully speculates that "Moses did well to conceal his face . . . for man shall not see the 'void' face-to-face and live" (133).

The Hebrew modernist further declares that units of language are "like the links in a suit of armor," clothing the poor conscious frailty who utters them from the darkness of imposing mystery. Outworn words and language systems alike yield to their successors at the precise moment when they are "no longer able to conceal and hide adequately" (135). For it is at that woeful moment of nudity that "Man, gazing for a moment through the open crack, finding to his terror that awesome void before him again, hurries to close the crack for a time—with a new word. He seizes the new talisman, like its predecessor; a proven momentary diversion—and is saved from the terror" (135). Bialik conceives of this process as a providential deferral of death, or rather successive cycles of linguistic endings and rebirths. The only fortunate aspect of this fateful business of deception is that the nightmarish moments "between concealments" when the abyss is actually exposed are comparatively rare. In Robert Alter's reading of Bialik's eerie formulation, he notices that in its apparent invocation of the Kabbalistic notion of "husks," the poet does not take comfort from the traditional mystical confidence in a concealment of the divine light of Creation: "'For man shall not look on me and live,' God says to Moses in Exodus, but here, in one of Bialik's boldest transpositions of traditional language, it is the void that speaks these words" (Alter, *Modern Hebrew Literature* 129). This is altogether a liturgy for a fallen universe. Subsequently, language, once the inexhaustible reservoir of meaning, is transformed into the lie that conceals the undoing of being.

Auster limns the essential quandary posed by the Jabèsian landscape of revelation and dismal concealment in terms that intensify my sense of its strong relation to Bialik's language: "Like the hidden God of classic theology, the text exists only by virtue of its absence" ("Introduction" x).

Or as Diamond puts it, "Jabès wanders in the same landscape his ancestors traversed in Biblical times, except that now there is no Promised Land on the horizon" (598). Yet just as with Kafka, a faint hint of messianism, and thus hope, lingers throughout *The Book of Questions:* "I know you, Lord, in the measure that I do not know you. For you are He who comes." But it survives as a weak hint in Jabès's post-Holocaust consciousness. The word endures but its landscape is bleak. An acute sensory deprivation always pervades Jabès's desert, all is becalmed by drifting sand. In nothingness and absence, consciousness strains for traces of the real. Knowing the bad news about both an absconded deity and the human condition after Auschwitz, Jabès can only declare, "I would now celebrate trees, / if there were anywhere but desert." and "Immortal for death. / Sand is our inheritance." (*If There Were Anywhere but Desert* 99).

6 *Wilderness as Experience and Metaphor*

> Hmēd [a Bedouin member of the Sinai Mzeina tribe]: In the beginning, when all these *tawatīt* (turkeys) started coming, I said, "They must be looking for manganese or oil, even gold, maybe." But after a while, I wasn't so sure. They didn't change anything, they just took a little of this, a little of that, maybe a souvenir for their government. But they continue, each time taking just a bit. Who knows, maybe this desert has some things hidden in it.
>
> —quoted in Smadar Lavie (*Poetics of Military Occupation* 101)

> We invited him to sit with us and drink Turkish coffee from the pot he had prepared for us, hoping to hear from him authentic stories about opium fields in the mountains, not about history, from which we, as Israelis, had fled south.
>
> —Oz Shelach (*Picnic Grounds: A Novel in Fragments* 3)

In the early 1960s the Knesset member Yizhar Smilansky (b. 1916), better known as S. Yizhar, one of Israel's most highly regarded literary figures, issued this impassioned call for the nation to preserve its deserts and other natural areas:

> It is impossible for man to remain without vistas that have not been mended by his own hand. It is impossible to exist in a place where everything is organized and planned unto the last detail, until all remnants of the original image, the natural and organic signs of the earth's creation,

> are erased. It is a necessity for man to have a place to go to shake himself off and refresh himself from the city, from the built, from the enclosed, from the delivered and to absorb the refreshing contact with the primal, with the open, with the "before the coming of mankind"—if there ever was such a time. A land without wildflowers through which winds can blow is a place of suffocation. A land where winds cannot blow without obstruction will be a hotel, not a homeland. (Tal 163)[1]

What now seems most noteworthy about Yizhar's unprecedented plea for an authentic "homeland" rather than a tourist site (which was subsequently quoted by an approving David Ben-Gurion) is his emphatic valuation of Israel's most hostile spaces as essential assets that were to be cherished as if somehow key to a healthy nation's cultural future. Or as one young starry-eyed Sabra of the same period wrote in a letter describing a school trip meant to strengthen a sense of connection between the new Zionist generation and the rural landscape: "How we rambled and roamed among the ruins . . . and everything around full of faint hints and fragments of echoes of distant and early days that have passed over this wonderful land of ours" (quoted in Almog 168).

The Israeli literature we have examined seems to be vital, if in some ways surprising, outcomes of Yizhar's intuition that the young nation's desolate places would somehow prove critical to Israel's critical consciousness and identity. And from a more distant perspective, the imaginations of Jabès and Zelitch too seem dependent on an enduring relation to the ethical imperatives that are bound up in Judaism's understanding of such space. If the Jewish experience in antiquity (some might say its mythic time), may be defined by the limitless expanses that gave rise to the simplicity of the oneness of the divine, it is equally true that subsequent Jewish history inhibited intercourse between the Jewish life contained and protected and the world beyond. As the psychoanalyst Shmuel Erlich observes: "Walls and fences are symbolically and poignantly an intrinsic part of Jewish experience and history—from the walls of Jericho to the destruction of the Temple walls, from ghetto walls to the barbwire electric fences of concentration and extermination camps. It is hard, with the exception of a few isolated instances, to find stretches of Jewish history in which walls and fences did not figure prominently into the Jewish landscape."[2] Hence we arrive at the moment of the highly successful television show *Northern Exposure,* in which the New Yorker Dr. Joel Fleischman plunges unhappily into the rustic setting of Cicely, Alaska; viewers were amused by the show's comic premise that the modern Jew is fated to be ill at ease at best outside the urban environment.

Of course this was but the latest incarnation of an image made famous by Woody Allen's shticks, where the *unheimlisch* countryside is the source of uncanny horrors for the nebbishy urbanites he favors. Both Fleischman and Allen embody repetitions of the Bible's own incongruous levity in highlighting the Israelites' moans and groans; neither the ancient Hebrew, after four centuries sojourning in Egypt, nor the Jewish New Yorker is prepared for an austere environment of open space. Moreover, some of the Jewish canon's most thoughtful literary luminaries perpetuate the notion of a Jewish dalliance with nature as one endowed with necessarily fatal consequences. For instance, in Cynthia Ozick's foreboding short story "The Pagan Rabbi," a brilliant scholar, obsessed with transcending his "corporeality," attempts to join his soul with the spirit of nature which, he hallucinates, is embodied in a sapling in a deserted urban park. The story ends tragically when, having forsaken Jewish community for an attempted copulation with the spirit, the young rabbi realizes the enormity of his idolatrous error and hangs himself from a limb of his sylvan mistress. Ozick, an ardent Zionist, may be exploring her ambivalence over the fact that one of the chief values of classic Zionist education was to instill a love for nature, which by some accounts has resulted in a nearly civic religion of nature-worshippers even on sacred days, including Yom Kippur.

Exile, immigration, and the traversing of boundaries were always at the heart of the Jewish adventure in modernity. Retold through the prism of the desert, the writers we examined have found exciting ways to recast these experiences. Taking their cue from the Hebrew Bible's richly conflicted, ambivalent renderings of the relation between desert and sovereign space, Jewish writers have rediscovered the ways in which those ancient tensions invigorate contemporary realities. Crossing symbolic borders, the Jewish writer's contemplative encounter with the desert has engendered new possibilities, recognitions of alternative realities that violate the normative boundaries of Jewish geography. As we have seen, they offer us unexpected confluences of here and elsewhere, rootedness and wandering, Diaspora and Zion. In the desert narrative, the Jewish subject pauses, sometimes for many long years, in an almost archaeological excavation uncovering buried layers of self that have been hidden from view or confused with the culture of the state. Sometimes a puzzle to others and even to themselves, the desert affords the characters examined here both self-recognition as well as opportunities to examine alternative routes not yet taken. To put this in other words: the desert not only crystallizes the urgency of re-visioning the other and reappraising the self, but it affords a space for transformation outside of the particularism of the Zionist, or any other exclusionist, narrative. In this regard, the potent metaphor and actuality of the desert may ultimately contribute to what Eyal Ben-Ari and Yoram Bilu call "the gradual erosion of the . . . attachment to territories and locations in Israeli public discourse," an essential factor in the painful but necessary peace process now underway between Israel and Palestine (245). In these fictions, the desert becomes a metaphysical idea that is both a process and a place. But what is so difficult about the intense yearnings expressed by the protagonist in the desert is that they are often so inchoate; pilgrimages without the consolation of a definite object.

Consider the fragment quoted from Oz Shelach, where the anonymous collective "we" (which seems to stand for Israelis in general) have fled to spend several days on a desert beach to escape "history" in Sinai. Ironically, this group's servile Bedouin waiter turns out not to be the romantic figure he is mistaken for, but rather signifies a much more troubled history:

> The Bedouin waiter was not a Bedouin. In the beginning he had been a teacher and at twenty-two, overnight, left his work and his village, Sa'sa', in the Galilee, heading north, then zig-zagging northeast and northwest until, after some months, stopping at 'Ayn Al-Helweh refugee camp in Lebanon. He told us, in English learned from tourists, about stealing across the border back into what had become our country, to work in the fields of his village, which were by then the fields of a kibbutz, which bore the same name Sa'sa'; then stealing across the border to Egypt. (3–4)

In Shelach's Kafkaesque fragment, the desert fails to fulfill the expectations of those seeking escapist fantasy, presenting instead the truth of a repressed political reality. The idle vacationers are uncannily confronted by the painful history of the "land of milk and honey" they sought consolation from in the wilderness, ironically reversing the Exodus narrative that launched the Jewish entanglement with the desert to begin with. Full circle. But more hopefully, the desert here has a special role, perhaps allowing identities usually contained and sheltered from one another to encounter the Other in a potentially revelatory exchange about repressed histories.[3]

A stubborn shard of foreboding otherness, the desert serves as a ubiquitous, troubling presence for the modern Hebrew literary imagination, which continues to cast it as the site of naked conscience. In Israel's literary culture, each subsequent desert narrative has contributed to an ongoing moral stock taking, a reassessment of the Zionist master narrative that participates in an expansive artistic focus on the relation between landscape and ideology.[4] For Oz, Grossman, and Hareven, the desert affords a diasporic aesthetics of temporal, spatial, and existential forms of exile not usually afforded by the parameters of modern Hebrew culture. In their conflictual relations to polarized spaces—fortified state and unyielding wilderness—the protagonists of their works experience powerful feelings of displacement, of being exiled from the place that was intended to end all exiles. There are signs that this expansive metaphor continues to thrive as a central trope of expression for some of Israel's youngest and most gifted writers and filmmakers, perhaps whenever a pressing inner reality demands a realm outside the Zionist metaplot. In Orly Castel-Bloom's *Haikhan Ani Nitzet?* (Where am I? [1990]), the narrator flounders between postmodern malaise and comic absurdity: "It was probably at the beginning of winter. A thunderstorm raged outside. But it had nothing to do with my state of mind, which was as indifferent as a dried-up well in the desert" (22). Despairing of even participating in the nostalgia for Zionist history that illuminates Grossman's and Oz's novels, Castel-Bloom invokes the desert as the ache of cultural emptiness.[5] Moreover, it must be stressed that for numerous Moroccans and other new immigrants who were unceremoniously hauled off to remote Negev development towns where they were subsequently neglected by the state for years, the desert represents the fragmentation of their identities. On the other hand, in Doron Eran's remarkable film *God's Sandbox* (2002), the Sinai, long ago relinquished by Israel, returns as a heavily eroticized landscape of nostalgia that shelters a utopian cross-cultural romance between a free-spirited woman and the son of a Bedouin sheik. And in Misha Shulman's *Desert Sunrise,* a new play staged at the time of this writing, a Palestinian shepherd and an Israeli soldier take refuge together at night in a desert wadi, eventually achieving mutual understanding and even forgiveness.

There are also signs that *tiyulim* (hikes) to the desert have a special, almost ritualistic role, in the contemporary Israeli relationship to the land's indeterminacy. For instance, on a Saturday in November 1989, several thousand Israeli members of the Society for the Protection of Nature in Israel as well as numerous youth movements whose members were raised on a number of wilderness outings, gathered to protest against the air force's plan to expropriate a sizeable area in the Arava to transform it into a closed area for military maneuvers. The explanatory leaflet distributed by the organizers read: "This is an area of unique natural resources and primeval scenery as yet untouched by man. . . . It is completely unacceptable that due to outside interests and alien considerations the citizens of Israel should be forced to give up this priceless scenic heritage. . . . We [Society for the Protection of Nature] call on you to come and join us and help remove the threat" (Ben-David 129–30). As

Orit Ben-David observes of Israeli "nature lovers," they "have an almost fanatical wish to preserve sites in the framework of nature, and not let society control them, keeping those sites as 'no man's land'" (142).

In recent years, such interest in the spiritual values of landscape has taken a slightly different but equally stirring form in the Diaspora, spawning Jewish spiritual adventure programs in North America with evocative monikers such as "The Adventure Rabbi," "Burning Bush Adventures," "Kosher Treks," "MannaOutdoor.Com," "and TorahTrek." Such ever-proliferating groups offer families and singles opportunities to study sacred texts and kabbalistic lore in America's wild places as well as biblical deserts such as the Sinai and the Negev. Rather than merely cashing in on the fast-growing trends of adventure travel and eco-tourism, the founders of such enterprises take their Jewish mission very seriously. As Rabbi Mike Comins remarks of such enterprises, "If you ask people where they experience God, at a synagogue or a national park, the majority will tell you in the mountains or by a stream." Wary of the pitfalls of American Jewry's insular and static congregational life, he cautions that "if a person's peak spiritual experience is not connected to Judaism, there's a terrible disconnect and it does damage to our attempts to raise the next generation."[6]

This new awareness may owe to the influence of Israel on generations of visiting North American youth. As Alon Tal explains in *Pollution in a Promised Land,* the only comprehensive environmental study of the history of Israel's troubled land use, "the passion for intimacy with the land of Israel continues to influence much of Israel's population. It explains why the Society for the Protection of Nature quickly became the largest membership organization in the country. One hears this consciousness in folk songs. One sees it when looking for a vacant stretch of beach at Lake Kinneret, or for an empty trail during an Israeli holiday; everybody is trying to get in touch with the land" (32). This idealization of Israel's empty and wild places has deep roots in modern Zionist childhoods, where Israeli youth movements bring hundreds of thousands of young people out of the claustrophobic Israeli cities into Israel's coastal areas, mountains, and deserts.[7]

In North America, the physical plane of this renewed acquaintance with spiritual adventure has its analogue in the resurgence of Jewish travel narratives to distant communities, arguably the most popular Jewish literary genre of the new century. In recent years, Jewish writers have returned to reinvestigate the Diaspora as a site of wanderings. The rich explosion of recent investigations into forgotten dimensions of the far-flung Jewish odyssey through time and space include essay collections and personal explorations with evocative titles such as *Tropical Diaspora, Jewish Communities in Exotic Places, Diaspora and Exiles, Still Moving: Recent Jewish Migration in Comparative Perspective,* and *Fragile Branches: Travels Through the Jewish Diaspora,* among many, many others. Of these, Bruce Feiler's *Walking the Bible* (2001) is a particularly ambitious exploration, largely because it returns to the beginnings of it all; most of it is set against the epic Jewish wanderings from what is now Turkey to Egypt, the Sinai, Jordan, and Israel. Indeed, Feiler's searching account of what he discovered on his desert journey is a fitting subject for the conclusion to this study.

It would appear that even among writers in the Diaspora, the Jewish literary and spiritual imagination continues to depend on the dialectic of city and wilderness.[8] Nowhere is this ethos more evident than in Feiler's *Walking the Bible.* In his meanderings, Feiler was almost constantly in the good hands of Avner Goren, a seasoned archeologist and Sinai specialist, who also mentored me as a desert guide many years ago.[9] Perhaps the greatest value of Feiler's journey (and a humbling lesson for literary critics who spend whole careers in musty archives and libraries), is its striking assertion that reading (biblical) stories in the place of their occurrence can matter a great deal in the successful apprehension of their meaning. For example, where else but amidst the archeology of ancient Egypt would one be so viscerally struck by the sheer *textuality* of that culture, which the Hebrews fled and yet re-envisioned in remote places. At the site of Kom Ombo, north of Aswan, Feiler notices how "hieroglyphs climb the walls, ring the columns, and line the lintels" leaving him dazzled both by the monumental ascendancy of language over nature and by the implications for understanding the nascent Hebrew culture's relation to story immediately prior to its desert sojourn:

> As I stared into the script, like being swallowed in a three-story dictionary, I tried to think of other buildings with so much writing on them. Not Greek temples. Not Gothic cathedrals. Not Japanese shrines . . . The only thing one can conclude is that language was such a novelty, such a profound revision of how people viewed the world, that builders wanted to inundate visitors with the force of language in the same way that the river inundated people with the force of life. . . . The volume of words on the public monuments of ancient Egypt is comparable to that other magnum force of Egypt, the flood. . . . The world's first pulp novels were carved on the walls of Egypt's temples. (143, 144)

Feiler further posits that, in mimicking nature, Egyptian language entered into its most essential phases of development and hegemony, for "if language is going to triumph over nature, it first must become nature—use those pictograms themselves; then divert attention from nature—use those pictograms to tell stories; then dominate it—erect tall buildings that show the triumph of stories over nature" (143). Perhaps it was due to the monumentality of this overshadowing linguistic experience, the awesomely public inscription of the Egyptian version of reality, that the Hebrews required such a radically unmediated encounter with a place of unadorned absence, a silence and withdrawal in which the nation could (re)construct its own cultural narrative. And perhaps precisely for that reason, unlike the patriarchs at the Cave of Machpelah, Aaron, Moses, and Miriam each had to be buried in unknown desert graves, so that the people make a clean break from the Egyptian cult of the dead and refrain from fetishizing human leadership.

Throughout, Feiler exuberantly praises the lucidity of what he considers the desert's "voice." With excitement that grows increasingly infectious, Feiler feverishly promises the armchair traveler that should he or she actually "[c]ome face-to-face with the high mountains of southern Sinai . . . whatever one's orientation, one pauses with anticipation. The Bible says that when the Israelites beheld Mount Sinai they 'trembled.'" For in his excited confession: "at the moment I could understand why" (255). Feiler's heartfelt and homespun imagery serves to delineate the revelation that many have encountered after days in desert stillness: "I felt myself slide farther away from the rigid, controlled person I was at the beginning. . . . I was less of an upright wooden chair . . . and more of a roll-out carpet. I was conforming to the land" (298). At such moments of somewhat easily earned rapture this rambling narrative may seem a tad predictable in its strategic junctures of spiritual epiphanies. Like its sequel *Abraham,* it self-consciously strives with uneven results to create convincing grounds for interfaith understanding. *Walking the Bible* is most stirring when Feiler records the words of wayfarers and politicians he encounters on his trek, such as Abu Tayeh, the Jordanian diplomat and grandson of a Bedouin prince who served in military campaigns with Lawrence of Arabia.

At first discomfited by the distance between his own fevered enthusiasm and his wealthy host's distant, officious manner, Feiler observes an immediate transformation the instant the subject of the desert is broached. The Jordanian tells Feiler instructively that "[t]he Jewish tribes, led by Moses, came from the most advanced civilization, in Egypt. They crossed the desert to the Promised Land, where they civilized again. But during their journey in between they were Bedouin. And look what happened to them. The desert, because of its uncertainty, forces you to feel more attached to the higher power" (401). One cannot but be moved by the striking ways that Feiler's Arab and Israeli interlocutors, divided by violent politics, often resemble one another. For instance, back in Israel, a professor of anatomy and anthropology at Tel Aviv University insists that one of the greatest of the "larger truths" to be gleaned about the ancient world is the role of the desert in shaping the sacred imagination: "It makes sense to me that the desert is where most of the great religions were born. . . . More than any other place, it gives you time for thinking about spiritual things" (410). In many ways, Feiler's book sheds less light on the Bible's narratives than it does on the desert as a spiritual presence perhaps with the power to vanquish the violence that festers in the region that borders it. Feiler is most persuasive when he pauses to gauge his own response. Mere weeks into his journey into landscapes in which he never quite feels at ease, Feiler grapples for the words to express a quiet sense of awe at the change in perspective he observes in himself: "The desert destroys affectation; it demands authenticity. The Sinai, in particular, poised between Africa and Asia, compels a certain clarity. Come with a vague sense of identity; leave with a deeper sense of self. If God knew this, as the Bible suggests, he may, indeed, have known everything" (200).

It was with some degree of poignancy that I recognized these sentiments as the essence of the inchoate sensations that first lured me to the desert environment as a teenager. It makes great sense to me that Feiler, a Jewish American, and Goren, an Israeli, chose to end their adventure not in Jerusalem, nor merely in the indeterminate desert, but of all places on windswept Mount Nebo (located in Jordan), the second mysterious mountain of the wilderness epic, from which Moses exits his own and his people's story, after being allowed by God only to view—and not cross into—the Holy Land. The pre-eminent site of non-arrival. It is here that Feiler's off-the-cuff encounters with scholars and laymen culminates in a meditation of surprising intimacy and power. Musing over his manifest attraction to individuals who identify themselves foremost as desert enthusiasts rather than as representatives of Egypt, Israel, or Jordan, individuals self-conscious of inhabiting a space that has nurtured a variety of faiths, Feiler offers a rhapsodic plea for an alternative Middle East that is at once utopian and irresistible:

> If I could feel a growing openness in myself, if I could sense a similar feeling in . . . countless other people we met, if I could picture a world full of ecumenical desert people, in touch with their inner selves, riding a wave of sand-hewn memories to international peace and togetherness, then surely it could happen. Surely we could forget the centuries of wars that have been fought over these stories. Surely we could forget the millennia of bad faith that have been engendered by these stories. Surely we

> could remove these stories from politics, religion, and geography, and view them instead as a universal sourcebook offering readers a guide to spiritual emancipation and personal fulfillment. (370)

Reading Feiler in relation to the other Jewish writers highlighted in this study, it is clear that the desert's strangeness is primarily a medium for various kinds of social recognition and self-recognition. Indefinite nostalgia and search for an "authentic" self are important motivating factors, indeed essential symptoms, of the desert narrative.

When it brushes up against the nation's vast, unyielding spaces, Zionism undergoes a strange transformation, as if chastened by the greater epic of silence and emptiness. There, the desert gazes on its captivated Jewish subject with the same commanding gaze as the biblical imaginary, and the hapless Jewish soul, longing only to disengage himself from the unending violence and disillusionment, is captured by something far more powerful. With the re-emergence into national space, solidarity replaces solitude but a different citizen-subject materializes. In this study we have explored how traumas that the Israeli narrative subject carries into the desert subside as what some might consider an expanding consciousness (or others might call a recidivist diasporic desire) takes over. After grappling with a threatened loss of selfhood and the limits of being, the protagonist emerges, if not triumphant, with a sense of heightened awareness and conscience.

There are signs that the ever-struggling nation, so poignantly beset with crises of identity and security, has begun to re-examine its ambivalent relation to its desert spaces. Increasingly, Israeli artists are drawn to the physical and mental space of the desert, visiting Bedouin encampments, sometimes taking more difficult journeys to the refugee camps of Palestinians.[10] Somehow, the exodus from Egypt, the story of Passover, remains embedded in all this. These artistic visions may owe in part to the fact that in the modern history of Arab-Israeli relations, there have been few periods of the kind of harmony and justice that seemed to prevail in the period of Israel's occupation of the Sinai from 1967 to 1982. Though they built a road that made much of the Gulf of Aqaba accessible and created some modest farming and tourism enterprises in those years, the Israelis treated the traditional Bedouin society they found there with justice and even compassion. For their part, though often shocked and dismayed by the intrusion of naked European and Israeli tourists in the vicinity of their fishing villages, the Bedouin enjoyed unprecedented economic well-being as they cooperated in Israeli tourism initiatives. Still, as Smadar Lavie ruefully notes, the Zionist romance with the Sinai nomads during the years of occupation had its shortcomings, perhaps exemplified by "the Israeli approach of wanting the Bedouin's flimsy shanties well away from the scenic asphalt tourist route, but refusing permission for permanent housing in order to keep the alluringly nostalgic shanties, as relics of Moses' forty years in the Sinai wilderness" (*Poetics of Military Occupation* 83).[11]

In Israel proper, there are of course far fewer harmonious contact zones (to borrow Mary Louise Pratt's astute phrase), as Shelach's narrative fragment suggests. Beyond the interminable conflict between Palestinians and Israelis exhibited in daily headlines, a quieter but long-festering campaign of land confiscation and cultural hegemony is currently being waged by Israel in the Negev against that Bedouin population's traditional relationship to the desert. As David Shipler suggests, due to the pressures of security and Jewish settlement, the ancient tribal system of the desert has proved all too vulnerable to the will of Western "justice":

> The ultimate legal argument—that the Bedouins had a right to graze their goats and wander on the desert land—was usually made in vain, for no title deeds have existed in the culture of the wilderness. Bedouins have simply known all their lives which clan and tribe live in which wadi; they have nothing on paper to state the obvious. And so the concept of formal land ownership . . . enforced by the Israeli structure of law and authority, has excluded the semi-nomads and left them practically defenseless in the courts, which have interpreted rules that are irrelevant to the Bedouin's ways. (366)

Besides its harsh impact on the lives and livelihoods of the Negev Bedouin, one might argue that, by radically expunging nomadism, Israel is effectively vanquishing vital cultural traces of its own desert past—arguably as valuable as any archaeological site or museum space. In what Shipler calls "a clash between antiquity and modernity, a conflict once again between the desert and the settled agrarian life," (367) the ideological stakes (Israel's self-definition in essence) appear to be very high. Observing the "schizophrenic" dimensions of this tension, Shipler notices that whereas "in Sinai, relations were admiring, paternalistic, respectful," increasingly, relations in the Negev desert adjacent to Beersheba were marked by "tense, condescending, and abusive" attitudes "as Israeli authorities have chased the tribesmen off their lands, confiscated their goats, confined them to reservations, and denigrated their way of life" (358).

But the Zionist mission to transform Israel's desolate regions into green spaces remains a core mission of Israel's settlement, intrinsic to Zionist ideology and rhetoric. And there may be something ultimately redemptive in this role for the present crisis. Even before a sixty-six-inch diameter pipe (the largest in the world) known as the Yarkon-Negev Project first began to carry water to remote Negev settlements in July 1955, the irrigation and domestication of the desert had the highest priority in Israel's early years.[12] But today, in spite of Ben-Gurion's passionate urging and his personal example (in 1953 he and his wife Paula moved south to Kibbutz Sdeh Boker where they are buried on an inspiring outcrop overlooking the empty surrounding desert), the Negev has suffered staggering neglect while billions have been invested in illegal settlements in Judea, Samaria, and the Gaza Strip. Despite constituting half of Israel's land mass, it houses less than 10 percent of the population. Hence, the fate of natural ecosystems notwithstanding, it would appear that the desert still seems for many to be the unfulfilled political dream, not only of Ben-Gurion Zionism, but of the crisis of the present moment. Many Israelis, who saw in the aftermath of Saddam Hussein's fall an opportunity to achieve peace with the Palestinians, thought the time was ripe to evacuate the settlements in the occupied territories and resettle those Jews in the Negev. In turn, this open landscape seems to promise (to use Smadar Lavie's evocative phrase) new "geographies of identity." The latter might yet reverse the tragic hijacking of the Jewish nation's values and future by a few thousand fanatic settlers.

As Professor Avishai Braverman, president of Ben-Gurion University of the Negev, commented in a revealing interview, "After the war in Iraq, this opportunity is being created. Israel has nothing to look for to the east. It's clear that the settlement enterprise in Judea and Samaria is finished. Where will all these young people go in the future, where will all the energies be channeled? The south is the new Zionism. . . . Ben Gurion called on the golden youth to follow him to the Negev. They didn't come; now they will be willing to come, if we take the right steps" (Ben-Simon 4). As of this writing, there have indeed been promising steps taken in this direction. A group of young Israeli entrepreneurs have self-consciously sought to fulfill Ben-Gurion's (who once remarked that "[t]he Negev will be the test of the People of Israel") legacy in creating Kfar Adiel in the southern Negev, which will provide incentives such as full scholarship and subsidized housing to attract young people willing to settle and in return provide volunteer hours in nearby development towns.[13] And Braverman, whose university has recently opened a branch in Eilat at the southern edge of Israel, dreams of the construction of a common campus that would benefit Jordanian and Israeli students. Braverman may very well see his vision realized, for Israel and Jordan are teaming up to create what is intended to be the Middle East's most advanced scientific research institution. The Bridging the Rift Center, a 150-acre project currently being developed by Cornell and Stanford Universities, will include a vast "Library of the Desert," focusing on the life forms found between the Dead Sea and the Red Sea and will eventually catalog all the world's DNA and attract scientists working in disciplines such as physiological ecology, genomics, and bioinformatics. Initially offering fellowships to Jordanian and Israeli scientists, the center ultimately aspires to promote scientific research as an instrument to promote peace throughout the Middle East. And there is also room for optimism in the innovative activities of the Arava Institute run by Kibbutz Ketura, located fifty kilometers north of Eilat, which for the past nine years has brought together Palestinian, Jordanian, Israeli, as well as North American students (Jews, Christians, and Muslims) to work on desert ecology as well as issues of Arab-Jewish coexistence. It is moving to consider that even at the height of the recent Intifada, Arabs and Jews participated in the institute's unique program known as the Peacebuilding and Environmental Leadership Seminar, and many of them experienced close contact with "the other" for the first time in their lives.

As with so many other spheres of Israeli life, there are conflicting visions about the uses of the desert in resettlement and restructuring the nation's priorities, running the gamut from tourist dreamscapes to industrial parks and visions in between. For every practical planner like Braverman, there seems to be an even more visionary counterpart, like the journalist Tsur Sheizaf, who sees the Negev as a harbinger of a rejuvenating new Israeli relation to place, a healthy society's necessary "mental horizon" offering "people the peace they need to deal with congested urban society. Not every corner of this country has to be settled. We need the open spaces to keep a sound mental balance, and it would be a wise thing to define the Negev this way officially" (Gilad 2).

The Swedish adventurer and writer Sven Lindqvist observes that "in the desert all changes have already occurred. Nothing grows, nothing dies, nothing decays. Everything has gone. Only eternity remains" (68) There are good reasons that the desert, as untamed space, got under the skin of rational Zionists like David Ben-Gurion and other philosophical and pragmatic architects of the nation, for, in spite of the boldest efforts to conquer and subdue, it posed a resilient realm in which the eternal and mythical stubbornly remained impermeable to nationalist jurisdiction. In Hareven's novellas, the sweeping immediacy of the desert as an omnipresent epic is a presence that reminds modern Israelis of their origins, encompassing a complex set of ideas that hold promise for the moral restructuring of the modern Zionist dream. As the Israeli ecologist Alon Tal remarks of the attractions of an expanse that offers both the promise of renewed life and emptiness: "The Israeli instinctively returns to this natural world, finding rest from the cacophony of city life, much as the prophets did when seeking inspiration in days of old. There is no better place . . . to purge defeatist impulses from the human heart" (431). And perhaps some of the darkness of contemporary Israeli reality is alleviated by the success story of the Egyptian-Israeli military agreement in the Sinai Peninsula, which has successfully demilitarized the large, empty desert spaces that separate the population centers of Israel and Egypt. Instead of being occupied by the armies that waged several costly wars in the last century, the Sinai has reverted to its traditional uses by smugglers and Bedouin.

Here I would invite the reader to consider the implications of my argument that the contemporary engagement with the desert past is by no means limited to literary discourse. For the desert still permeates Jewish lives in the far-flung realities of contemporary life in a surprisingly visceral but often unrecognized way outside the Passover story. Indeed, I would argue that though contemporary Judaism often seems a badly fissured community containing many political and religious divisions, the primal experience of wandering the desert remains the vital glue unifying the Jewish relation to time and space. For instance, when a couple is married under a *chupah,* they stand within a loose structure, open on all four sides, symbolizing the hospitable dwelling of Abraham's desert tent. The Jewish liturgical calendar is ostensibly dominated by three great festivals (Passover, Shavuot, Sukkoth) that affirm the centrality of Jerusalem, but each of these makes powerful gestures to the nomadic life of Israel in the desert.[14] And, as Amos Oz observes of ancient Hebrew, a language having no present tense, we are forced to imagine a condition of permanent, vigilant hospitality: "'And Abraham *sitting* in the entrance to the tent' . . . like the stage directions of a play: 'Every time the curtain goes up, we see Abraham sitting in the entrance to his tent.' For all eternity, He sat, he sits, he will sit forever and ever in the entrance to that tent" (*Black Box* 127). The fundamental aesthetic and metaphoric properties of this tradition are surfacing in unexpected quarters. There are signs that the city/wilderness dialectic remains at the creative core of other Jewish visionary narratives who envision ways that the primordial desert experience might enliven contemporary urban realities. For example, in New York City, the architect Bonnie Roche describes her purpose in a proposal for Congregation B'nai Jeshurun inspired by the biblical description of the *Mishkan* (Tabernacle) and its mobile court: "At the center of steel and stone in our modern cities stands the same individual that once stood in the shadows of the ancient desert. This individual yearns for the same spiritual rootedness to a universe larger than oneself. This cry for a glimpse of the ineffable is becoming increasingly audible as a public voice in the canyons of our urban environments" (342).

Roche speculates whether the ancient metaphors of the desert experience might not illumine the sacred in secular cities, awakening the "spiritual capital" that otherwise "lies latent" (342). She posits that, like the ancient Israelites in the desert, we must construct "places that have a continuous presence in the collective consciousness, with forms that remain silent, incomplete, waiting for human beings to enter . . . uncovered and transformed in the center of our urban terrain, we must, as the ancients did, cease and pause for breath after we have constructed. . . . This dialectic tension in the context of our urban built environment is the reconciliation between souls and forms" (351). Rather than regard the remote Israelite past as unbridgeable, she suggests we are intended to take its communal infrastructure as seriously as its moral laws. Why else, Roche ponders, would so much of Exodus be "dedicated to the most intricate and detailed descriptions of the building, contents, materials, assemblage, and even timing of the assemblage of the Mishkan along this journey" (343). This seems a strikingly fitting paradigm, for after all, the Jewish American experience has proved to be strikingly nomadic. Whereas other immigrant groups of the same historical era, such as Irish and Italians, have often remained rooted in a locale due to the structure of geographic parishes, Jewish synagogues proved to be freestanding organizations, unfettered by a hierarchy from above. The synagogue membership could sell its buildings, rebuild, and move on to suit its demographic needs and the movement from the city into the beckoning suburbs.

Taking the strange logic of linking the urban present to the ancient desert even further, one has to bear in mind the fact that, as Belden Lane observes, "the impulse of modernity . . . emphasize[s] the universal rather than the vernacular, the anonymous instead of the personal, the freedom of uninterrupted space as opposed to the particularity of place" (235). Hence, for the urban Jewish architect, it is clear that the same desert design that was at the heart of the people's growth as a community offers a spiritual value "significant beyond its literal physical attributes" (343). The Mishkan of the wilderness has enduring relevance for the crisis of modern civilization:

> What we once knew in the ancient world, more than ever, has relevance today; that the ancient Mishkan, the tent assembled and disassembled for forty years throughout the journey . . . was critical to creating and holding a newly formed community from a nomadic people in a land that was ownerless and free. The Mishkan became a vehicle for spiritual rootedness within nomadism, within mobility. (342)

Still, one might reasonably wonder just precisely what the ancient choreography of desert movement has to do with the contemporary urban life of Jews and others. Roche addresses this by drawing on the thought of a range of thinkers who have considered the perils and promises of modern life as disparate as Abraham Joshua Heschel and Oswald Spengler. Roche affirms the achievement of the city dweller in having transcended the peasant's rootedness in limitations (though she does not see the two locked in enmity but rather as complementary paradigms), whether of planting, soil, or seasonal cycles. In contrast, the birth of cities left us free to "imagine, through the abstract life of the mind, a built world manifesting a universe greater than oneself. The intellectual construct of the collective, which we know as urban landscape, freed us, made us limitless and again nomadic" (Roche 343). Yet Roche also pays close heed to Heschel's warning that "life goes wrong when the control of space, the acquisition of things of space, becomes our sole concern" (3). As an architect, Roche sees the essential qualities of the ancient Mishkan—"impermanence, mutability, and openness"—as necessary spiritual counters for the contemporary nomadic condition of secular materialism (Roche 350). In the desert, the Israelites took a respite from the highly technical civilization of the Egyptians, learning the moral lessons of living genuinely in what Heschel calls the "realm of time": "The danger begins when in gaining power in the realm of space we forfeit all aspirations in the realm of time, where the goal is not to have but to be, not to own but to give, not to control but to share, not to subdue but to be in accord" (3).

Inviting us to consider our modern condition "as nomads in the desert of our cities," Roche proposes that whereas "our cities are sinuous constructions of constant reminders of the things of space," city dwellers need to recover a world more intellectually and spiritually expansive than the limits set by the "built urban wilderness" (344–45), for "our cities, though intricately layered, have become a singular idea, a space-oriented world devoid of the distinctions of time. . . . Its spaces are static, its architecture is immutable. Our urban complexities are losing the living dynamic, the constant dialogue between space and time" (345).

As Roche suggests, the Jewish desert experience remains a beacon moored deep within culture. If it is dormant, it nevertheless has the power to inspire our society's most visionary imaginations to renew humanity's intimate relation with the dimension of time as well as space, allowing for the prospect of political and spiritual transformations even in the pressured density of the urban environment.

Perhaps most of all, Jews living in the land of Israel have a special duty to come to terms with the wilderness ethics of displacement embedded in our deepest rituals. In her consideration of the cultural poetics of the festival of Sukkot, with its strange requirement that one dwell for a week in a temporary, rough dwelling evoking the desert experience, an ethical imperative to find oneself disrupted in one's territorial complacency, Zali Gurevitch argues that:

> The hallmark of this ritual is nonpermanence. The permanent dwellers of the land are required to leave the permanence of their homes and sit in a *sukka* to return symbolically to life in the desert. In this way, in the midst of the tranquility of nativity and the celebration of the yield of the (owned) land, the desert is commemorated and revived as an antithetical myth of the place. Dwellers of the land must come to grips again with their essential strangeness in the land. The necessity of place is thus counterpointed with a ritual of temporariness and of movement that highlights non-place and the freedom from captivity in place. (213)

As I hope my readers have seen, writing about the desert's empty spaces often enables an indelible expression of the Jewish writer's self. The desert stands on the edge of a precipice of Jewish thought that is still moved by its silences, stirred by its emptiness, and above all by the ethical ancient legacy it has bequeathed its careful listeners. I have been thinking all along of the desert texts we have explored as *sukkot* of disruptions, taking postoccupation Israelis, diasporic Jews, and all others out of the indolence of the oppressive sovereignty of identity, nationality, and borders, into a shelter of non-place, awakening all of us toward, as Emmanuel Levinas has it, a more "difficult freedom."

NOTES

Preface

1. The passage continues: "and if the force of the human world's attraction remains great enough to draw him back to the border and keep him there as crushed, no less great is the pull of his own world, the one where he is free, where he has the liberty he speaks of with a tremor, a tone of prophetic authority which contrasts with his habitual modesty." See Maurice Blanchot, *The Space of Literature,* 71.

2. Canaanism perceived Zionism as a mere outgrowth of exilic Judaism. Renouncing the "moribund" religion (as well as Christianity and Islam), it sought a return to the ancient, mythic roots of the ancient Israelites; rather than choose between exilic Judaism or Zionist ideology, its proponents sought an authentically organic role model for the present. The Canaanites were a small but very dynamic group of modernist artists and writers who argued that the Jews of Israel needed to see themselves sharing with the Arab occupants of the land a common descent from the people who lived there prior to the founding of the ancient "Israeli" commonwealth. Their political program proved utterly ineffectual (an unwieldy blend of the militant Right's territorial expansionism with the militant Left's rejection of Zionism for its ethnic exclusionism). But the Canaanites left a lasting impact on Israeli art and literature. At various moments, the lingering effects of their influence on the writers I consider will be apparent in this study.

3. The Arava constitutes more than a hundred miles of the Jordan rift valley between the Dead Sea and the Gulf of Eilat (Aqaba). In the Bible, the term "Arava" is often used as a synonym for "desert." Separating the hills of the Negev from the loftier summits of the Edom Mountains in Jordan, it has a hot climate with little annual rainfall. The road to Eilat passes through this dry expanse and in ancient times copper ore was mined from the Nubian sandstone at Wadi Timna. Today its agricultural communes raise dairy cattle and sheep, grow winter vegetables (melons, onions, peppers, tomatoes), cultivate date, mango, and other hot-climate orchards, and even farm fish in desert ponds. Desert eco-tourism is also an important growing enterprise in the region.

4. Sadly, though, I now look back on those years through the prism of my colleague Mike Comin's admonishment that "the desert does not indulge those who cannot tell reality from a mirage. Take your rationalizations to the desert and they will lead you to your death. Pretense is not an option."

5. There is a similar passage in the Babylonian Talmud, Erubin 54a, in the name of Rav Mattena: "*Im mesim adam atsmo kedmidbar zeh shehakol dashin bo,*

talmudo mitqayyen beyado, veim lav, eyn talmudo mitqayyem beyado" (If a man makes himself like this wilderness which everybody treads on, his learning stays with him, and if not, his learning does not stay with him). In the rabbinic imagination, the humility required of making one's self like the wilderness enlarged one's consciousness and agility with what one learned. I am grateful to Alan D. Cosse for these references.

Chapter 1: Representing Desert Wilderness in Jewish Narrative

1. The term for "desert" in biblical Hebrew is "*midbār*," which originally alluded to all agriculturally unexploited areas or even the desolated sites of once-inhabited settlements. For an excellent discussion of the etymology of the term, see Shemaryahu Talmon's comprehensive essay "The Desert Motif in the Bible and in Qumran Literature."

2. As Gordon Brubacher in *Eerdmans Dictionary of the Bible* puts it in his judicious reading of a range of biblical accounts, "life in the desert teaches important lessons about faith and ethics. Surviving in this unforgiving environment requires both specialized knowledge and the discipline to apply it. Yet no amount of skill and discipline will guarantee survival, so desert life requires that people help each other, and it also generates more direct trust in God. The desert seems to facilitate revelation. People hear the voice of God more clearly, unimpeded by civilization or their own rationalizations" (340).

3. For example, at a May 18–19, 2003, interdisciplinary conference, "Cultural Cartography and Constructions of Identity," held at Stanford University, an exciting range of Jewish scholars from the social sciences and the humanities traced the ethical and ethnic significance of space in presentations ranging from rabbinic urbanism in the Diaspora to the cultural construction of public and private space in Zionist settlement.

4. The term "Diaspora" first appears in the Septuagint, the Egyptian Jewish translation of the Hebrew Bible into Greek, in 250 B.C.E. The literal translation, "to be scattered" (like seeds), derives from the Hebrew of Deuteronomy 28:64, *v'hefitzcha* ("you will be scattered"). Today, when speaking in the Jewish context, it is most often used by those for whom the condition of living outside the Jewish homeland does not necessarily engender a feeling of exile or disenfranchisement.

5. For recent examples, see Ezrahi's *Booking Passage*; Andrew Furman's *Israel Through the Jewish American Imagination* (Albany: State University of New York Press, 1997), and my own *Diaspora and Zionism in Jewish American Literature: Lazarus, Syrkin, Reznikoff, Roth* (Hanover: University Press of New England, 2002).

6. Moreover, as the biologist Michael Mares observes, "We developed our most human characteristics in a dry savannah. . . . It is the need to organize families, tribes, and societies in the face of an unpredictable environment that helped form societal structures over the millennia. . . . Deserts, with their clear air and limitless vistas, taught people to organize, for desert survival requires organization. Indeed, the harsh surrounding desert that placed a limit on the green oases of life may have permitted the growth of dense human populations within the cir-

cumscribed area of the Fertile Crescent" (2–3). It is no coincidence that the very phenomenon of codified law, the first textual realization of the moral imagination that later inspired Hebraic monotheism, was stirred up and created by exigency of daily struggle, famines, and droughts in the semiarid region of the Tigris and Euphrates.

7. Here, and throughout this book, I am inspired by critical discussions of the subversive Mosaic tradition, which, scholars argue, stresses loss of roots, wandering, and dispossession, opposing the royalist Davidic tradition. As Harry Berger Jr. declares, "The Old Testament ideologeme . . . sets the tent against the house, nomadism against agriculture, the wilderness against Canaan, wandering and exile against settlement, diaspora against the political integrity of a settled place" (123).

8. Interestingly, early Zionist generations represented themselves as *dor ha'midbar* (the generation of the desert) "who were born in freedom and conquered the promised land [and] sought to disclaim the history of the Palestinian presence in the land, depicting the Zionists as the redeemers of the land." See Rachel Feldhay Brenner, *Inextricably Bonded,* 6–7.

9. I am indebted to Ariel Hirschfeld's translation of these lines in his splendid analysis of Zionist Orientalism. See "Locus and Language," 1020–22.

10. The translation from "To the Sun" is Robert Alter's from Alan Mintz's edited collection *Reading Hebrew Literature,* 64–72. I am indebted to Arnold Band's meticulous explication in an essay that appears in the same volume, 81–91.

11. For a comprehensive discussion of interpretations of the "desert motif" and the "nomadic ideal" in biblical research, see Shemaryahu Talmon 31–34. In part, his study constitutes an investigation of claims by scholars that prophets such as Isaiah, Jeremiah, and Hosea evoke the desert as a sort of nomadic "zeal for freedom . . . opposed to the monarchical regime" (54).

12. As Rabbis Matthew and Miriam Berkowitz observe, "Isaac cannot change his neighbors, but by changing his own actions, he shifts an entire situation. Sensitivity and creativity help him break a destructive cycle. He is committed to living in the land of his father, yet he digs his own wells. He holds to a vision and compromises on the strategy. Isaac's quest for a life that honors his roots and nourishes his future leads him to Gerar, where a buffer is established between the two parties. Water represents life, yet when Isaac's water becomes a source of dissension, he understands that other waters must feed his vision. And so he digs until peaceful, life-giving waters are found. . . . What he does not do is resort to violence" (27). See my discussion of the poet Charles Reznikoff's dramatization of this narrative in *Diaspora and Zionism in Jewish American Literature,* 156–58.

13. As Belden C. Lane observes, defying oppression in Egypt and by extension every royal tradition of image or structure, the Hebraic desert "is a place where political priorities are realigned. To flee to the mountain is to identify with the marginalized, with those denied access to the empowerment of the state and thus subject to its wrath" (135).

14. Accordingly, I have confined this discussion to works available in English translation, reluctantly omitting important modern Hebrew works such as Meir Shalev's *His House in the Desert* (1998) as well as a number of Yiddish writers such as Zalmen Brokhes. Yael Chaver is currently writing a study of the latter's

Palestinian fiction of the 1920s, narratives often set in the desolate regions of the Judean Desert and the Dead Sea, featuring the exploits of "Jewish Bedouin."

15. Besides the devastating wasteland that often seems to dominate Deuteronomy, there is a competing tradition voiced in Deuteronomy 29:4 in which the desert is the site of supreme clarity and shelter for the evolving relationship between the human and the divine. See also Hosea's vision of the intimacy shared by God and Israel (Hos. 2:16–17) and Jeremiah (Jer. 2:2 and 31:1–2) for examples of creative stimulants for the contemporary visions analyzed throughout this study. For an exhaustive survey of the biblical term *midbār* and its uses, see Shemaryahu Talmon, "The Desert Motif in the Bible and in Qumran Literature."

16. In the archetypal moral dualism of Zoroastrianism, the schism between followers of truth and followers of deceit echoes the irreconcilable rift between the farmer and the violent predatory existence of desert tribes. Over the centuries, Chinese historical writing revisits the conflict between sedentary people (order and prosperity) and nomads (unproductive barbarism) and Chinese poets complemented that worldview with vivid evocations of the steppes and desert as melancholic expanses of desolation and death.

17. A notable exception may be found in the early Christian desert writers for whom, Lane says, "the self is a desert that must be stripped and made empty before God can be found at its center" (11).

18. Personal communication, February 10, University of Miami. Similarly, the Judean wilderness site of Masada, the Herodian fortress where Jewish defenders staunchly withstood Roman occupation before committing suicide, which performs such a primary commemorative role in Israeli political culture, formed the backdrop for the preeminent archetypal story of resistance and sacrifice. However, for many, Masada, as part of a script of seamless continuity between the ancient past and the return to the land after two millennia, poses difficult questions about a nation so officially linked to siege and suicide, which Meira Weiss has dubbed a "cult of the dead" (86). With this notable exception, the desert returns life to individuals in the most intimate sense, at the very moment that it prepares them to participate more fully in a renewed idea of the nation.

19. See *Mekhilta, Bahodesh,* 1, for the rabbinic commentary on Exodus 19:2.

20. For an overview of Levinas's engagement with the rabbinic tradition, see *Difficult Freedom: Essays on Judaism,* trans. Seán Hand (Baltimore: The Johns Hopkins University Press, 1990), and *Nine Talmudic Readings,* trans. Annette Aronowicz (Bloomington: Indiana University Press, 1994).

21. The spatial equivalent to the West's fear of the uncanny Other would seem to be desert space for, as Jonathan Rutherford argues, "[t]o the Western European eye, the desert seems an uncanny space, its borders marking out a margin between the habitable and the inhabitable." Like the encounter with the human Other, venturing into its space would seem to entail a deconstructive logic threatening established hierarchies: "Here lies the desert as a cultural metaphor . . . representing the margins of our culture and the knowledge and values that underpin it, it is also the place of their undoing . . . the [desert is] site of difference and the repository of our fears and anxieties" (9–10).

22. Levinas explicitly reads counter to Hegel, who sees Abraham as rupturing "the bonds of community and love." In Hegel's negative reading, "Abraham wandered here and there over a boundless territory, without bringing any parts of

it nearer him by cultivating or improving them. . . . He was a stranger on earth, a stranger to the soil and men alike." Hegel sees in Abraham's refusal to create any form of national or familial identification the destiny—"mean, abject, wretched"—of the Jews of Hegel's Europe (quoted in Presner 526).

23. My chapter on David Grossman considers an unusual literary antecedent: the Jewish nationalist verse of Hayim Nahman Bialik, which construes this as an inversion of those of his generation who, without divine injunction, insist on returning to the land.

24. See also Ella Shohat's Saidian analysis of an earlier period of filmmaking's representation of the Jewish settlement of Palestine, in her *Israeli Cinema,* where she finds, in films such as *Oded the Wanderer* (Dir. Nathan Axelrod, 1933) and *Sabra* (Dir. Alexander Ford, 1933), passive Arabs and enervated Oriental desert landscapes awaiting the rejuvenating effects of "Western penetration," 44.

25. Where the British frequently romanticized the Sinai and other Middle Eastern deserts, nineteenth-century French writers, including Eugäne Fromentin, Alphonse Daudet, Theophile Gautier, Guy de Maupassant, as well as Gustave Flaubert, turned to the Sahara.

26. In a revealing interview with both Oz and Grossman, Israel's two most vocal literary spokesmen of the left, *Haaretz* journalist Ari Shavit characterized their political visions in ways that may also illuminate intriguing differences in their literary imaginations: "Both admit the mistakes of the left, but insist on its justness. Oz advocates a unilateral withdrawal, Grossman is closer to the indefatigable diplomatic efforts of Yossi Beilin. Oz won't let go of a fundamental optimism, Grossman allows himself more pessimism. Oz's style is the aggressive selectivity of a writer-statesman, Grossman is more hesitant and personal. Oz's logic and rhetoric are impeccable; with Grossman the contradictions are captivating." See Shavit 7.

27. This illusion, perpetuated by many young men in pursuit of self, perhaps bears an odd similarity to the first scene of Disney's *Aladdin* (1992) where, in Alan Nadel's memorable observation, a sinister man in disguise, the fascistic Jafar, "has found a way to make the blank desert surface reveal its secret identity as a monstrous leonine head with a cavernous throat opening to a cave of wonders. Although the throat opening appears to be a fiery abyss, it actually disguises a stairwell to treasures" (Nadel 189). But in Disney's *Aladdin,* it is not the evil Jafar who can successfully penetrate the desert's secrets, but only "one who is worthy"—like so many of us, the Disney writers (numbering many Jews among them) conceived of pristine desert space as a place to instill, reward, or perpetuate the virtuous individual.

28. In modern Hebrew, "Ha-Makom" literally means the "place" or "location" but in rabbinic literature signifies "The Place," one of numerous metaphoric names for God. Ha-Makom names the physical, immanent aspect of God's presence as one might experience it under a clear night of stars in the countryside, upon an encounter with wildlife, on gazing on a sublime natural landscape, or other natural phenomenon.

29. In Jonathan Boyarin's analysis of the land-oriented ethos of the Zionist revolution, the cultivation of "knowledge of the land" was a sacred imperative toward regaining a vital connection to the ancient geography of the Jew's homeland ("In Search of 'Israeli Identity'" 195). The belief in the interrelatedness of reborn Jew-

ish bodies and Jewish culture was evocatively codified in the pioneering phrase of the Zionist settlements: Likhbosh et HaAdama BaRaglyim (conquer the land by foot). But if, as David Biale has argued, "Zionism meant both the physical rooting of [what were previously] the 'people of the air' (*Luftmenschen*) in the soil of Palestine and the reclamation of the body" (176), might not exposure to the desert's flux threaten the successful reconstitution of the Jewish national body? For more sympathetic treatments of the role of nature in the Israeli construction of identity, see Zerubavel, *Recovered Roots*, and Almog, *The Sabra*.

30. This retelling of the ancient story is an admirable exemplar of the fact that for the modern Hebrew-speaking Israeli, the Bible does not merely generate literary allusions or motifs but in fact *constructs* reality, enabling expression, culminating in a *social* reality.

31. *A Perfect Peace* 51. Subsequent references will be quoted parenthetically. When I first read Oz's novel many years ago, I was reminded of Wim Wender's classic film *Paris, Texas* (1984), which employs the American desert as both backdrop and metaphor for a vacant protagonist's search of a "lost" identity.

32. Stein notes the irony that "[o]f course, Jaffa was a thriving seaport at the time of Zionist settlement, as Jewish settlers were quick to discover . . . it is important to take seriously the ways in which the story of the empty . . . landscape, as told and retold . . . resonate with histories and contemporary fantasies of Palestinian dispossession" (17–19).

Chapter 2: Justice and the Old/New Jewish Nation

1. This creative and spiritual problem was anticipated as early as 1926. In Gershom Scholem's darkly candid assessment in a letter to Franz Rosenzweig regarding the renewal and secularization of Hebrew: "The Land is a volcano, and it hosts the language. . . . [But] what will be the result of updating the Hebrew language? Is not the holy language, which we have planted among our children, an abyss that must open up? People here do not know the meaning of what they have done. They think they have made Hebrew into a secular language and that they have removed its apocalyptic sting, but it is not so. . . . All those words which were not created arbitrarily . . . but were taken from the good old lexicon, are filled to the brim with explosive meaning. . . . God cannot remain silent in a language in which He has been evoked thousands of times to return to our life. . . . Would that the lightness of mind which guided us on this apocalyptic path not lead us to destruction" (27–29).

2. This discussion is greatly indebted to many of the insights Yael Feldman develops in her rich reading of the "psychopolitics" of *Thirst: The Desert Trilogy*, which appears in her groundbreaking study *No Room of Their Own* (159–76). Her discussion is the most comprehensive of this and other Hareven works to date, especially valuable for its analysis of Hareven's critical reception in Israel as well as the novelist's early career. Feldman, whose work has guided me a great deal, tells me that she feels that Hareven saw herself as staunchly "Zionist"; nevertheless, my own discussion emphasizes the ways her narrative might be put in dialogue with post-Zionism's questionings of identity and territorial justice.

3. One of the questions of the study reads as follows: "Suppose that the Israeli

army conquers an Arab village in battle. Do you think it would be good or bad to act toward the inhabitants as Joshua did toward the people of Jericho and Makkedah?" Among other conclusions, the study noted that "the overestimation of statehood as a supreme value and the idea that assimilation is the greatest evil, and the influences of militaristic values in ideological education, are further sources of discriminatory tendencies." See Gover 5–6.

4. For representative accounts that trace the supposed devaluation of the feminine from Sumerian myth through the Hebrew Bible, see Anne Baring and Jules Cashford's *The Myth of the Goddess: Evolution of an Image* and Merlin Stone's *When God Was a Woman.*

5. See Feldman's analysis of the trope of the *akedah* as it evolved in both Hareven's oeuvre and Israeli culture, 170–76.

6. For a recent novelistic retelling whose vision is highly commensurate with Hareven's sense of Abraham's family as a paradigm of spiritual and political dysfunction, see the Cambridge-based author Jenny Diski's *After These Things* (Little Brown, 2004).

7. The final two stanzas read:

> Isaac, as the story goes, was not sacrificed
> He had a long life, saw what pleasure had to offer,
> until his eyes went dark.
>
> But that hour
> he bequeathed to his descendants
> who are born
> with a knife
> in the heart.

My translation is a reworking of Naomi Tauber and Howard Schwartz's version in *Voices Within the Ark: The Modern Jewish Poets,* edited by Howard Schwartz and Anthony Rudolf, 98.

8. In *Al tishlakh yadkha el hanaar: Shirim vedivrei hagut al haakeda* (Lay not thine hand upon the lad: Poetry and essays on the binding of Isaac), edited by Aryeh Ben-Gurion. The anthology opens with Haim Be'er's essay "The Fire and the Wood" which describes the *akedah* as the deepest infrastructural paradigm of life and literature in Israel, illuminating its resonance through echoing traces of phrases such as "Lay not thine hand upon . . ." and "the fire and the wood." Be'er characterizes these as the *akedah*'s "eternal DNA coils."

9. Another memorable re-creation of the Genesis tale of the binding of Isaac may be found in Amos Oz's early short story about a passionate kibbutz patriarch and a son whose eagerness to satisfy his father's ambitious plans for the Day of Independence leads to his spectacularly horrific demise. "The Way of the Wind," *Where the Jackals Howl and Other Stories.*

10. Later succeeding Moses as the leader of the people, Joshua, together with Caleb, is the only leader out of the twelve representatives sent by Moses to explore the Promised Land to advocate the conquest of the land. See Numbers 13.

11. Though I am speaking here of contemporary Hebrew literature, it is noteworthy that in other prominent twentieth-century novels, such as Paul Bowles's *The Sheltering Sky* or Michael Ondaatje's *The English Patient,* the desert landscape is

subject to continual change, flux, and erosion in ways that urgently underscore their characters' inner revelations and adjustments to new realities.

Notably, these texts share the antinationalistic tendencies of Hareven's politically inflected midrash.

12. In contrasting a feminist perspective on the biblical text, Hareven is undoubtedly thinking of the harsh treatment of Moses' sister-prophetess. In Exodus, God punishes Miriam with leprosy for challenging her brother's authority, leading to her being quarantined outside the official camp of the Israelites. For many feminist biblical readers this is highly suggestive of an inherently androcentric ideology, where "[w]omen are at the boundary of the symbolic order, the border between men and chaos. As borderline figures, women partake of the properties of a border: they are neither inside nor outside" (Athalya Brenner 86). I would also argue that it is precisely such indeterminacy that inspires Hareven to articulate a feminist politics/poetics of wandering, and insider-outsider dwelling; these sustain a critique of both the origins of her tradition's gender biases and the symbolic male order of the violent present.

13. It is surprisingly useful to consider Hareven alongside Gertrude Stein, who, after returning from her thirty-one-year sojourn in France, thought she recognized the germ of European-style dictatorship tactics in the America of the Depression: "There is too much fathering going on now. . . . Everybody nowadays is a father, there is father Mussolini and father Hitler and father Roosevelt and father Stalin and father Lewis and father Blum and father Franco is just commencing now and there are ever so many more ready to be one. Fathers are depressing. . . . I say fathers are depressing any father who is a father and there are far too many fathers now existing. The periods of the world's history that have always been most dismal ones are the ones where fathers were looming and filling up everything" (quoted in Carson 53).

14. Hareven's critique might be considered alongside Amos Oz's troubled reflections some years ago on the legendary Moshe Dayan: "the charms of death inspire Dayan . . . one glimpses a poetical, romantic lust for death which I would gladly accept in a poet or author, but which inspires dread in me when it is expressed by a man who makes decisions concerning the lives and deaths of many people" (*Under This Blazing Light* 28–29).

15. I am grateful to an anonymous reader of an early draft of this essay for bringing to my attention the resounding echo of Freud's *Moses and Monotheism* at this intriguing moment in Hareven's novella.

16. Nash insightfully addresses the way Hareven's work encodes the word *aharayut* (responsibility) which itself contains the word *aher* (other), demanding concern for Other persons (224).

17. Interestingly, Israel's Supreme Court Justice Edmond Levy recently declared that "[a]n entire population has been designated as hewers of wood and bearers of water," in response to a report criticizing the country's institutions of higher learning for discriminating against minority groups, including Israeli Arabs. See Haim Watzman, "Israeli Supreme Court Declines to Intervene in Case Over University Admissions," *Chronicle of Higher Education* (February 11, 2004).

18. See Schwartz, *The Curse of Cain: The Violent Legacy of Monotheism.*

19. Certain recent trends in feminist biblical scholarship tend to support the notion of a biblical text that contains multiplicity. For example, *A Feminist*

Companion to Genesis (Sheffield: SAP Continuum, 1993) contains nine articles on the Creation stories alone.

Chapter 3: Desert Space and National Consciousness

1. From his earliest publication, *Where the Jackals Howl* (*Artzot Hatan* [1965]), this ethos has been present in Oz's work, as uneasy and unresolved tensions rather than as a linear trajectory of progress. Ever since the translation of early novels such as *Elsewhere, Perhaps* (*Makom Acher* [1966]) and *My Michael* (*Michael Sheli* [1968]), Oz has enjoyed a spectacular international career. As his close friend and contemporary, the novelist A. B. Yehoshua, once observed of his own career, Oz's oeuvre affirms "the ability to conquer one's terror, and record everything, including the most revolting truths in one's being" (Fuchs 50).

2. Readers interested in comparing this discussion to later representations of the Negev desert in Oz's oeuvre should also consider *Don't Call It Night (Al Tagidi Layla* [1994]), where a much older man, who more closely resembles the author himself, lives in the dusty Negev development town of Tel Kedar (pop. 9,000), more than an hour's journey from Beersheba, Israel's last densely populated city between the desert and Eilat on the Red Sea coast. Oz's most recently translated novel *Oto Ha-Yam* (*The Same Sea,* 1999) contains teasing references to the existential role of the desert in the writer's imagination.

3. English translation, Harcourt Brace Jovanovich, 1985. First published in Hebrew in 1982 (*Menucha Nechona*) by Am Oved. Textual references cited parenthetically.

4. Avraham Balaban observes that "for the writers of the 'Palmach Generation', human society was . . . [the] arena where conflicting forces clashed and where the protagonists' lives were shaped. It was this arena, with its dynamic social and cultural forces, that engendered the protagonists' problems, and it was within its boundaries that the problems had to be resolved. In the fiction published in Israel in the late 1950s and early 1960s, however, the existential horizon, the scope of yearning, became considerably higher. . . . Although the immediate social reality is still depicted and elucidated in the stories of that period, it serves only as a starting point for a quest of an entirely different nature" ("Secularity and Religiosity" 63).

5. Oz's story is of particular historical interest for the way it challenged the prevailing cultural equation of "Arab" and "savage passions" in films such as *The Great Promise* and *End of Evil,* mentioned in chapter 1.

6. "Coping With Conflict: Elizabeth Farnsworth Interviews Amos Oz" from *PBS Online NewsHour* (January 23, 2002) http://www.pbs.org/newshour/bb/middle_east/jan-june02/oz_1-23.html. See also Amos Oz's introductory essay in *Under this Blazing Light* 10. More recently, in June of 2004, he declared that "the calamity—and I don't use the word lightly—resides in the personal cowardice of the leadership groups. And also in the two leader figures. Sharafat, I call them. And of them it can definitely be said that like has found like. Because I have a deep suspicion that both of them prefer this reality to the post-solution reality. Neither of them knows how to live the morning of the day after the solution. That is also why it holds no attraction for them. What for you and for you and for me seems to be a new dawn is for them dusk." See Shavit 9.

7. Alternatively, there is Avner Holtzman's view that the classic narrative conflict in Oz's works is always between a messianic attraction to zealous militancy and a pull toward rationality. Holtzman regards this as a "religious" yearning for the peaceful synthesis of these warring cultural binaries. As we will see, this tension has crucial implications for how one interprets the conclusion of *A Perfect Peace.* See "Fima mekhake l'nes" (Hebrew).

8. Among these, Aschkenasy observes that "Oz's dialogue with the Bible, polemical, dialectical, comical, and ultimately conciliatory, began with his early publications in the 1960s . . . and continued throughout his literary career. In some ways this dialogue reflects changing attitudes in Israeli culture toward the Bible as a pedagogic tool for inspiring patriotic loyalty, and in other ways it anticipates, or even influences, cultural perceptions and processes" (123).

9. Mazor traces the bitter reference here to 1 Samuel 14 where Jonathan fails to hear his father Saul's order to his troops not to consume any food until victory. Upon hearing that his son has tasted some honey in the field, the king orders his execution, but Jonathan is saved by the active will of the people (Mazor 43). Aschkenasy concurs, seeing Oz's intentions throughout his development of this relationship as a "modern-day version of the tragic King Saul, who fell out of favor with God and failed to establish a dynasty," while his son, "lacking his father's political aspirations . . . yet still performing courageously on the battlefield is the modern counterpart of King Saul's heroic son Jonathan" (130).

10. Interestingly, in the final pages of the novel, Srulik, the conscientious kibbutz member who replaces Yolek as secretary by the novel's end, wonders to himself "with what weapon can we repel this interior wilderness?" (363). This figure, a member of Yolek's founding generation, is made even more sympathetic when he writes in his journal of his own alienation from the formulas of socialism: "I have lived my life here to the music of a marching band, as if death had already been abolished . . . and the whole universe nothing but a giant arena for political and ideological quarrels" (226).

11. For the historiography of this controversial slogan, see Garfinkle 539–50.

12. In the myth described in Jessie L. Weston's classic study *From Ritual to Romance,* the mystical relation between monarch and land is causal since "the loss of virility in one brings about a suspension of the reproductive processes of Nature in the other. The same effect would naturally be the result of the death of the sovereign upon whose vitality these processes depended" (23). For a provocative application of the Grail romance to the landscapes of Zionist cinema, see Ne'eman's essay "The Jar and the Blade: Fertility Myth and Medieval Romance in Israeli Political Films."

13. This seems to be a lightly mocking self-portrait, for in his youth at Kibbutz Hulda, Oz was a voracious reader of Spinoza. Balaban concludes that in those early years "Spinoza's pantheism appealed to Oz because it emphasizes the sanctity that permeates the world, and the harsh determinism that it implies. . . . But Oz did not find Spinoza's religious concepts wholly satisfactory. The harmonious totality that characterizes God in Spinoza . . . lacked the drama and the strife that were part and parcel of Oz's life experiences" ("Secularity and Religiosity" 69–70).

14. Balaban aptly observes how the two men "move in opposite directions: one moves outward from inside the circle, the other moves from the darkness beyond the circle inward toward the center. . . . In contrast to Yonatan, born on the kibbutz, trying to uproot himself from the soil of his homeland, Azariah, the persecuted refugee, wants to take root in that soil" *(Between God and Beast* 216–17).

15. For a comprehensive discussion of these issues, see Zvi Lavi, ed., *Kibbutz Members Study Kibbutz Children.*

16. The psalm reads, "I shall raise my eyes to the mountains whence shall come my help. My help comes from the Lord, the Creator of heaven and earth."

17. Interestingly, Almog observes that among the early Zionist youth marches, "the jewels in the crown . . . were the ones to Petra in Jordan. These became a kind of Sabra sport, a covert competition for breaking records of difficulty and danger" (183).

18. Here I vigorously dissent from Balaban's otherwise astute analysis for his utopian reading of Oz's representation of the kibbutzniks' relation to this disturbing site of absence: "the members of the kibbutz have a strange longing for the world of the Bible and its relics, apparently hidden in the abandoned Arab village [which] exhibits . . . a primal autochthonous essence, which umbilically binds them to the earth, uniting them with the primary, Biblical world " (*Between God and Beast* 119). This interpretation betrays Oz's ironic tone and distinct political critique of the Zionist settlers' nostalgia.

19. Elsewhere, Azariah, whose outsider status is accentuated when the reader learns he is a Holocaust survivor, denounces the young men of the kibbutz "who do nothing all day but talk about killing the Arabs. This is a snake pit, not a country. A jungle, not a commune. Death, not Zionism" (289).

20. It is as if Oz had this very character and scene in mind when he commented to an interviewer that "there will always be the fascination of blood and fire and death, and the enchantment of something bigger than life that you can melt into, and all your toil and tribulation will be swallowed by it and you'll be consumed in the flames. I always see this enchantment—always from afar. One must not get close." See "Amos Oz Talks about Amos Oz" 174.

21. Amos Oz, "The Quality of Equality," Center for Kibbutz Studies, Overseas Department of the United Kibbutz Movement. The essay was reprinted in the *Greater Phoenix Jewish Times,* Phoenix, Arizona (September 17, 1986), 15.

22. Even the graveyard of Sheikh Dahr, which ostensibly tests Yonatan's resolve and Zionism's self-satisfaction earlier in the novel, is symbolically erased by the forces of time and entropy: "In the courtyards of the Arab village the bougainvillea blazed through the stones, wild grape vines inched their tendrils up the smashed archways, acacia trees spread a fragrance"; as for Udi, his atrocious scheme to dig up a skeleton from the Arab graveyard and turn it into a scarecrow is forgotten in the harmonious and breezy resolution of the novel (344).

23. Even the title presumes this teleology: *A Perfect Peace* is a phrase from the Jewish service for the dead, strongly suggesting that Oz views his hero's quest for an alternative identity as a moribund illusion from the outset. Another popular Israeli novel written in the same period that presents the deserter theme is Yehoshua's novel *The Lover* (1977), in which Gabriel, a young man living in France, returns home to claim an inheritance, only to be conscripted into the Yom Kippur War. And in Oz's own *Elsewhere, Perhaps* (1973), originally entitled *Makom Acher* (*Sifriat Hapoalim* [1966]), a desertion of a poet by his wife is similarly resolved, in Oz's words, "with the formation of an unlikely extended family . . . a kind of comprehensive family of potential enemies" as if the prospect of a character being left permanently outside of the narrative of the collective is a paradigm the novelist (who acknowledges that desertion, or rather its resolution, is a theme that runs throughout his work) would rather not contemplate ("Amos Oz Talks about Amos Oz" 186).

24. Here I obviously diverge from Balaban's reading that from the journey to Petra, the hero no longer seeks "complete liberation from the restraints of culture and consciousness," but embraces "the acceptance of life in its full reality" (*Between God and Beast* 126).

25. In a rare moment of candor, Oz once remarked of being torn by his characters' own desires, who he often has stated have lives that elude his authorial control: "Most of the people I wrote stories about are 'relatives' of mine. We have many things in common, but most of them believe in things that I don't believe in. They believe in happiness. They want eternal love and absolute justice and freedom at all cost." Oz, perhaps wearing the skeptical mask of the postmodern literary luminary, says that "[t]hese are things I don't believe in," but nonetheless he concludes candidly that "[t]here is great seduction in them, and I am easily seduced." See "Amos Oz Talks about Amos Oz" 171.

26. Ironically, Alex Gideon, the political scientist who is the central character of Oz's epistolary novel *Black Box* (*Kufsah shehorah*), observes in his unpublished study of politics and violence: "The self—the focus of suffering. Redemption—annihilation of the self. Complete absorption in the masses" (175).

27. Indeed, Oz seems to ironically anticipate the reader's expectation of Yonatan's dramatic transformation in the way that other characters superficially perceive him: "He had grown a beard, turned brown and lean as a Bedouin" (369) and "resembled a young scholar of proud old rabbinical stock who was studying to become a rabbi" (370).

Chapter 4: Immobilized Rebels on the Outskirts of the Promised Land

1. Cited passages of Bialik's epic poem come from Ruth Nevo's unrivaled translation in Hayim Nahman Bialik, *Selected Poems.* My reading of Bialik's reworking of his source material is indebted to Ilana Pardes's insightful observations in *The Biography of Ancient Israel* 122–25, as well as Robert Alter's fine discussion in *Canon and Creativity* 114–149.

2. The talmudic reference may be found in B. Baba Ratha 74a.

3. The translation is Ruth Nevo's in *Chaim Nachman Bialik: Selected Poems* 109.

4. See Ariel Hirschfeld's illuminating explication of this countertradition in "Locus and Language" 1016.

5. David Grossman, "Seven Days: A Diary," *Death as a Way of Life* 145.

6. *Yani on the Mountain* was originally published as "*Yani b'Harim*" in *Ratz,* by David Grossman (Tel Aviv: Hakibbutz Hameuchad, 1983) and was translated by Dalya Bilu for *Six Israeli Novellas,* edited by Gershon Shaked.

7. To commemorate the twentieth anniversary of the Six-Day War and Israel's subsequent occupation of the Palestinian territories, the editor of the leftist *Koteret Rashit* sent the young, unknown writer to explore the troubled relations of its Jewish and Arab inhabitants. Arguably, without this unprecedented work of journalism, Grossman would be a little-known figure outside of Israel; it was on the strength of a serialized translation in *The New Yorker* that American publishers began to express interest in Grossman's fiction. Today *The Yellow Wind* is considered essential reading for any introduction to the Israel-Arab dispute.

8. Perhaps Grossman's character bears some degree of comparison with Alex Gideon, the friendless academic of Amos Oz's *Black Box,* who, at the end of his life recalls his military career in the Sinai desert as the most memorable of his life: "the most electric moments in my life were spent in the desert, charging and trampling under my tracks all that lay in my path, smashing with my gunfire whatever displayed signs of life, raising columns of fire and smoke . . . shaking the whole world with the roar of thirty engines" (93). In Oz's portrayal of Gideon's mournful imagination, the engines of war that electrified him as a soldier ironically occupy the place of the divine pillars of smoke and fire that led the Israelites in the wilderness. Years later, this aging university professor, now living in Chicago, imagines the violent display of a summer thunderstorm "as though my tank battles are pursuing me here all the way from the Sinai" (93). However, Grossman's character has dug himself into an underground lair that exceeds that of Oz's protagonist.

9. See Frankel and Teutsch, *Encyclopedia of Jewish Symbols,* 192.

10. In a recent interview for the left-leaning Israeli daily *Haaretz,* Grossman admonishes his fellow citizens "to ensure that not all our energies are diverted solely to building this armor that protects us from the outside. Because right now the feeling is that we are so focused on the armor that there is no human being left inside. My dream is for it to contain a human being. That the life here will be the life of human beings" (Shavit 7). It is striking that in another interview he remarks that in the process of writing "a novel, you must deconstruct yourself pitilessly, and disarm yourself from the defense mechanisms you laboriously built for so many years. From novel to novel, the defense filters that guard my emotions disappear, I become exposed and vulnerable" (Negev 37).

11. This incident seems nakedly autobiographical; Grossman once told an interviewer that he first began to have a terrifying awareness of death, the knowledge that everyone dies, at four years old: "It scared me terribly, and since then I've been living with a constant awareness of death. I live as if I'll die tomorrow. . . . I'm stingy with my time, which makes me unbearable in the eyes of many people. We're emerging out of a darkness of a million years, then there's a short flash of light and then we sink again into eternal darkness." But along with this morbidity, Grossman acknowledges that such awareness seems to be a boon to his art: "Finality is a very rich fuel" (Negev 142).

12. In my reading, both Oz's and Grossman's protagonists strikingly conform to Balaban's analysis of those of Amalia Kahana-Carmon's novels, who, when the reader first encounters them, "typically" embody a "state of death-in-life. The new human contact that the protagonists establish helps restore them back to life, alluding thereby to a possible connection with a transcendental sphere" ("Secularity and Religiosity" 67).

Chapter 5: Sinai of the Diasporic Imagination

1. For additional worthy and representative examples of this growing genre, see Deena Metzger's *What Dinah Thought* (New York: Viking, 1989), Anita Diamant's *The Red Tent* (New York: Picador, 1998) and Marek Halter's *Sarah* (New York: Crown, 2004).

2. *Philadelphia Inquirer* and *Kirkus Reviews,* quoted on the flyleaf of the first edition.

3. One of the most infamous figures of the Five Books of Moses; the earth is said to have opened up and swallowed Korah as well as his followers when he challenged the authority of Moses and Aaron in the wilderness (Num. 16:17).

4. Zelitch seems to have in mind the description of a "great and terrible wilderness, an arid wasteland with poisonous snakes and scorpions" in Deuteronomy 8:15.

5. My analysis of Zelitch's violent and indifferent desert is much informed by B. Jill Carroll's argument in *The Savage Side: Reclaiming Violent Models of God.* Carroll offers a strong defense of the Jewish philosopher Emmanuel Levinas, as well as the Pulitzer Prize–winning author Annie Dillard, against "the models of God that have emerged from a dominant strand of contemporary religious thought," which she decries as "reductionist, utilitarian, and domesticate the concept of 'God.'" In place of "God as mother, lover, and friend," she proposes that we come to terms with a model that resists "the violence" "committed by feminist theologians against deity by domesticating deity" that would necessarily acknowledge that "if nature is to be seen as in any way representative of deity . . . then the beautiful *and* the horrifying aspects of nature are to be considered in constructing the doctrine of God" (1, 3–4).

6. Cf. Hareven's female character Moran in "After Childhood": "She would rather God stayed away from her. Let him ignore her in his heaven, because the gods burned all when they came. They brought death and sickness and madness and drought. It's all we can do to make good what they ruin" (183).

7. For an exemplary reading in this mode, see Yaira Amit, *Hidden Polemics in Biblical Narrative* (Boston: Brill Academic Publishers, 1998).

8. By this phrase I intend to stress the immediacy of community that would be the likely outcome of a prolonged wilderness sojourn rather than the abstraction of a nationalist identity. As esteemed biblical archeologist Yohanan Aharoni speculates: "The long line of march according to Numbers 33 summarizes the extended period of wanderings in a geographical annotation, but one need not assume that it reflects a single and unified historical journey. A large number of men could not have existed in the southern deserts in one assembled group, but rather they were forced to scatter with their herds . . . over a wide area, just as the Bedouin are accustomed to doing today" (200). Hence it seems apt that the desert experience that Zelitch (like Hareven) portrays is not really a time of cohesion and cultural homogeneity but rather nomadism.

9. Edmond Jabès's major works include the seven-volume *Livre des Questions* (1963–1973) and the three-volume *Livre des Ressemblances* (1976–1980). I rely throughout this discussion on Rosmarie Waldrop's splendid translations.

10. For a striking comparison, consider the Jewish Romanian writer Norman Manea's summing up of his family's diasporic fate in the nightmare of the twentieth century: "Now she [his mother] resides on a hilltop in Suceava, and her husband is dying in Jerusalem. A grave for their son awaits him in the nondenominational cemetery of Bard college" (quoted in Redlich B4).

11. Jabès, "This Is the Desert, Nothing Strikes Root Here," 252.

12. Similarly, in an interview with Bracha Ettinger Lichtenberg, he recalls coming into realization "that the Jew's real place is the book. In the book he questions himself, in the book he has his freedom, which has been forbidden him everywhere. . . . Moses, in the act of breaking the tablets, gave the word a human origin" (Jabès, "This is the Desert, Nothing Strikes Root Here, 248, 250).

13. I am indebted to Gary Mole's insightful argument that Moses' breaking of the tablets provides Jabès with the aesthetics—and ethics—of fragmentary writing: "By conceiving of the breaking of the tablets . . . in terms of the dialectic of creation (the book) and destruction (silence), where the destruction of the book (the law) is situated by the chosen people, Jabès would also suggest that Moses himself is subverted by the Jewish people, taught a lesson that nothing can precede writing . . . the people have the freedom to read the book that dictates laws that are undermined by interpretation" (86).

14. Emmanuel Levinas, *Difficile liberté: Essais sur le judaisme* (Paris: Ėditions Albin Michel, 1963), 165.

Chapter 6: Wilderness as Experience and Metaphor

1. Yizhar's earliest work is infused by the landscape of arid southland where he was raised in prestate Palestine. His magnum opus, *Yemei Tsiklag* (The Days of Ziklag, 1958), explores the physical and metaphysical ordeal of soldiers taking an enemy stronghold in the Negev during the War of Independence.

2. Erlich further observes the consequences of diasporic anxiety for the peculiar cultural forms of Jewish nation building: "The new campus of the Hebrew University is constructed as a hilltop fortress enclosed within walls, as are many Jerusalem structures. The pre-state Jewish settlements, built clandestinely in defiance of the British mandate's censure and opposition, were part of an era and ethos of resettling the land aptly termed 'Wall and Tower'" (15).

3. Significantly, though Shelach's entire family was killed by an Egyptian soldier while vacationing at the Ras Burqa beach on the Sinai coast in an infamous incident October 1985, he makes no reference of any kind to that event, as if wary of further contributing to the memory of an event that continues to polarize Arabs and Jews skeptical about a lasting peace between Egypt and Israel.

4. In Israeli cinema, bold visual articulations of this relationship can also be witnessed in films such as *Hamsin* (Daniel Wachsman, 1982), *The Smile of the Lamb* (Shimon Dotan, 1986), *Avanti Popolo* (Rafi Bukai, 1986), and *God's Sandbox* (Doron Eran, 2002), which explores the power relations between Arabs and Jews in a mystical desert landscape.

5. Perhaps in part this is the writers' response to the overdetermined nature of the Zionist possession of the Negev through language. As Attias and Benbassa point out, though Israel's desert is largely "devoid of a historic tradition," in the early years of statehood, "Hebrew names were given to some 533 geographic sites, between Eilat in the south and the Ein Gedi-Gaza line in the north. Of these, 120 took historical names and 50 were named after biblical characters; for the remainder, Arab names were translated. . . . The language of the Bible . . . thus redeemed and sanctified everything that could not be inserted into historical continuity. It purified the land and guaranteed its conquest via naming, as if physical conquest could not suffice" (167).

6. Personal communication. See also Keys 13.

7. On the other hand, early Zionist culture, so committed to settling the land, often succumbed to binary oppositions. Early Zionist films often portrayed Arab villages as essentially desert, in contrast to the green orchards and fields of the young kibbutzim, as if the natives had no agriculture of their own. For an excel-

lent critique of this dichotomy, see Ne'eman, "The Jar and the Blade: Fertility Myth and Medieval Romance in Israeli Political Films."

8. Here I am much taken by Robert Alter's extended analysis of Judaism's unease with the spiritually eviscerating encroachment of the urban in his *Canon and Creativity:*

> Kafka's reading [of Genesis's story of the Tower of Babel] embraces a second urgent theme of the original biblical story—its antiurbanism. The ancient Hebrew writer, from his perspective in a little nation of pastoralists and agriculturalists, viewed the urban concentration of power, technology, and population of the great surrounding empires as an expression of humankind's morally dangerous grandiosity. Kafka, writing in an urban and technological environment three millennia removed from the setting of Genesis 11, shares this fundamental perception of the biblical text. Indeed, he amplifies its resonance by concluding his reflection on an apocalyptic note: the intolerable conflicts of urban existence engender a longing for release through destruction, "for a prophesied day when the city would be destroyed by five successive blows from a gigantic fist." (The image of the menacing clenched fist, no doubt psychologically derived from the looming power of the paternal body, is quintessential Kafka.) In this fashion the biblical Babel, upon which modern Prague or any counterpart elsewhere in Europe has been superimposed, also becomes a medieval city that "has a closed fist on its coat of arms." The paradoxical effect is that the authority of the canonical text, its universal relevance, is confirmed even as it is drastically revised.

9. Goren also makes memorable appearances in Lesley Hazelton's wonderful *Where Mountains Roar: A Personal Report from the Sinai and Negev Deserts.*

10. For an overview of this trend, see Shapira, *Routes of Wandering: Nomadism, Voyages and Transitions in Contemporary Israeli Art.*

11. With a steely resistance to sentimentalizing even her own experience of living many years in complete acceptance among the Mzeina tribe, Lavie concludes: "After all, we are but trivial beings who disintegrate into small particles in the shadow of the Arab-Israeli conflict" (*Poetics of Military Occupation* 289).

12. As early as Theodor Herzl's 1902 utopian-futurist novel *Altneuland,* Zionist dreamers and planners have envisioned the Jordan River's potential for providing water to the arid regions of the country and even more grandiose projects such as a canal from the Mediterranean Sea which, dropping to the lowest spot on the planet, the Dead Sea, would drive massive electrical turbines. Ben-Gurion's ambition to create a green Negev motivated numerous Israelis' personal dreams and settlement projects.

13. In late 2003, the founder of the group, Matan Dahan, reported that the $7 million project had received two-thirds of its support from the government and the Jewish Agency and that additional villages for young people in the Negev were in the planning stage. See Friedman 60.

14. Attias and Benbassa observe how "Passover in the spring commemorates the exodus from Egypt. [Shavuot], fifty days later, commemorates the giving of the Law at Sinai. The Festival of Booths (Sukkoth) at the start of autumn is meant to lead to a rediscovery of the precariousness of life in the desert . . . for seven days, Israel must quit its stone houses and live in tents, in remembrance of the tents God gave the Hebrews as homes when they left Egypt" (19).

WORKS CITED

Adorno, Theodor. *Minima Moralia: Reflections from Damaged Life.* London: New Left Books, 1951.

Aharoni, Yohanan. *The Archaeology of the Land of Israel: From the Prehistoric Beginnings to the End of the First Temple Period.* London: Westminster Press, 1982.

Alcalay, Ammiel. *After Jews and Arabs: Remaking Levantine Culture.* Minneapolis: University of Minnesota Press, 1993.

Almog, Oz. *The Sabra: The Creation of the New Jew.* Translated by Haim Watzman. Berkeley: University of California Press, 2000.

Alter, Robert. *Canon and Creativity: Modern Writing and the Authority of Scripture.* London: Yale University Press, 2000.

———. ed. *Modern Hebrew Literature.* West Orange, N.J.: Behrman House, 1975.

Amichai, Yehuda. "Interview." In Joseph Cohen, *Voices of Israel: Essays on and Interviews with Yehuda Amichai, A.B. Yehoshua, T. Carmi, Aharon Appelfeld, and Amos Oz.* Albany: State University of New York Press, 1990.

Arendt, Hannah. *Eichmann in Jerusalem: A Report on the Banality of Evil.* London: Penguin Books, 1994.

Aschkenasy, Nehama. "Deconstructing the Metanarrative: Amos Oz's Evolving Discourse With the Bible." *Symposium.* 55.3. Fall 2001: 123–34.

Attias, Jean-Christophe, and Esther Benbassa. *Israel, the Impossible Land.* Translated by Susan Emanuel. Stanford, Calif.: Stanford University Press, 2003.

Auster, Paul. "An Interview with Edmond Jabès." *The Sin of the Book: Edmond Jabès.* Edited by Eric Gould. Lincoln: University of Nebraska Press, 1985, 3–25.

———. "Introduction." *Edmond Jabès. If There Were Anywhere but Desert:* viii–xiv.

———. *The Invention of Solitude.* New York: Penguin, 1998.

Bachelard, Gaston. *The Poetics of Space.* Translated by Maria Jolas. New York: Orion Press, 1964.

Balaban, Avraham. *Between God and Beast: An Examination of Amos Oz's Prose.* University Park, Pa.: Pennsylvania State University Press, 1993.

———. "Secularity and Religiosity in Contemporary Hebrew Literature." *Middle Eastern Literatures.* 15.1. 2002: 63–79.

Baring, Anne, and Jules Cashford. *The Myth of the Goddess: Evolution of an Image.* London: Viking Arkana, 1991.

Ben-Ari, Eyal, and Yoram Bilu, eds. *Grasping Land: Space and Place in Contemporary Israeli Discourse and Experience.* Albany: State University of New York Press, 1997.

Ben-David, Orit. "*Tiyul* (Hike) as an Act of Consecration of Space." In Eyal Ben-Ari and Yoram Bilu, eds., *Grasping Land: Space and Place in Contemporary Israeli Discourse and Experience*, 129–45.

Ben-Ezer, Ehud. ed. *Sleepwalkers and Other Stories: The Arab in Hebrew Fiction.* London: Lynne Rienner Publishers, 1999.

Ben-Gurion, Aryeh, ed. *Al tishlakh yadkha el hanaar: Shirim vedivrei hagut al haakeda.* Tel Aviv: Keter Publishing House, 2002.

Ben-Simon, Daniel. "Deserted Dreams." *Haaretz,* May 7, 2003.

Berger, Harry Jr. "The Lie of the Land: Text Beyond Canaan." *Representations* 25. Winter 1989: 119–38.

Berkowitz, Matthew and Miriam. "Isaac's Statesmanship." *The Jerusalem Report.* December 1, 2003: 27.

Biale, David. *Eros and the Jews: From Biblical Israel to Contemporary America.* New York: Basic Books, 1992.

Bialik, Hayim Nahman. *Chaim Nachman Bialik: Selected Poems.* Translated by Ruth Nevo. Jerusalem: Dvir, 1981.

———. "Revealment and Concealment in Language." In *Modern Hebrew Literature,* edited by Robert Alter. New York: Behrman House, 1975.

Bilu, Yoram. With Eliezer Witztum. "War-Related Loss and Suffering in Israeli Society: An Historical Perspective." *Israel Studies* 5.2. 2000: 1–31.

Blanchot, Maurice. *L'Entretien infini.* Paris: Gallimard, 1969.

———. *L'Espace littéraire.* Paris: Gallimard, 1986.

———. *The Space of Literature.* Translated by Ann Smock. Lincoln: University of Nebraska Press: 1982.

Boyarin, Daniel. *Intertextuality and the Reading of Midrash.* Bloomington: Indiana University Press, 1990.

Boyarin, Jonathan. "In Search of 'Israeli Identity': Anecdotes and Afterthoughts." In *Palestine and Jewish History: Criticism at the Borders of Ethnography.* Minneapolis: University of Minnesota Press, 1996.

———. "Ruins, Mounting Toward Jerusalem." In *Wrestling with Zion: Progressive Jewish-American Responses to the Israeli-Palestinian Conflict,* edited by Tony Kushner and Alisa Solomon. New York: Grove Press, 2003, 323–36.

Brenner, Athalya. *A Feminist Companion to Exodus-Deuteronomy*. Sheffield, England: Sheffield Academic Press, 1994.

Brenner, Rachel Feldhay. "'Hidden Transcripts' Made Public: Israeli Arab Fiction and Its Reception." *Critical Inquiry* 26. Autumn 1999: 85–108.

———. *Inextricably Bonded: Israeli and Jewish Writers Re-Visioning Culture.* Madison: University of Wisconsin Press, 2003.

Brubacher, Gordon. "Desert." In *Eerdmans Dictionary of the Bible,* edited by David Noel Freedman, Allen C. Myers, and Astrid B. Beck. Cambridge: William B. Eerdman's Publishing Company, 2000, 338–40.

Brueggemann, Walter. "Trajectories in Old Testament Literature and the Sociology of Ancient Israel." In *The Bible and Liberation: Political and Social Hermeneutics,* edited by Norman K. Gottwald and Richard A. Horsley. Maryknoll, N.Y.: Orbis, 1993, 201–26.

Butler, Judith. *Bodies That Matter: On the Discursive Limits of "Sex."* New York: Routledge, 1993.

Carroll, B. Jill. *The Savage Side: Reclaiming Violent Models of God.* New York: Rowman & Littlefield, 2001.

Carson, Luke. *Consumption and Depression in Gertrude Stein, Louis Zukofsky and Ezra Pound.* New York: St. Martin's Press, 1999.

Chateaubriand, François-René de. *Oeuvres romanesques et voyages.* Vol. 2. Edited by Maurice Regard. Paris: Gallimard, 1969.

Chevalier, Jean, and Alain Gheerbrant. *Dictionaire des symbols II.* Paris: Seghers, 1974.

Childs, Craig. *Soul of Nowhere: Traversing Grace in a Rugged Land.* Seattle, Wash.: Sasquatch Books, 2002.

Cohen, Joseph. *Voices of Israel: Essays on and Interviews with Yehuda Amichai, A. B. Yehoshua, T. Carmi, Aharon Appelfeld, and Amos Oz.* Albany: State University of New York Press, 1990.

Cohen, Josh. "Desertions: Paul Auster, Edmond Jabès, and the Writing of Auschwitz." *Journal of the Midwest Modern Language Association* 3.1. Fall 2001: 95–107.

Cousineau, Thomas J. *Ritual Unbound: Reading Sacrifice in Modernist Fiction.* Newark: University of Delaware Press, 2004.

Diamond, James S. "The Post-Secular: A Jewish Perspective." *CrossCurrents.* Winter 2004: 580–606.

Dillard, Annie. *Holy the Firm.* New York: Harper and Row, 1977.

———. *Pilgrim at Tinker Creek.* New York: Harper and Row, 1974.

Disraeli, Benjamin. *Tancred, or The New Crusade.* 2 vols. London: 1847.

Duncan, Robert. "Afterword." In Edmond Jabès, *If There Were Anywhere but Desert: The Selected Poems of Edmond Jabès,* 105–24.

Edwards, Diane T. "From Garden to City: Closure in the Bible." In *Mappings of the Biblical Terrain: The Bible as Text,* edited by Vincent L. Tollers and John Maier. Lewisburg, Pa.: Bucknell University Press, 1990, 102–17.

Erlich, Shmuel. "In Keeping Terrorists Out, Security Fences Israelis In." *Forward.* September 12, 2003: 15.

Ezrahi, Sidra DeKoven. *Booking Passage: Exile and Homecoming in the Modern Jewish Imagination.* Los Angeles: University of California Press, 2000.

———. "Sacred Space." *Tikkun.* January/February 2002: 19–20.

Feiler, Bruce. *Walking the Bible: A Journey by Land through the Five Books of Moses.* New York: HarperCollins, 2001.

Feldman, Yael S. *No Room of Their Own: Gender and Nation in Israeli Women's Fiction.* New York: Columbia University Press, 1999.

Frankel, Ellen, and Betsy Platkin Teutsch. *The Encyclopedia of Jewish Symbols.* London: Jason Aronson, 1992.

Friedman, Matti. "'If Young People Don't Do It, No One Will.'" *The Jerusalem Report.* December 29, 2003: 60.

Fuchs, Esther. *Encounters with Israeli Authors.* Marblehead, Mass.: Michah Publications, 1982.

Garfinkle, Adam M. "On the Origin, Meaning, Use, and Abuse of a Phrase." *Middle Eastern Studies* 27. October 1991: 539–550.

Gertz, Nurith. "From Jew to Hebrew: The 'Zionist Narrative' in the Israeli Cinema of the 1940s and 1950s." In *In Search of Identity: Jewish Aspects in Israeli Culture,* edited by Dan Urian and Efraim Karsh. London: Frank Cass, 1999, 175–99.

———. "Space and Gender in the New Israeli and Palestinian Cinema." *Prooftexts* 22. 1/2. Winter/Spring 2002: 157–85.

Gilad, Moshe. "Starry Skies and Wide Open Spaces." *Haaretz.* May 7, 2003.
Gover, Yerach. *Zionism: The Limits of Moral Discourse in Israeli Hebrew Fiction.* Minneapolis: University of Minnesota Press, 1994.
Grossman, David. *Death as a Way of Life: Israel Ten Years After Oslo.* Translated by Haim Watzman. New York: Farrar, Straus and Giroux, 2003.
———. "Fictions Embraced by an Israel at War." *New York Times.* October 1, 2002.
———. *Someone to Run With.* Translated by Vered Almog and Maya Gurantz. New York: Farrar, Straus and Giroux, 2004.
———. *Yani on the Mountain.* Translated by Dalya Bilu. In *Six Israeli Novellas,* edited by Gershon Shaked. Boston: Verba Mundi 1999.
Gurevitch, Zali. "The Double Site of Israel." In Eyal Ben-Ari and Yoram Bilu, eds., *Grasping Land: Space and Place in Contemporary Israeli Discourse and Experience,* 203–16.
Handelman, Susan A. *Fragments of Redemption: Jewish Thought and Literary Theory in Benjamin, Scholem, and Levinas.* Bloomington: Indiana University Press, 1991.
———. "'Torments of an Ancient Word': Edmond Jabès and the Rabbinic Tradition." In *The Sin of the Book: Edmond Jabès,* edited by Eric Gould, 1985. 55–91.
Hareven, Shulamith. *Thirst: The Desert Trilogy.* Translated by Hillel Halkin. San Francisco: Mercury House, 1996.
———. *The Vocabulary of Peace: Life, Culture, and Politics in the Middle East.* San Francisco: Mercury House, 1995.
Hazelton, Lesley. *Where Mountains Roar: A Personal Report from the Sinai and Negev Deserts.* New York: Holt, Rinehart, Winston, 1980.
Heschel, Abraham Joshua. *The Sabbath: Its Meaning for Modern Man.* New York: Farrar, Straus and Giroux, 1951.
Hirschfeld, Ariel. "Locus and Language: Hebrew Culture in Israel, 1890–1990." In *Cultures of the Jews: A New History,* edited by David Biale. New York: Schocken Books, 2002. 1011–60.
Holtzman, Avner. "Fima mekhake l'nes." (Fima waits for a miracle). Hebrew. *Haaretz.* February 15, 1991.
Jabès, Edmond. *The Book of Dialogue.* Translated by Rosmarie Waldrop. Middletown, Conn.: Wesleyan University Press, 1987.
———. *The Book of Margins.* Translated by Rosmarie Waldrop. Chicago: University of Chicago Press, 1993.
———. *The Book of Questions: The Book of Questions; The Book of Yukel: Return to the Book.* Translated by Rosmarie Waldrop. Middletown, Conn.: Wesleyan University Press, 1991.
———. *The Book of Questions: Yael Elya Aely El, or the Last Book.* Vols. 1 and 2. Translated by Rosmarie Waldrop. Middletown, Conn.: Wesleyan University Press, 1991.
———. *The Book of Resemblances: The Ineffaceable, the Unperceived.* Translated by Rosmarie Waldrop. Middletown, Conn.: Wesleyan University Press, 2000.
———. *The Book of Shares.* Translated by Rosmarie Waldrop. Chicago: University of Chicago Press, 1989.
———. *From the Book to the Book: An Edmond Jabès Reader.* Translated by Rosmarie Waldrop. Middletown, Conn.: Wesleyan University Press, 1991.

———. *From the Desert to the Book: Dialogues with Marcel Cohen.* Barrytown, N.Y.: Station Hill Press, 1990.

———. *If There Were Anywhere but Desert: The Selected Poems of Edmond Jabès.* Translated by Keith Waldrop. Introduction by Paul Auster. Afterword by Robert Duncan. Barrytown, N.Y.: Station Hill Press, 1988.

———. "An Interview with Edmond Jabès Conducted by Jason Wiess." *Conjunctions* 9. 1986: 140–41.

———. *Le Parcours.* Paris: Gallimard, 1985.

———. *Le Livre de Yukel.* Paris: Gallimard, 1964.

———. *The Sin of the Book: Edmond Jabès.* Edited by Eric Gould. Lincoln: University of Nebraska Press, 1985.

———. "This Is the Desert, Nothing Strikes Root Here: A Talk with Bracha Lichtenberg Ettinger." In *Maslulei nedudim,* edited by Sarit Shapira. Exhibition Catalogue. Jerusalem: Israel Museum, 1991.

Jacobson, David C. *Modern Midrash: The Retelling of Traditional Jewish Narratives by Twentieth-Century Hebrew Writers.* Albany: State University of New York Press, 1987.

JPS Hebrew English Tanakh: The Traditional Hebrew Text and the New JPS Translation. Second Edition. Philadelphia: The Jewish Publication Society, 1999.

Kartun-Blum, Ruth. *Profane Scriptures: Reflections on the Dialogue with the Bible in Modern Hebrew Poetry.* Cincinnati, Ohio: Hebrew Union College Press, 1999.

Kenan, Amos. "Interview with Dan Omer." *Prozah.* August–September 1977: 4–13.

Keys, Lisa. "Off the Beaten Trail, Adventurers Seek Out a Rocky Mountain *Chai.*" *Forward.* December 27, 2002: 1, 13.

Kluback, William. *Edmond Jabès: The Poetry of the Nomad.* New York: Peter Lang, 1998.

Kunitz, Stanley. *The Testing Tree.* Boston: Little Brown, 1971.

Lane, Belden C. *The Solace of Fierce Landscapes: Exploring Desert and Mountain Spirituality.* Oxford: Oxford University Press, 1998.

Lavi, Zvi, ed. *Kibbutz Members Study Kibbutz Children.* New York: Greenwood Press, 1990.

Lavie, Smadar. "Blowups in the Borderzones: Third World Israeli Authors' Gropings for Home." In *Displacement, Diaspora, and Geographies of Identity,* edited by Smadar Lavie and Ted Swedenburg. Durham, N.C.: Duke University Press, 1996, 55–96.

———. *The Poetics of Military Occupation: Mzeina Allegories of Bedouin Identity Under Israeli and Egyptian Rule.* Los Angeles, University of California Press, 1990.

Lazarus, Josephine. "Zionism and Americanism." *Menorah: A Monthly Magazine for the Jewish Home.* May 1905: 262–68.

Leveen, Adriane, "Falling in the Wilderness: Death Reports in the Book of Numbers." *Prooftexts: a Journal of Jewish Literary History.* 22.3. Fall 2002: 245–72.

Levenson, Jon D. *Sinai and Zion: An Entry Into the Jewish Bible.* Minneapolis, Minn.: Winston Press, 1985.

Levinas, Emmanuel. *Difficile liberté: Essais sur le judaisme.* Paris: Editions Albin Michel, 1963.

———. *Du sacré au saint. Cinq nouvelles lectures talmudiques.* Paris: Minuit, 1977.

———. *En découvrant l'existence avec Husserl et Heidegger.* Paris: Vrin, 1988.

———. "Meaning and Sense." In *Collected Philosophical Papers.* Translated by Alphonso Lingis. Dordrecht: Martines Nijhoff Publishers, 1987.

———. "The Trace of the Other." In *Deconstruction in Context: Literature and Philosophy,* edited by Mark C. Taylor. Chicago: University of Chicago Press, 1986.

Lichtenberg, Bracha Ettinger. "'This is the desert. Nothing strikes root here': A Talk with Edmond Jabès." In *Routes of Wandering: Nomadism, Voyages and Transitions in Contemporary Israeli Art.* Israel Museum: Jerusalem, 1991, 246–56.

Lindqvist, Sven. *Desert Divers.* Translated by Joan Tate. London: Granta Books, 2002.

Loshitzky, Yosefa. *Identity Politics on the Israeli Screen.* Austin: University of Texas Press, 2001.

Luz, Ehud. *Wrestling with an Angel: Power, Morality, and Jewish Identity.* Translated by Michael Swirsky. New Haven, Conn., and London: Yale University Press, 2003.

Mares, Michael A. *A Desert Calling: Life in a Forbidding Landscape.* Cambridge, Mass.: Harvard University Press, 2002.

Mazor, Yair. *Somber Lust: The Art of Amos Oz.* Translated by Marganit Weinberger-Rotman. Albany: State University of New York Press, 2002.

McClung, William A. *The Architecture of Paradise: Survivals of Eden and Jerusalem.* Berkeley: University of California Press, 1983.

Minh-ha, Trinh. "Cotton and Iron." In *Out There: Marginalization and Contemporary Cultures,* edited by Russell Ferguson, Martha Gever, Trinh T. Minh-ha, and Cornel West. New York: The New Museum of Contemporary Art, 1990, 327–35.

Mintz, Alan. *Reading Hebrew Literature: Critical Discussions of Six Modern Texts.* Hanover, N.H., and London: Brandeis University Press/University Press of New England, 2003.

Mitchell, W. J. T. "Imperial Landscape." In *Landscape and Power,* edited by W. J. T. Mitchell. Chicago: University of Chicago Press, 1994, 5–34.

Mole, Gary D. *Levinas, Blanchot, Jabès: Figures of Estrangement.* Miami: University Press of Florida, 1997.

Morrow, Susan Brind. *The Names of Things: Life, Language and Beginning in the Egyptian Desert.* New York: Riverhead Books, 1997.

Motte, Warren F. Jr. *Questioning Edmond Jabès.* Lincoln: University of Nebraska Press, 1990.

Nadel, Alan. "A Whole New (Disney) World Order." In *Visions of the East: Orientalism in Film,* edited by Matthew Bernstein and Gaylyn Studlar. New Brunswick, N.J.: Rutgers University Press, 1997: 184–203.

Nash, Stanley. "Character Portrayal and Cultural Critique in Shulamit Hareven's Work." *Modern Judaism* 16. 1996: 215–28.

Ne'eman, Judd. "The Jar and the Blade: Fertility Myth and Medieval Romance in Israeli Political Films." *Prooftexts* 22. 2002: 141–56.

Negev, Eilat. *Close Encounters with Twenty Israeli Writers.* London: Vallentine Mitchell, 2003.

Niditch, Susan. *Ancient Israelite Religion.* Oxford: Oxford University Press, 1997.

Ondaatje, Michael. *The English Patient.* New York: Vintage, 1992.

Orpaz, Yitzhak. *The Secular Pilgrim.* Tel Aviv: Hakibbutz Hameuchad, 1982.

Ouaknin, Marc-Alain. *The Burnt Book: Reading the Talmud.* Translated by Llewellyn Brown. Princeton, N.J.: Princeton University Press, 1995.

Oz, Amos. "Amos Oz Talks about Amos Oz: 'Being I, Plus Being Myself'—An Interview with Hillit Yeshourun." In Yair Mazor, *Somber Lust: The Art of Amos Oz.* Albany: State University of New York Press, 2002: 159–94.

———. *Black Box.* New York: Random House, 1988.

———. *Don't Call It Night.* Translated by Nicholas de Lange. New York: Harcourt Brace & Company, 1994.

———. *Panther in the Basement.* Translated by Nicholas de Lange. New York: Harcourt Brace & Company, 1998.

———. *A Perfect Peace.* Translated by Hillel Halkin. New York: Harcourt Brace Jovanovich, 1985.

———. *A Tale of Love and Darkness.* Translated by Nicholas de Lange. Harcourt Brace & Company, 2004.

———. *Under This Blazing Light.* Translated by Nicholas de Lange. Cambridge: Cambridge University Press, 1995.

———. "The Way of the Wind." In *Where the Jackals Howl and Other Stories.*

———. *Where the Jackals Howl and Other Stories.* Translated by Nicholas de Lange and Philip Simpson. New York: Harcourt Brace Jovanovich, 1981.

Pardes, Ilana. *The Biography of Ancient Israel: National Narratives in the Bible.* Los Angeles: University of California Press, 2000.

Peperzak, Adriaan. *To the Other: An Introduction to the Philosophy of Emmanuel Levinas.* Indiana: Purdue University Press, 1993.

Pinar, William. *Curriculum: Toward New Identities.* New York: Garland, 1998.

Presner, Todd Samuel. "Jews on Ships; or, How Heine's *Reisebilder* Deconstruct Hegel's Philosophy of World History." *PMLA* 18.3. May 2003: 521–36.

Redlich, Shimon. "The Right of Return: *The Hooligan's Return: A Memoir* by Norman Manea." *Haaretz.* April 30, 2004: B4.

Reinhartz, Adele. "Margins, Methods, and Metaphors: Reflections on *A Feminist Companion to the Hebrew Bible.*" *Prooftexts.* 20. 1&2. Winter/Spring 2000: 43–59.

Roche, Bonnie. "The Mishkan as Metaphor-Form and Anti-Form: On the Transformation of Urban Space." *CrossCurrents* 52.3. Fall 2002: 342–52.

Rosenak, Michael. "Paths to Holiness." *The Jerusalem Report.* May 3, 2004: 25.

Rosenzweig, Franz. *The Star of Redemption.* Translated by William H. Hallo. Notre Dame, Ind.: Notre Dame Press, 1985.

Rushkoff, Douglas. *Nothing Sacred: The Truth about Judaism.* New York: Crown Publishers, 2003.

Rutherford, Jonathan. "A Place Called Home: Identity and the Cultural Politics of Difference." In *Identity: Community, Culture, Difference,* edited by Jonathan Rutherford. London: Lawrence and Wishart, 1990, 9–27.

Sacks, Jonathan. *The Dignity of Difference: How to Avoid the Clash of Civilizations.* New York: Continuum Books, 2002.

Safran, Alexandre. *Israel in Time and Space: Essays on Basic Themes in Jewish Spiritual Thought.* Jerusalem: Feldheim, 1987.

Said, Edward. *Orientalism.* New York: Vintage Books, 1979.

Scholem, Gershom. "Thoughts About Our Language. (1926)" In *On the Possibility of Jewish Mysticism in Our Time and Other Essays.* Philadelphia: Jewish Publication Society of America, 1996, 27–29.

Schwartz, Howard, and Anthony Rudolf, eds. *Voices Within the Ark: The Modern Jewish Poets.* New York: Avon Books, 1980.

Schwartz, Regina M. *The Curse of Cain: The Violent Legacy of Monotheism.* Chicago: University of Chicago Press, 1997.

Schweid, Eliezer. "The Construction and Deconstruction of Jewish Zionist Identity." In *Ideology and Jewish Identity in Israeli and American Literature,* edited by Emily Miller Budick. Albany: State University of New York Press, 2001, 23–43.

Shands, Kerstin. *Embracing Space: Spatial Metaphors in Feminist Discourse.* London: Greenwood Press, 1999.

Shapira, Sarit. *Routes of Wandering: Nomadism, Voyages and Transitions in Contemporary Israeli Art.* Exhibition catalogue. Jerusalem: Israel Museum, 1991.

Shavit, Ari. "Elective Affinities/Reality Bites." Interview with Amos Oz and David Grossman. *Haaretz.* June 18, 2004.

Shelach, Oz. *Picnic Grounds: A Novel in Fragments.* San Francisco: City Lights Foundation Books, 2003.

Shiffman, Smadar. "Meir Shalev's Ambiguous Use of Biblical Allusions." *Israel Studies Forum* 19.2. Spring 2004: 75–87.

Shipler, David. *Arab and Jew: Wounded Spirits in a Promised Land.* New York: Penguin Books, 2002.

Shohat, Ella. *Israeli Cinema: East/West and the Politics of Representation.* Austin: University of Texas Press, 1987.

Silberstein, Laurence J. *The Postzionism Debates: Knowledge and Power in Israeli Culture.* Routledge: New York, 1999.

Spinoza, Baruch. "Theological-Political Treatise." In Daniel H. Frank, Oliver Leaman, Charles H. Manekin, *The Jewish Philosophy Reader.* Routledge: New York, 2000, 306–38.

Stein, Rebecca. "Israeli Leisure, 'Palestinian Terror,' and The Question of Palestine (Again)." *Theory & Event.* 6.3. 2003: 1–21.

Stone, Merlin. *When God Was a Woman.* New York: Harvest Books, 1978.

Tal, Alon. *Pollution in a Promised Land: An Environmental History of Israel.* Berkeley: University of California Press, 2002.

Talmon, Miri. "Here, There, and Nowhere: Representations of Space and the Negotiation of Identity in Israeli Cinema and Television of the 1990s." In *Arts et Identite Regionale,* edited by P. Carmingnani and T. Jappy. Pepignan: Presses Universitaires de Perpignan, 2001, 187–205.

Talmon, Shemaryahu. "The Desert Motif in the Bible and in Qumran Literature." In *Biblical Motifs: Origins and Transformations,* edited by Alexander Altmann. Cambridge: Harvard University Press, 1966.

Thesiger, Wilfrid. *Arabian Sands.* New York: Viking Press, 1985.

Tuan, Yi-Fu. "Desert and Ice: Ambivalent Aesthetics." In *Landscape, Natural Beauty and the Arts,* edited by Salim Kemal and Ivan Gaskell. Cambridge: Cambridge University Press, 1993, 139–57.

Watzman, Haim. "Israeli Supreme Court Declines to Intervene in Case Over

University Admissions." *Chronicle of Higher Education*. February 11, 2004: A37.

Weiss, Meira. *The Chosen Body: The Politics of the Body in Israeli Society*. Stanford, Calif.: Stanford University Press, 2002.

Weston, Jessie L. *From Ritual to Romance*. Garden City, N.Y.: Doubleday, 1957.

Williams, George H. *Wilderness and Paradise in Christian Thought*. New York: Harper and Brothers, 1962.

Zelitch, Simone. *Moses in Sinai*. Seattle: Black Heron Press, 2002.

Zerubavel, Yael. "The 'Mythological Sabra' and Jewish Past: Trauma, Memory, and Contested Identities." *Israel Studies* 7.2. 2002: 115–44.

———. *Recovered Roots: Collective Memory and the Making of Israeli National Tradition*. Chicago: University of Chicago Press, 1995.

Zornberg, Avivah Gottlieb. *The Particulars of Rapture: Reflections on Exodus*. New York: Doubleday: 2001.

INDEX

RANEN OMER-SHERMAN is the author of *Diaspora and Zionism in Jewish American Literature* as well as numerous articles on Jewish and comparative literature. He currently teaches literature at the University of Miami and has taught at the University of Notre Dame and the University of St. Louis in Madrid, Spain. His activities as an Israeli soldier, kibbutz member, and desert guide have been a strong influence on this study.

The University of Illinois Press
is a founding member of the
Association of American University Presses.

Composed in 9.5/12.5 Trump Mediaeval
by Celia Shapland
for the University of Illinois Press
Manufactured by Thomson-Shore, Inc.

University of Illinois Press
1325 South Oak Street
Champaign, IL 61820-6903
www.press.uillinois.edu